IMAGES
of America

SEAGOVILLE

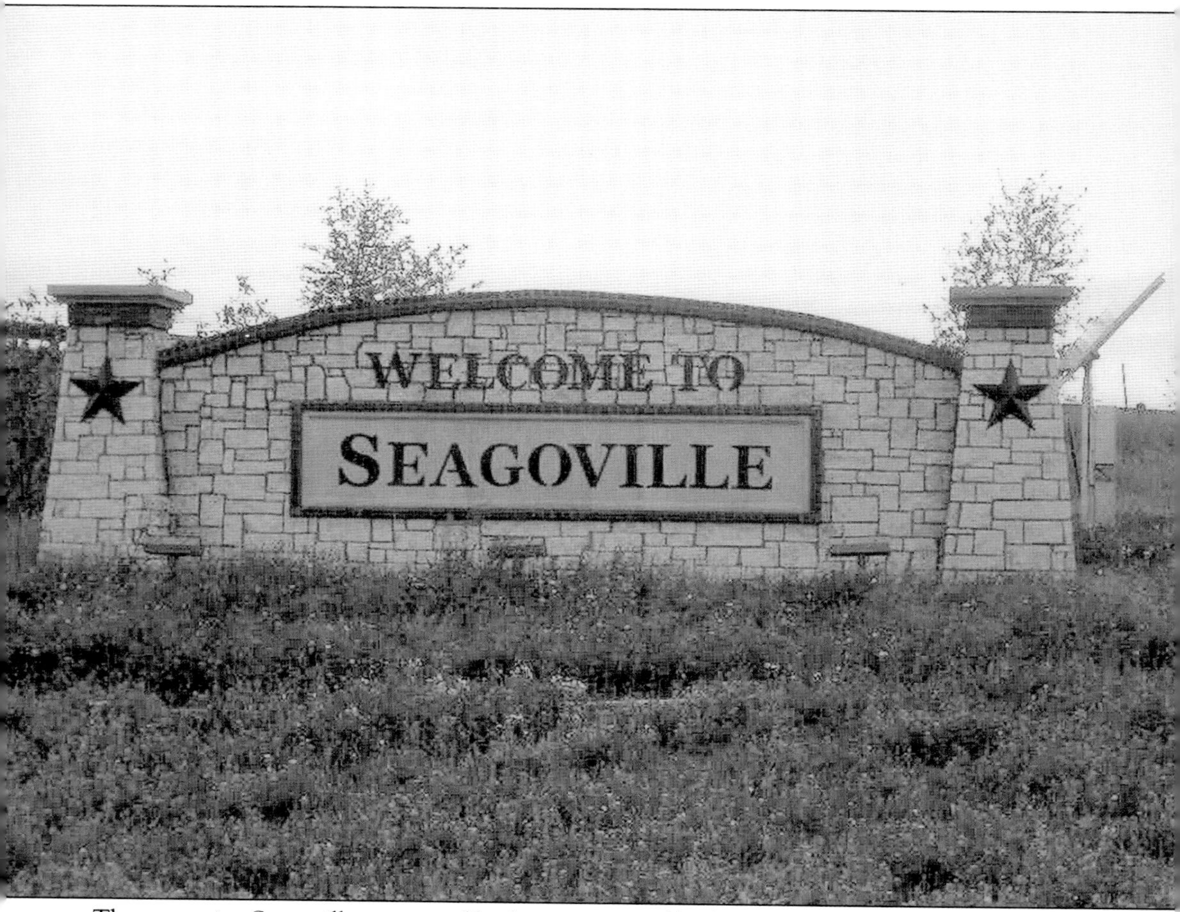

Those entering Seagoville are greeted by this sign, erected by the Texas Department of Transportation with the City of Seagoville's cooperation. The lone star represents the state of Texas and is on the state flag. The Texas state flower, bluebonnets, bloom in profusion in the spring. The state motto of Texas is "Friendship," which aptly relates to Seagoville. (Courtesy of Billie Frank Phillips.)

On the Cover: The Seagoville Dragonettes, Texas state basketball champions of 1949, departed on March 30th for Des Moines, Iowa. They were to play the Iowa state champions, the Wellsburg Maroons. Traveling by train and dressed in cowgirl regalia were the 13 players, team manager, and coach Jimmy Phillips. In the background are the many Seagoville supporters who accompanied the team to Iowa. The starting team of the Seagoville Dragonettes were Lola Wilson, Patsy Anderson, Vera Patterson, Wanda Nelson, Madge Sorrells, and Patsy Pharr accompanied by coach Jimmy Phillips. Other team members were Doris Krone, Derethia Satterwhite, Bobbie Page, Jeannine Smith, Lucy Dickerson, Melba Lanier, Monita Swaim, and Nelda Ritchie. (Courtesy of the Phillips family.)

IMAGES
of America

SEAGOVILLE

Billie Frank Phillips

ARCADIA
PUBLISHING

ISBN 978-0-7385-7863-7

Published by Arcadia Publishing
Charleston, South Carolina

Printed in the United States of America

Library of Congress Control Number: 2010934337

For all general information, please contact Arcadia Publishing:
Telephone 843-853-2070
Fax 843-853-0044
E-mail sales@arcadiapublishing.com
For customer service and orders:
Toll-Free 1-888-313-2665

Visit us on the Internet at www.arcadiapublishing.com

A Tribute to Billie Frank Hurt Phillips

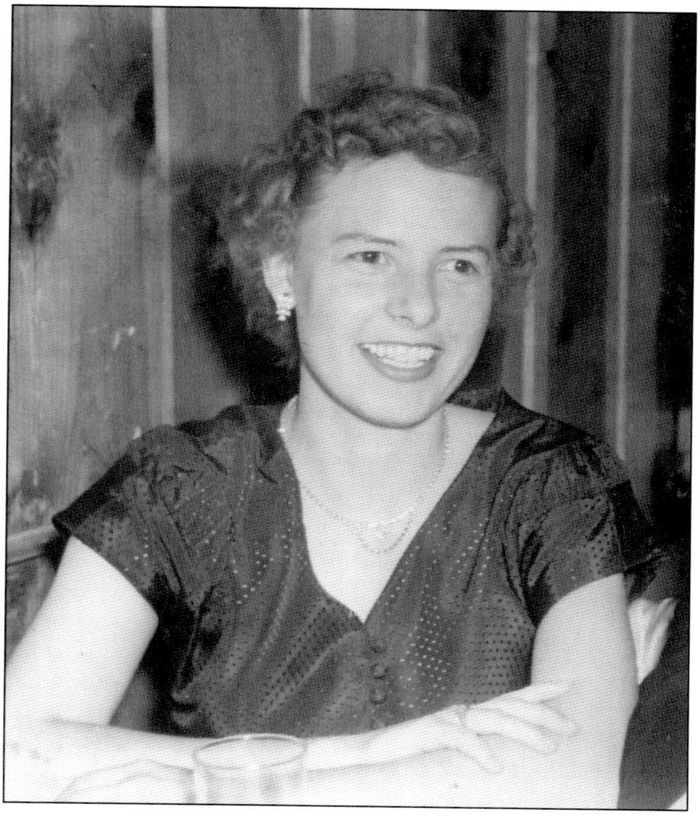

It is agreed that Billie Frank was a dominant force in *preparing* the history of Seagoville. What was not known by even most members—all but one—was that in the last few meetings she was silently suffering from the demon that would soon claim her life. She had a lot of determination—she pushed to get the history written and she pushed to save her beloved Old Red Schoolhouse. Hopefully her work from above will save Old Red. Billie also wanted this book to be dedicated in memory of Hattie Mae Harrell who was a lifelong resident, postal carrier, and a member of the Seagoville Historical Commission. Both will be greatly missed.

Contents

Acknowledgments

Thank you to the many folks who helped in accumulating materials for this book: Neal and Lois Wooley, Reagan L. Glenn, Jerry Waldrum, Alfred Machala, Jerry Miller, Delta and Melba Mathis, Barbara and Rodney Yarbrough, Dorothy Risinger, Kathryn Ballard, Floy Ballantine, Kalton Burt, Beatriz Araiza, Nobie Patterson, and Betty Starnes. Gratitude is also extended to the members of the Seagoville Historical Commission—Carol Franks, Gwen Gaida, Wayne Phillips, and Mary Gaida, whose tireless efforts made this book possible.

Thank you, Kristie Kelly and Scott Davis, editors at Arcadia, for all your help, advice, and support.

Introduction

Long before anyone ever heard the name of Seagoville, Native Americans found the area to be an excellent source for game, water, shelter, and wood for their bows. The East Fork of the Trinity, which runs into the Trinity River near Seagoville served as a source of water, and the very rich bottomlands developed into some of the world's best and most fertile soils, of much value to agriculturists in later years. The first citizens were primarily subsistence farmers or businessmen such as T. K. Seago, for whom the town is named.

Cotton was for years the most important crop, requiring the services of two cotton gins. The North Texas Gin Company was managed by Clarence Murphrey, and the Southern Gin Company was managed by Bob Randerson. Seagoville's first cotton gin had been erected by B. F. Pick. The roads between Dallas and Seagoville would be filled in early morning and late evening during cotton-picking time. Seagoville was at one time home to one of the largest farms in the state of Texas, the Cobb farm, and later boasted one of the largest and best herds of Jersey cattle. In the mid-1930s, a federal farm project was established on a 70-acre farm northwest of town. Vegetables were harvested and sent to the Seagoville Community Cannery for processing. The cannery processed 25,000 cans of food in four months. It retained 12,500 cans as a fee for labor and materials; the remaining 12,500 cans were returned to the producer.

Seagoville became home to many famous people over the years. Chill Wills, born in Seagoville, was a Western movie star who appeared with such actors as John Wayne, Spencer Tracy, and Clark Gable. Wills was also the voice for several cartoon and movie characters, including Francis the Talking Mule. Bonnie and Clyde found temporary homes in Seagoville and the surrounding area and often drove to the back of Jim Hurt's hamburger stand for some of his famous burgers. Warner Brothers used two locations in Seagoville for the movie *Route* 66. And the city received much recognition in the 1940s and 1950s for its girls' basketball team's successes. The Dragonettes even made a trip to Iowa to play the Iowa champions.

An interesting aspect of the roots of several families in Seagoville is that they came in with a company building the Trinity River levee. The L. A. Price Construction Company of Illinois was responsible for bringing the Maroney, Ballantine, Pollan, Waldrum, and Roy Smith families. Another business of interest is Gibson Discount Centers. Its first outlet center was in Seagoville as was the manufacturing plant. Many families such as the Perrins and Massies came with and worked for the Gibsons. The Federal Correctional Institution brought in many folks through the years. This institution was started in 1937 as an all-women's prison and served as a detention station for Japanese during World War II. The U.S. Army Reserve Center is located on Simmonds Road. In 1991, after several years of being a training facility, the facility and medical center were expanded. The medical center is also the headquarters of the 807th Medical Brigade, which participated in Operation Desert Storm.

A Walmart Supercenter opened in April 2004. The store, along with Coca-Cola and Dr. Pepper, gave $25,500 in grants to local and area organizations. Other businesses also constructed in the shopping area are Bealls, Cato Fashions, Dollar Tree, Colortime, Domino's Pizza, Hibbert Sports, Rose Nails, Sally Beauty Supply, the Dental Place, Wendy's, and Eastern Buffet. Seagoville has many more businesses located all over the area.

Seagoville has always been full of sound and solid citizens in all walks of life. They have always strived to have the best in education, religion, and government. This is illustrated in the parks, playgrounds, schools, and churches located in the area. Seagoville has seen much change and growth throughout the years but still strives in today's world to be a nice community in which to live and play.

An attempt here is made to present an accurate, informative, and interesting history of Seagoville. No individual or group will see things in the same way. Obviously, some will think something else should have been included or what was written was not quite right. Any reader will know that from the 1870s to the present, there are going to be some omissions and discrepancies. Even the Seagoville Historical Commission (who helped work on this project) had some differences of opinion. But here it is. It was a lot of fun! And I hope you like it.

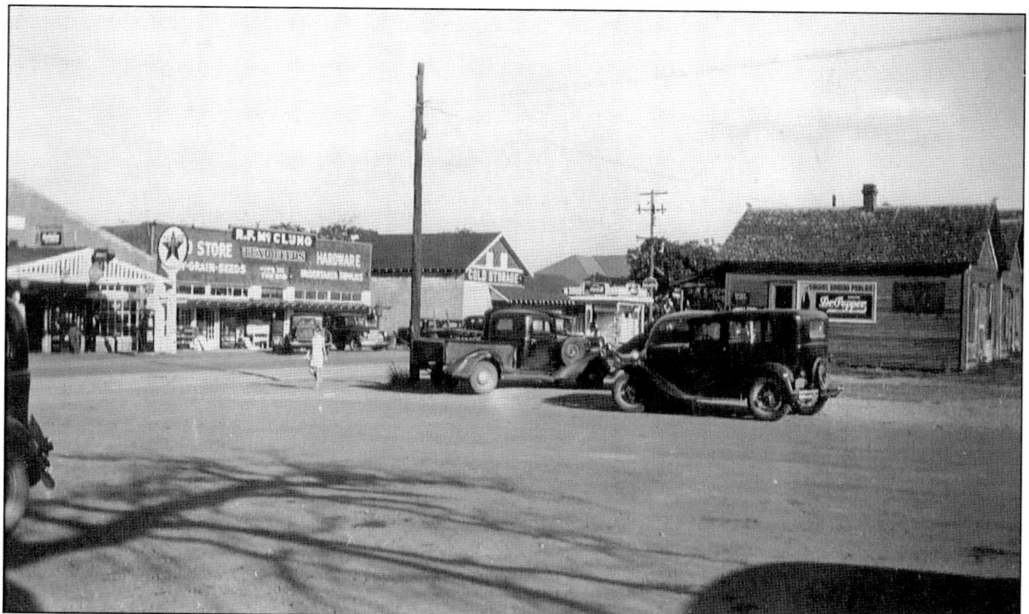

This charming 1935 photograph of Seagoville shows Elm Street looking east. The wooden building on the right is Dr. Oscar Glenn's office. Across the street are, from left to right, Buck Ballard's Garage, R. F. McClung's General Store and Hardware, the Ice House, and Seagoville Methodist Church. (Courtesy Billie Frank Phillips.)

One

Geological Survey

Seagoville could not become a village until a foundation was formed. This began millions of years ago. Many geological periods have passed, including the Cambrian with its diversification of life. The later Triassic period saw the arrival of dinosaurs and primitive mammals, while the Cretaceous included the uplifting of the Rocky Mountains and the mass extinction of the dinosaurs. The familiar ice age peaked in the Pleistocene epoch. During past glacial periods, as the freezing and thawing process continued, the area was also under an inland sea. Glaciers moved back and forth, dragging rocks that broke into small material creating the alluvial soil, soil that is transported by water or ice from other areas. The Three Forks of the Trinity was also formed by glaciation. Man made his appearance in this continuing era known as the Cenozoic. This was the beginning of a uniqueness known nowhere else—the cross timbers, the Blackland Prairie, and the Grand Prairie.

There are 20 soil types in the area. These types range from very fine sand to dark clay. The area is fortunate in having the Seagoville series soil in the Trinity bottomland that is characterized by a nearly brown soil with a mixture of clay and sand. In the East Fork bottom is the Trinity series, also deep and very fertile. The Axtell soil is the primary type in the uplands and is a fine sandy loam. There are also areas of Houston black, Burleson, and Wilson clay soils within a 20-mile radius around Seagoville.

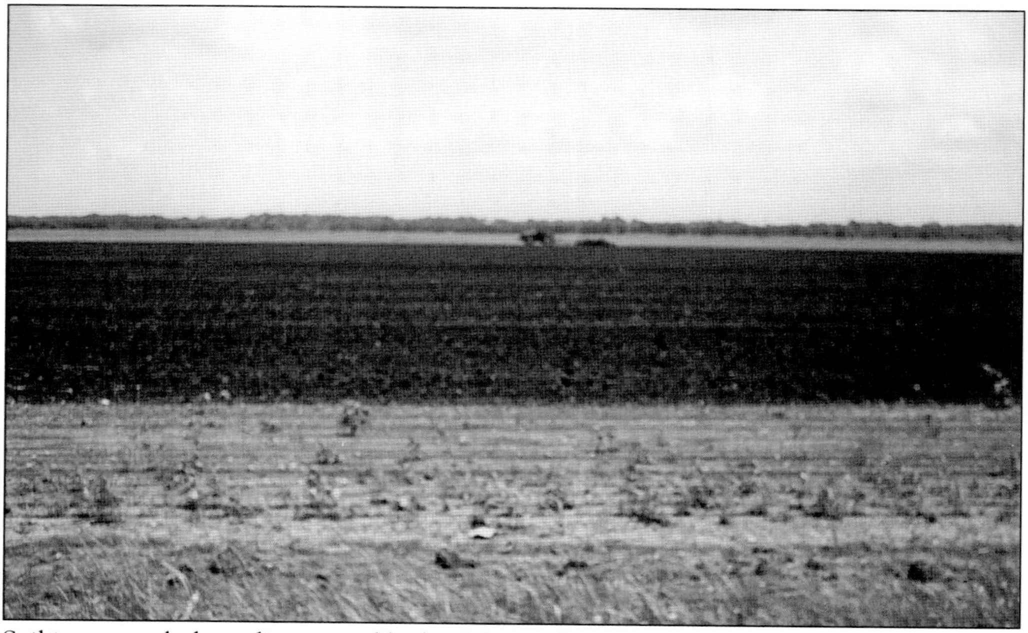

Soil is a natural, three-dimensional body of the earth's surface capable of supporting plants and having properties resulting from the integrated effect of climate and living matter acting on earthy parent materials, as conditioned by relief over periods of time. Shown here is a tractor tilling the Seagoville clay bottomland. Areas range from 25 to several thousand acres. Seagoville soil is used for cropland and has high potential. (Courtesy of Billie Frank Phillips.)

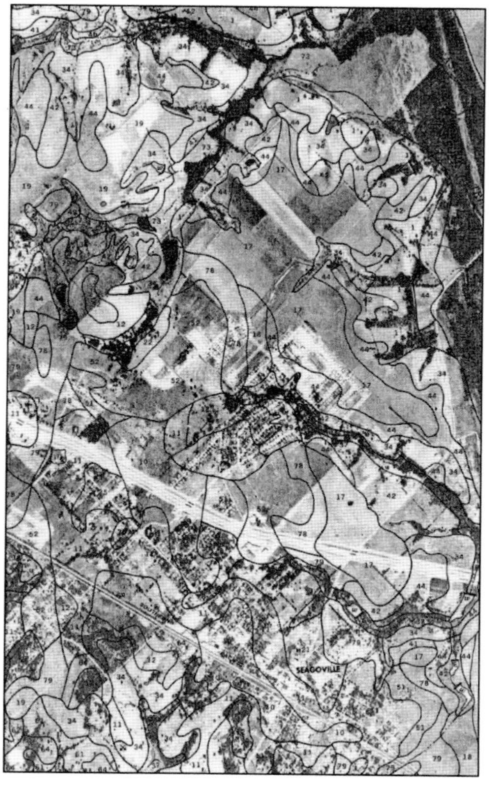

This map shows the 20 different types of soil that surround Seagoville. The Seagoville series is found just south of North Kaufman Street to a 3-mile stretch north of Malloy Bridge Road. Other series include Silawa, Silsted, Branyon, Burleson clay, Ferris, Heiden, Crockett fine loam, Axtell, and Alloga silty clay. These are important to the cultivation of soybeans, maize, and hay crops. (Courtesy of United States Department of Agriculture Soil Conservation Service, soil survey of Dallas County, 1975.)

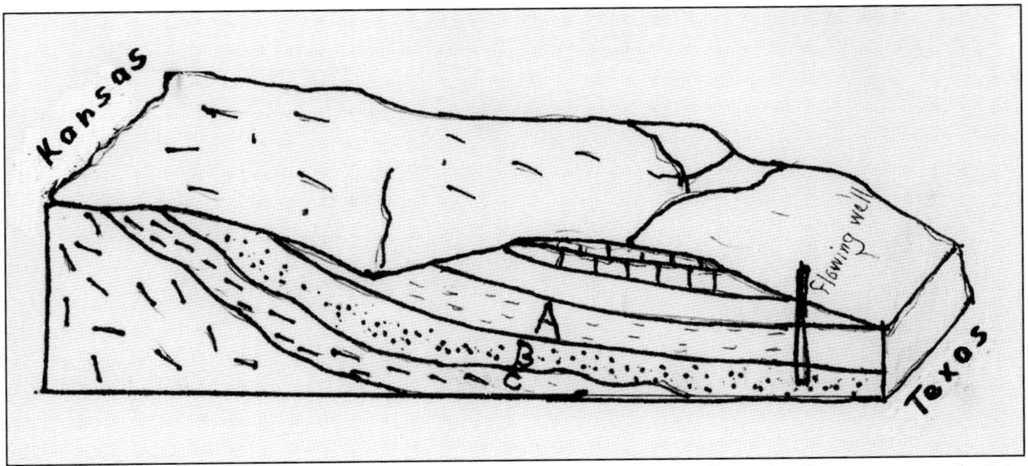

Seagoville got its first artesian well in 1912. A contract was entered into by the citizens and a Mr. Weatherford of Ferris to drill a well, and $3,000 was raised by selling $50 shares. The well was 1,700 feet deep, and water was piped to a trough on the edge of Kaufman and Elm Streets. The stream can be seen flowing out of an elevated pipe (below) that had a cut-off valve and was used to fill barrels loaded on wagons driven up on a platform erected opposite the well. The water was so warm that animals drinking from the trough would have to be pulled away. The well was used until the 1950s when man-made lakes began to supply water to the area. Water in the Seagoville well originated in aquifers in Kansas, as shown in the ground water map above. (Courtesy of R. L. Glenn and Billie Frank Phillips.)

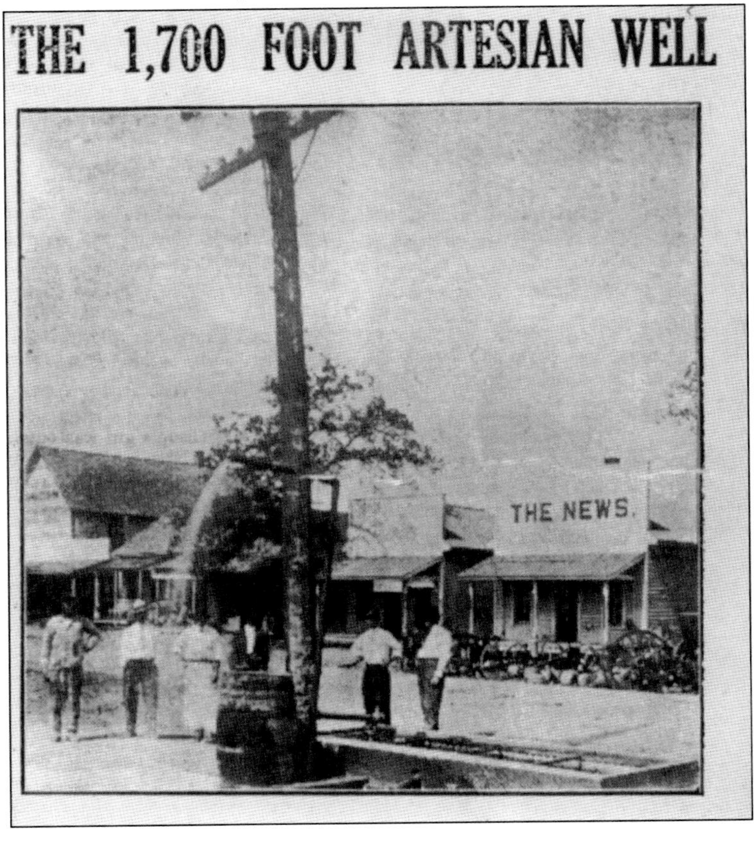

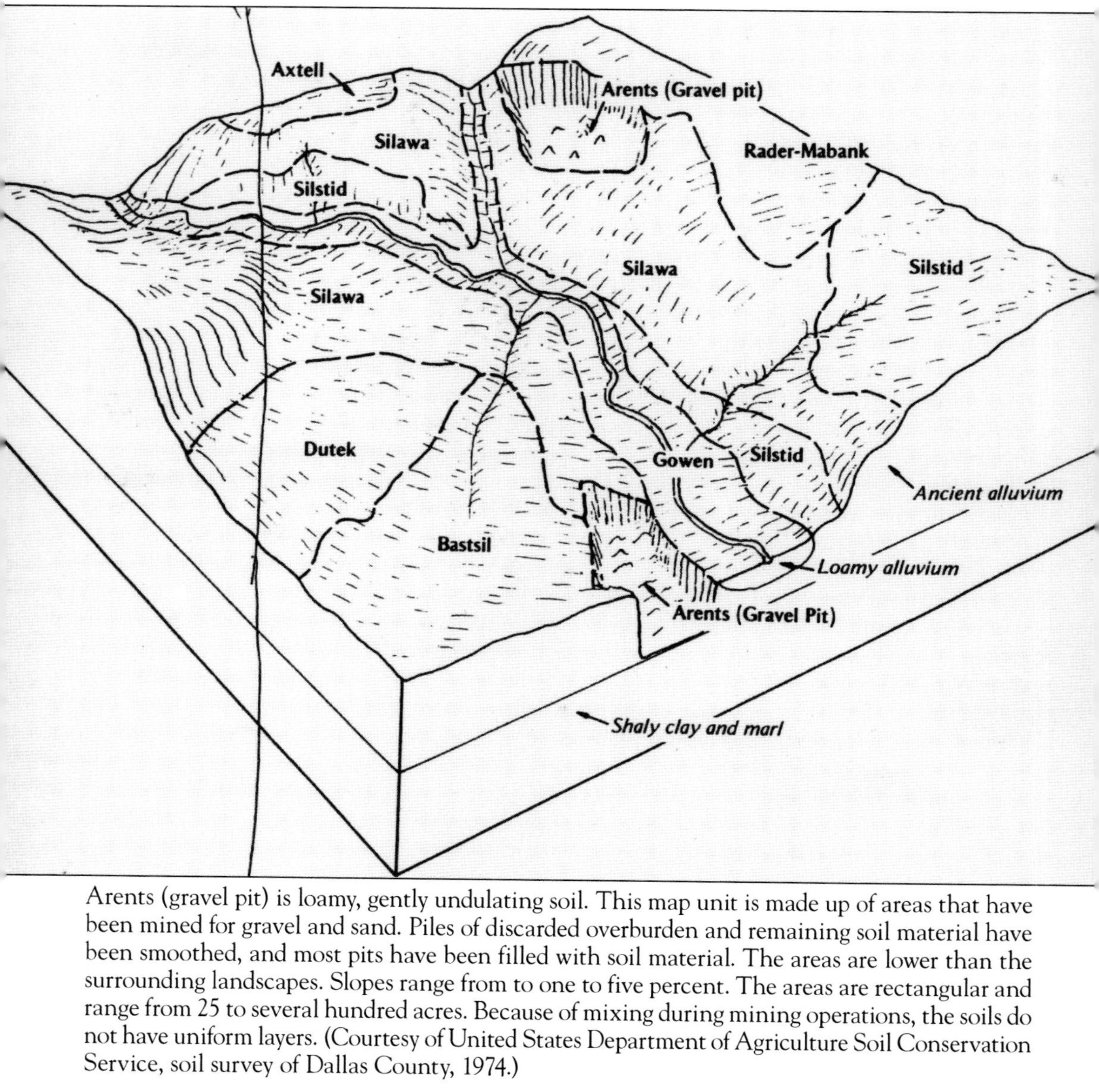

Arents (gravel pit) is loamy, gently undulating soil. This map unit is made up of areas that have been mined for gravel and sand. Piles of discarded overburden and remaining soil material have been smoothed, and most pits have been filled with soil material. The areas are lower than the surrounding landscapes. Slopes range from to one to five percent. The areas are rectangular and range from 25 to several hundred acres. Because of mixing during mining operations, the soils do not have uniform layers. (Courtesy of United States Department of Agriculture Soil Conservation Service, soil survey of Dallas County, 1974.)

Two

NATIVE AMERICANS

The Indian era is the period from the earliest archeological evidences of man to the arrival of the first European explorers in 1519. The most predominant Native Americans in this area were the Caddoan speakers, including the Caddo, Hainai, and Wichita; they were related to the Pawnee.

Caddoan speakers of east, northeast, and north Texas formed the largest cultural group of Native Americans in the region when the Europeans arrived in the area known as the Three Forks of the Trinity River. The Caddos were advanced, having permanent homes and their own form of government. They were inclined to farm and not as nomadic as many Plains Indians. It was certainly a suitable area for them, as there was ample wood for their fires, grass and water for wild animals, and very fertile lands for pumpkins, squash, corn, tobacco, or whatever crops they chose. The Caddos and their relatives that were prominent in this area were also traders. They held fairs and gatherings to barter with the western Native Americans. Their pumpkins, nuts, and bois d'arc to make bows were favored items for trade.

The Caddos are sometimes subdivided into the Hainai in the lower half of the Texas Pine Belt–Nacogdoches area, the Caddo proper living in northeast Texas, and, according to some sources, the Wichita in the Middle Red River Valley on the Trinity headwaters. This last group is accepted as a branch of the Caddo stock, although their dialects undoubtedly varied considerably, and their habits were more nomadic. Most authorities agree that there were not more than 30,000 Caddos in the Middle Red River Valley in the Trinity headwaters area at any given time.

The Caddoan was among the most important linguistic stocks in North America in point of speakers or territory. Of the 30,000 Caddos in the three subgroups listed above, 10,000 lived in and around the area known as the Three Forks of the Trinity River for almost three centuries. The last known trade fair gathering witnessed by Europeans was in 1790.

Native American artifacts have been found in the Seagoville area by the Wade, Rucks, Harlan, and Grammer families.

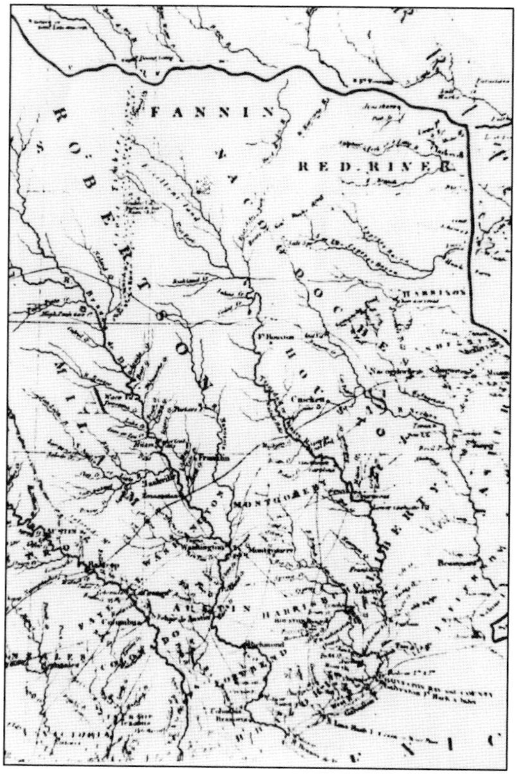

The excellent land of the Three Forks of the Trinity River is noted in this East Texas detail from John Arrowsmith's map of Texas, made in London in 1841. This chart shows Native American villages, rivers, roads, and the 1839 route of General Rask's army to Fort Houston on the Trinity River. (Courtesy of Seagoville Library, historical map collection.)

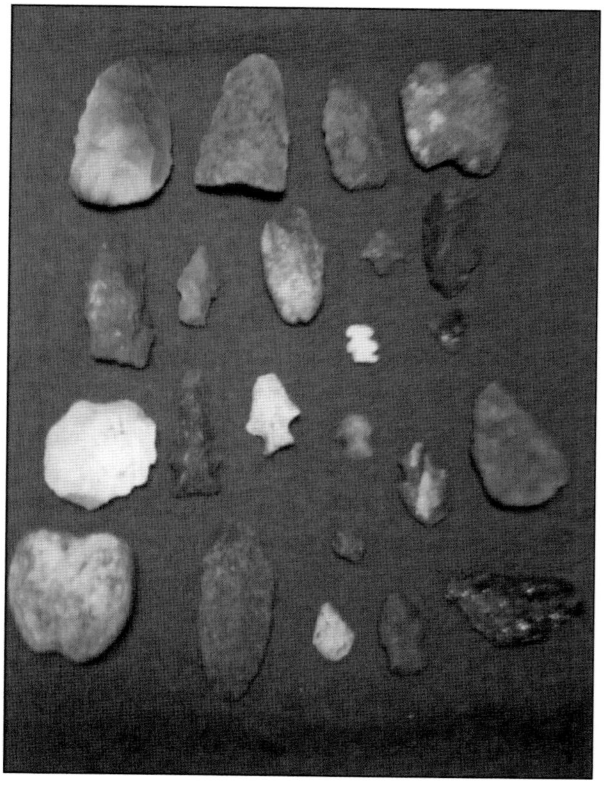

These arrowheads show the separate tips or points of arrow shafts the Native Americans in the Seagoville area used. The white and gray to black are flint; yellow-brown, green, and red are jasper. Because of their hardness and toughness, chert and flint were used by early man for manufacturing blades, scrapers, and knives. Many other forms of stone have been found, such as obsidian, which probably had been traded as far away as Mexico. (Courtesy of the Phillips family.)

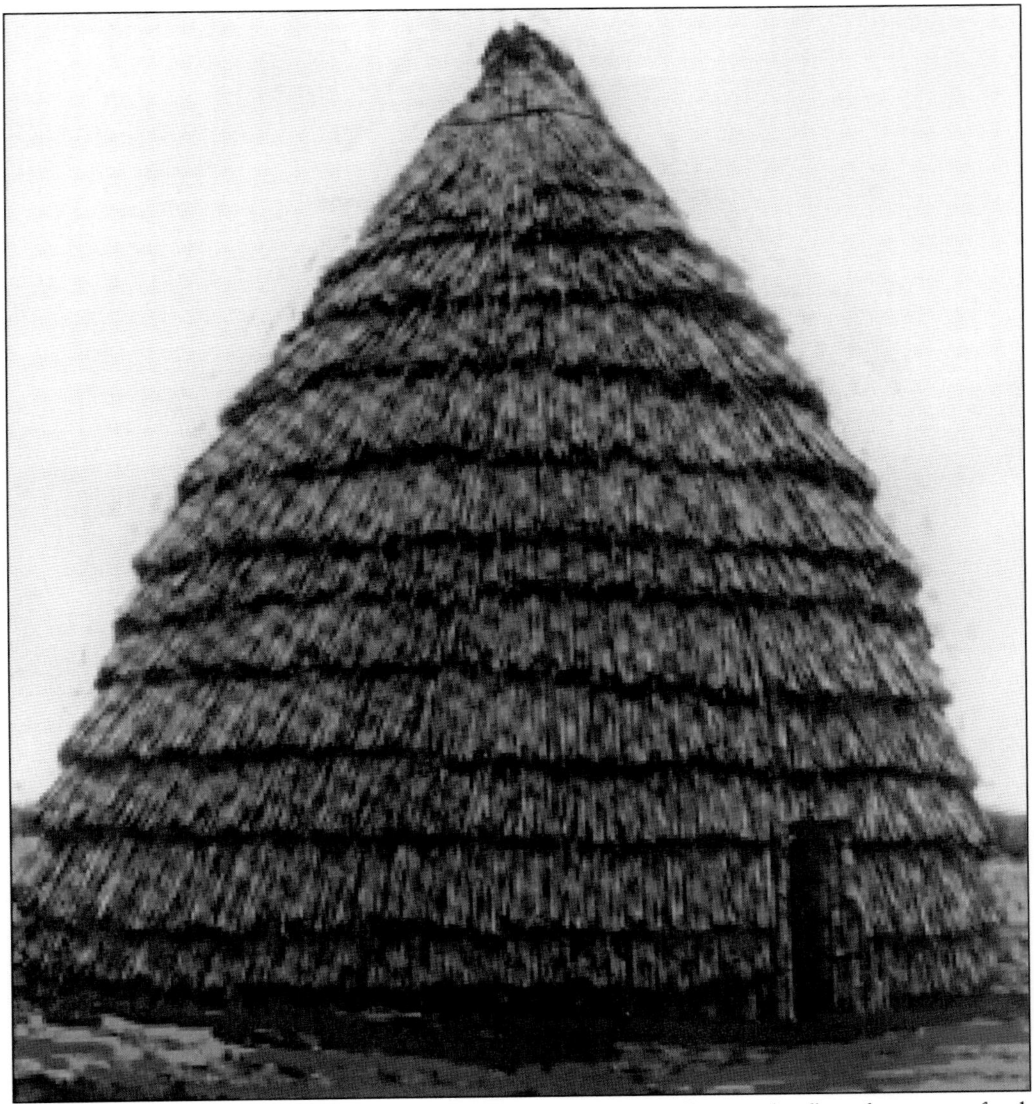

The Caddos were nearly modern in their homes as they had cellars in the floor for storing food. They preferred building on a bluff or mound overlooking a stream. The homes were constructed of large and small poles and thatched with mud and buffalo grass. Sometimes two families related through the female line occupied the same home. Early European visitors complimented the Caddos on their cleanliness and orderliness. (Courtesy of texasindians.com.)

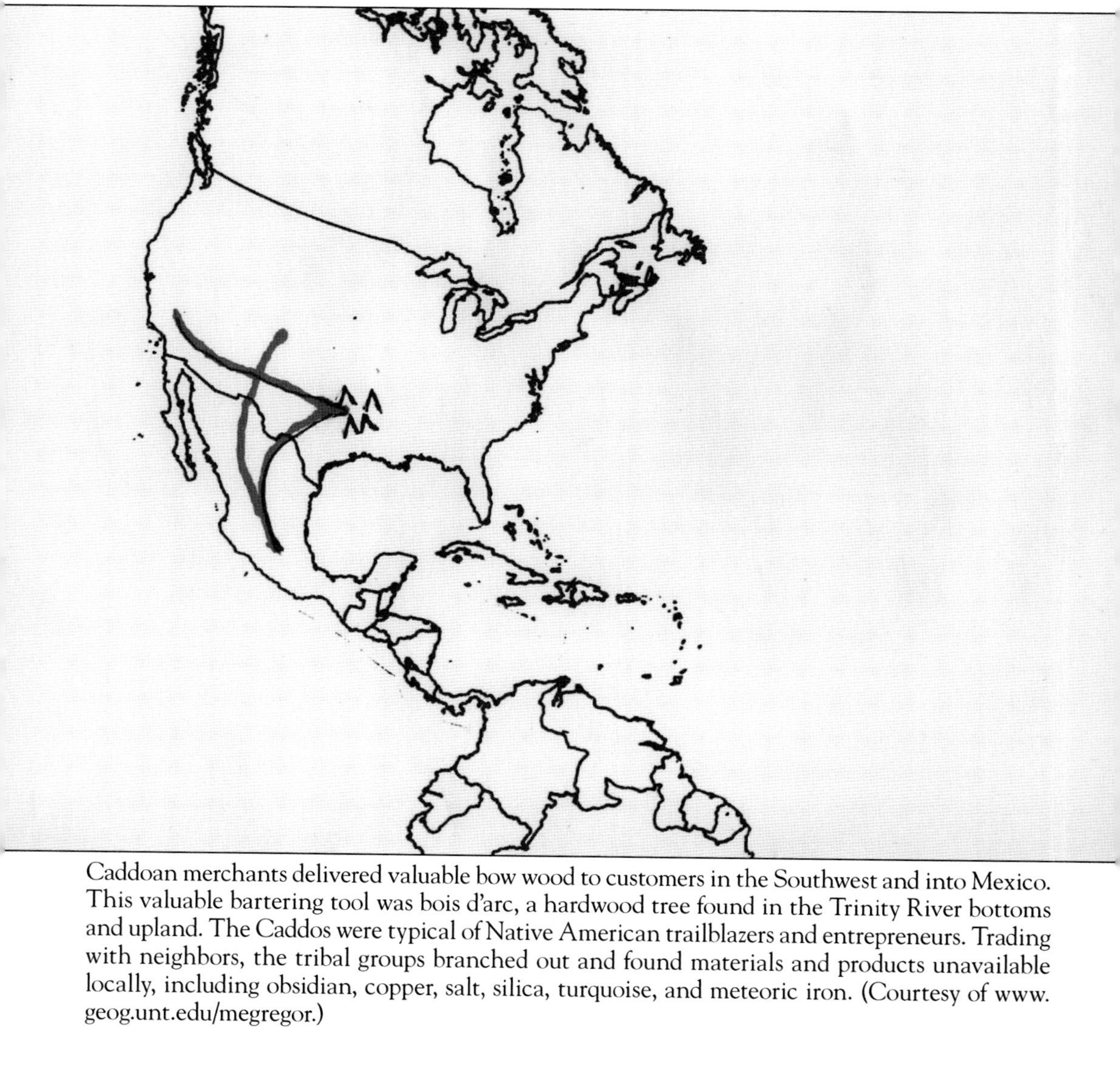

Caddoan merchants delivered valuable bow wood to customers in the Southwest and into Mexico. This valuable bartering tool was bois d'arc, a hardwood tree found in the Trinity River bottoms and upland. The Caddos were typical of Native American trailblazers and entrepreneurs. Trading with neighbors, the tribal groups branched out and found materials and products unavailable locally, including obsidian, copper, salt, silica, turquoise, and meteoric iron. (Courtesy of www.geog.unt.edu/megregor.)

Three

Founding

The founding of Seagoville is attributed to Tillman Kimsey Seago, son of Isaac and Lucinda Seago. He moved to Texas in 1851 and established Seago in 1879. T. K. Seago was the first postmaster, owned the first dry goods store, and donated the land that brought the Texas and New Orleans Railroad (T&NO) to town. He stayed in Seago until 1887.

The Texas and New Orleans Railroad was a branch of the Southern Pacific Railroad that first came through Seago in 1880. By 1905, the railway had turned the city into a new industrial frontier with a thriving rail terminal center. Before the advent of the rails, there were locks on the Trinity River about 8 miles from Seago, and freight was received via the river on barges.

The first official plat of Seago was recorded in the Dallas County deed records in 1883. In 1910, the Post Office Department added the *ville* to Seago because there was another Texas town with a similar name, Sego, which caused a lot of postal confusion. A second plat was filed in 1926, at which time the city was incorporated with a population of 296.

The first telephones were on a line between the homes of the Ard, Hawthorne, Griffin, and Crawford citizens of Seagoville. There was no central office at the time, so each home had a ring when a call was being received. Electricity came to Seagoville in 1925. The first industry was a bois d'arc mill. Men rode on horseback to the bottomlands, picked the bois d'arc apples when they were ripe, and delivered them to the mill to be sliced and placed in the vat. The vat would crush the apples and separate the pulp from the seeds. The seeds would then be removed and dried for selling at $18 per pound. People from as far away as Indiana and Ohio would come to the mill to buy the seeds, used to grow hedges for use as fences for farm property. Bois d'arc apple hedges had been in use for many years prior to barbwire and were extremely hard to destroy. Once a hedge was in place it was usually left untouched until the age when bulldozers could be used to take them down.

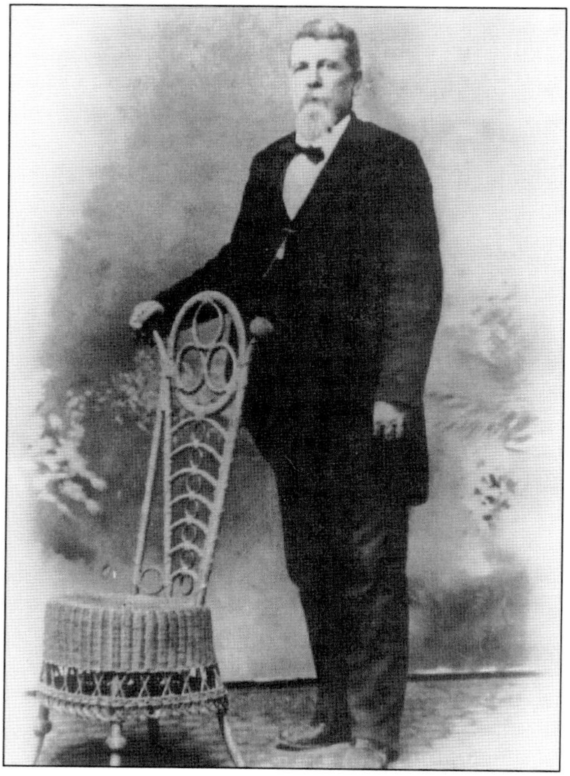

T. K. Seago was born July 29, 1836, in Cherokee County, Georgia. In 1861, he enlisted in the 3rd Texas Calvary and served throughout the Civil War. After the war, he was engaged in farming and carpentry and later moved to Comanche County and purchased good farmland there. Seago served in the Texas Legislature in 1894. He died on September 17, 1904, and is buried in Comanche County, Texas. (Courtesy of Seagoville Library Archives.)

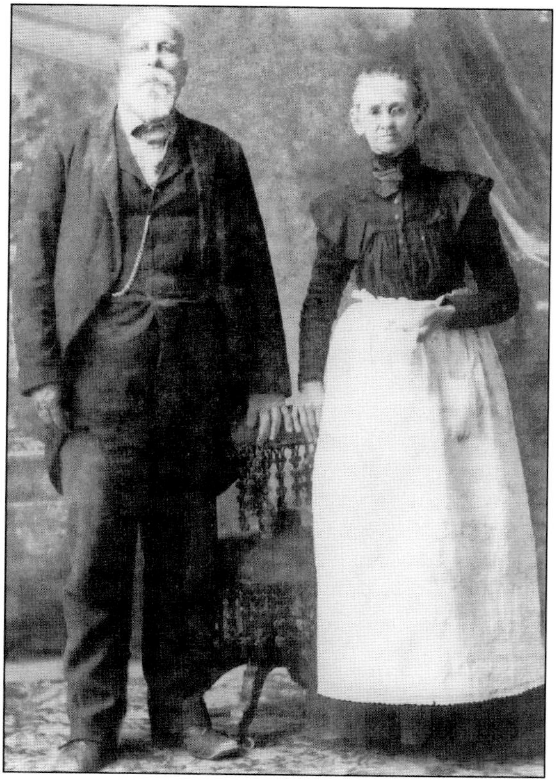

T. K. Seago and Matilda Elvira Davenport were married on January 28, 1955, in Cass County, Texas. She was born in Georgia about 1839, the daughter of P. G. and Sarah (Cradille) Davenport. T. K. and Matilda had eight children—Sarah, Tillman B., Jennie, Lilla, Annie, Ada, Eunice, and Benjamin Lee. (Courtesy of Seagoville Library Archives.)

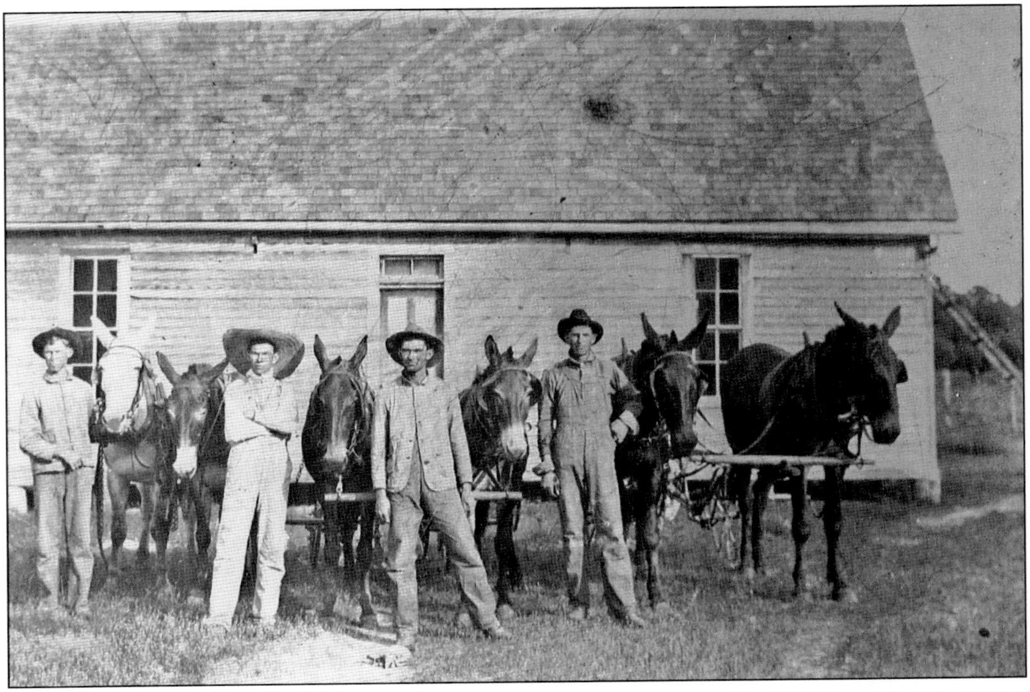

Pictured above are Ben H., Walter, and J. Lawrence Fly and friend Joe Petty. The Fly brothers were the sons of J. L. Fly and later became prominent citizens of Seagoville. Their father was an early pioneer in Seagoville, a merchant, and a justice of the peace. J. Lawrence became assistant attorney general of the United States and was assigned to the case involving the Tennessee Valley Authority construction of dams on the Tennessee River. Later he was appointed as head of the Federal Communications Commission by Pres. Franklin D. Roosevelt and was also a member of a New York law firm. Walter became a Dallas attorney, and Ben H. (pictured at right) became a Dallas County judge. (Courtesy of R. L. Glenn and Gwen Robinson Gaida.)

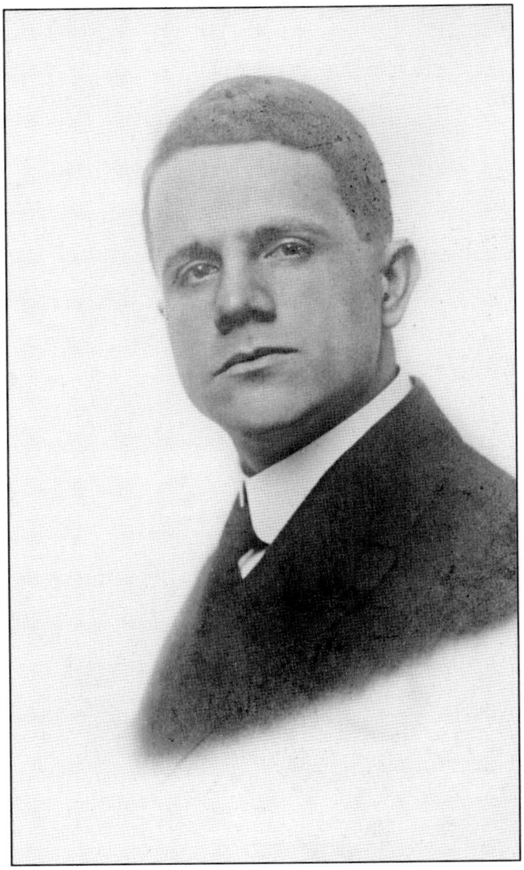

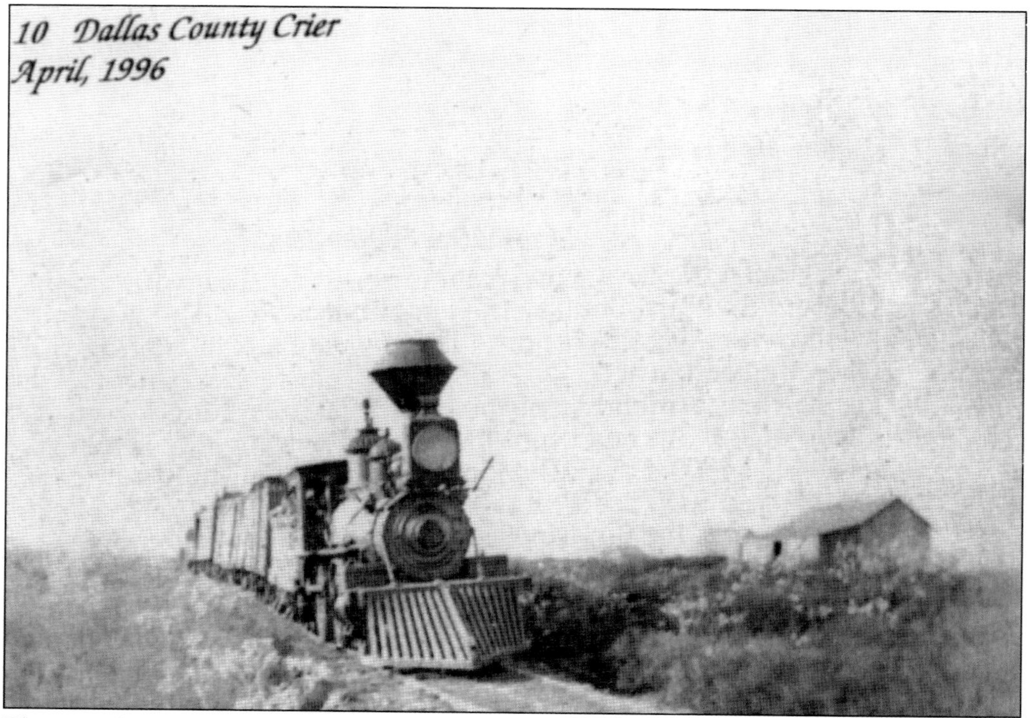

This was the first train to run through Seagoville. The Texas Trunk Train ran from Dallas to Kaufman, a distance of 37 miles at the high speed of five miles an hour. C. C. Cobb sent farm products to Dallas by train. In 1905, the Texas and New Orleans Railroad, a branch of the Southern Pacific, helped the city to become an industrial frontier in the Blackland cotton belt. (Courtesy of Coppell Advocate.)

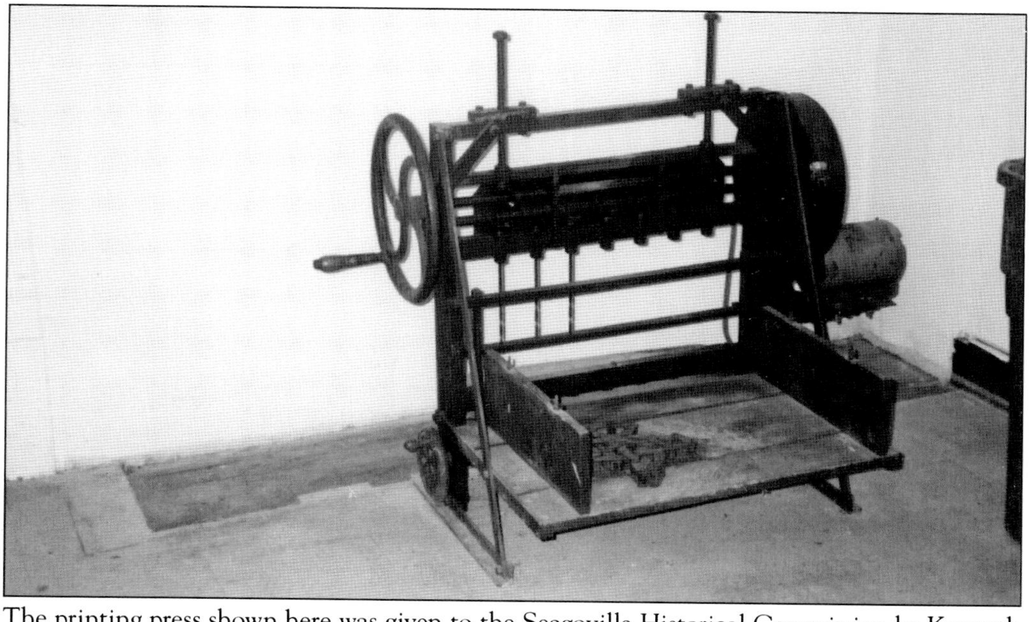

The printing press shown here was given to the Seagoville Historical Commission by Kenneth Lassiter when he retired from the Southern Pacific Railroad. Southern Pacific used the press to publish its newspaper and announcements from the early 1900s. (Courtesy of Carol Franks.)

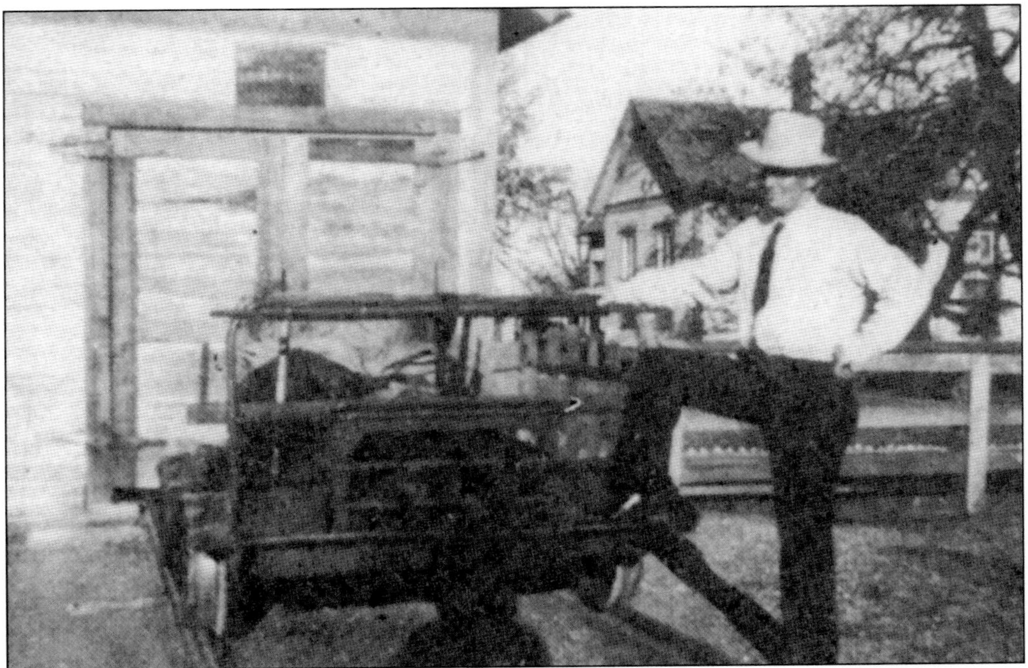

John G. McMillan served as section foreman of the Southern Pacific Railroad in Seagoville from 1925 to 1940. He is shown in front of the shop on South Kaufman Street with one of the railcars. In the background is the section foreman's house where McMillan and his family resided. The house was painted a railroad yellow. (Courtesy of Neal Wooley.)

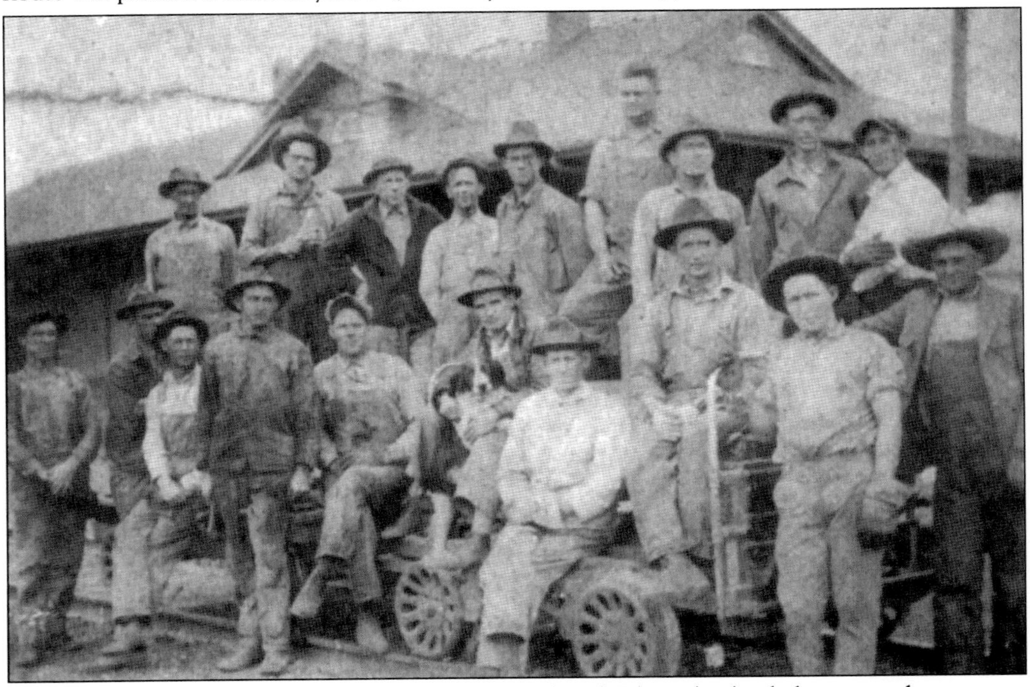

These are some of the men who worked on the railroad. They also loaded items such as cotton on the dock for shipment on the trains. The railroad station is in the background. (Courtesy of Neal Wooley.)

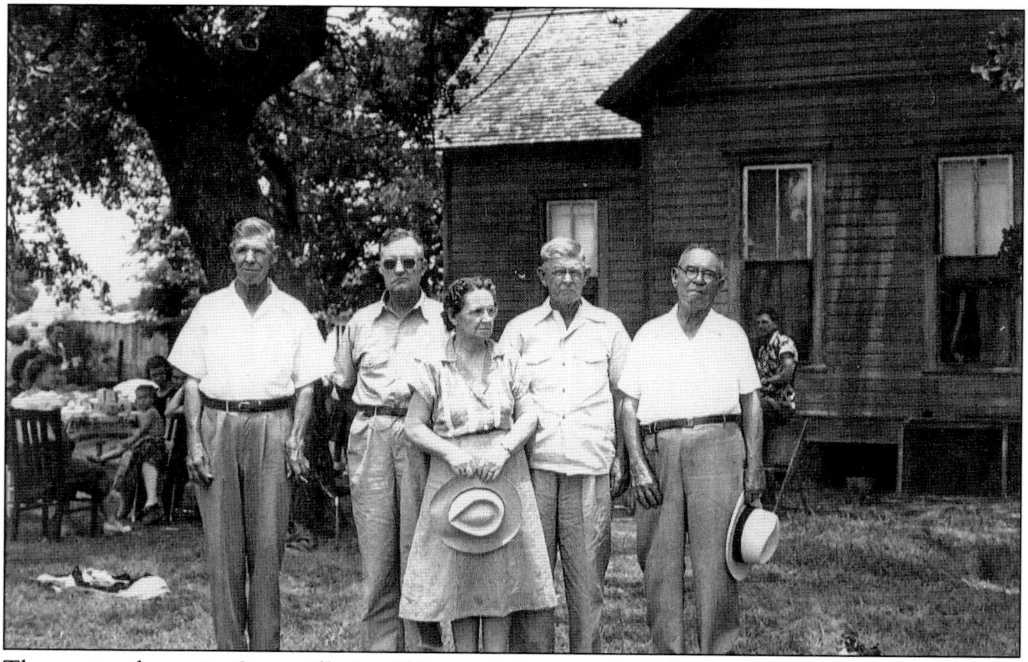

The section house in Seagoville is still located close to where the depot stood before being torn down. Renovations took place many years ago when Ada Petty purchased the structure for a home. It was always a neat place. Petty lived there until her death in 1980. (Courtesy of R. L. Glenn.)

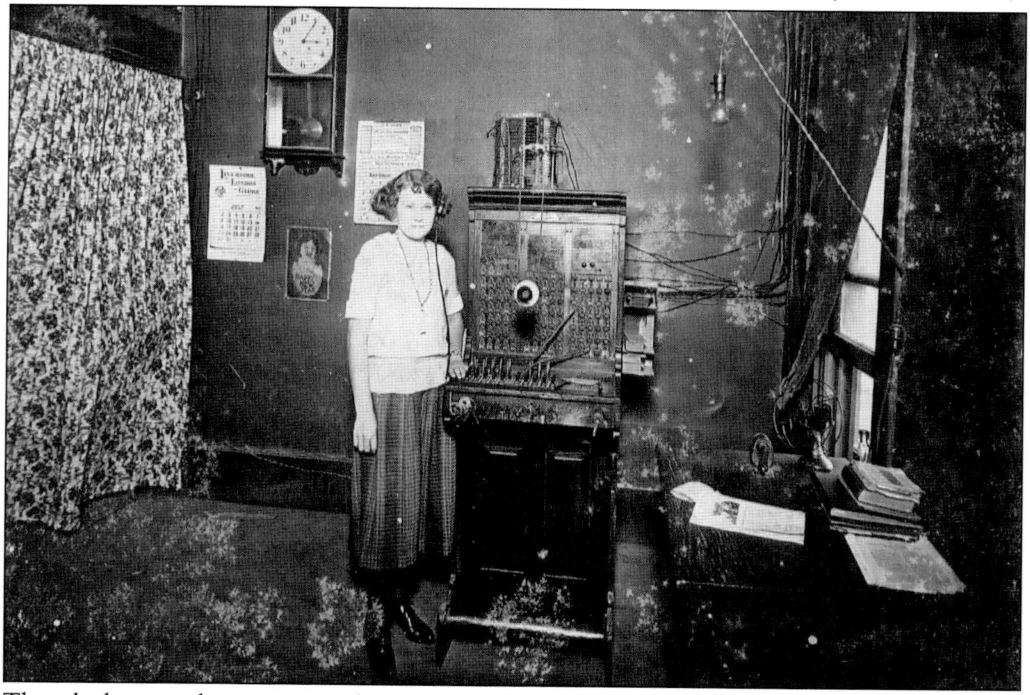

The telephone exchange was run by a Miss Marshall in 1921 in a building facing the depot. There were 16 subscribers. Later Mattie Hitt was the telephone operator in a small house on Kaufman Street through the 1930s into the 1940s. In the 1940s, Gulf States Telephone Company came in and callers could dial their own numbers. (Courtesy of R. L. Glenn.)

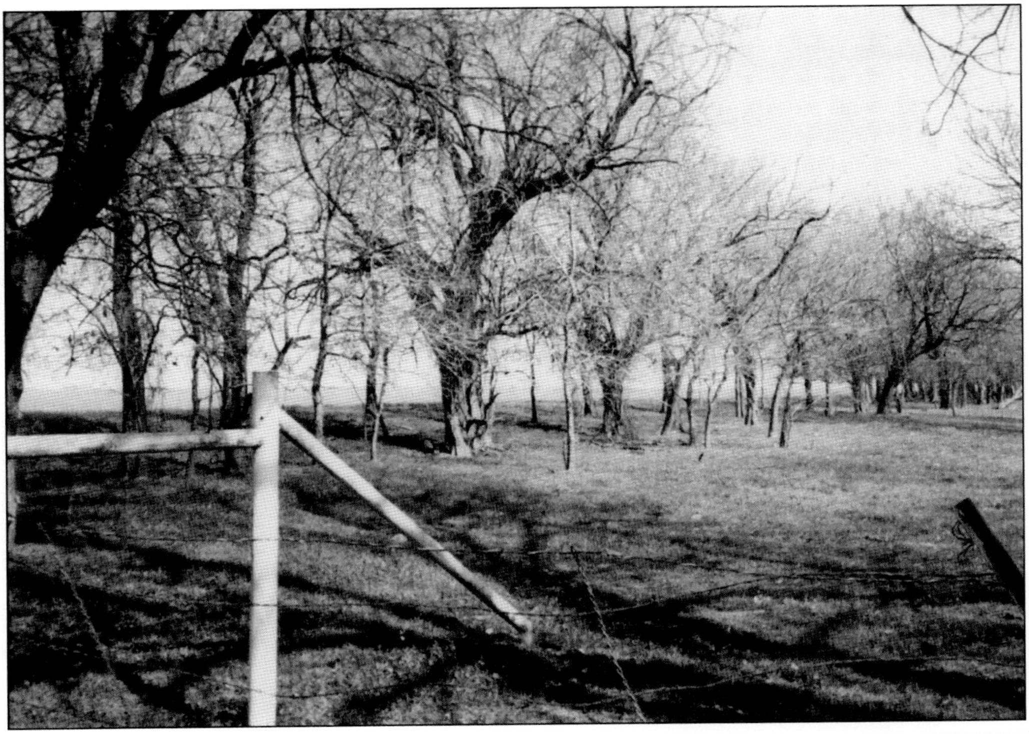

Historians say that the very first business in Seagoville was that of processing bois d'arc seed for the purpose of planting hedges for fences. This preceded the manufacture of barbed wire. Dried apples were crushed by a horse walking round and round with a pole attached to a crushing mechanism in a vat. The seed would drop to the bottom. It was said the seed would bring $18 per pound in 1869–1870. Bois d'arc was also used for paving streets and as blocks for houses. The contract pictured at right calls for bois d'arc sprouts to be used. They likely came from Seagoville. It is also likely that the seeds were used in the Midwest or other areas too far to haul sprouts. Planted 145 years ago, the hedge in the picture above was thinned and lost the ability to obstruct cows. (Courtesy of the Phillips family.)

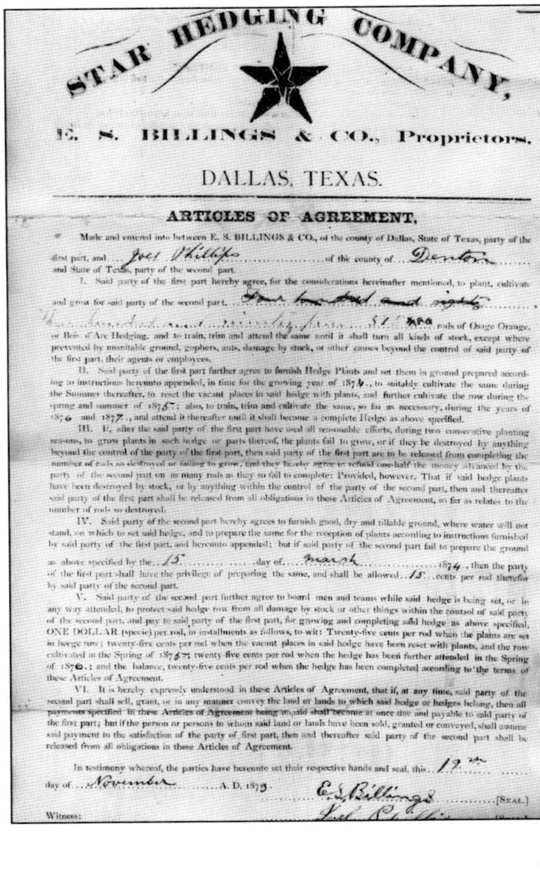

STAR HEDGING COMPANY,

E. S. BILLINGS & CO., Proprietors.

DALLAS, TEXAS.

ARTICLES OF AGREEMENT,

Made and entered into between E. S. BILLINGS & CO., of the county of Dallas, State of Texas, party of the first part, and Joel Phillips of the county of Denton and State of Texas, party of the second part.

I. Said party of the first part hereby agree, for the considerations hereinafter mentioned, to plant, cultivate and grow for said party of the second part, Four hundred and eighty ... 480 rods of Osage Orange, or Bois d'Arc Hedging, and to train, trim and attend the same until it shall turn all kinds of stock, except where prevented by unsuitable ground, gophers, ants, damage by stock, or other causes beyond the control of said party of the first part, their agents or employees.

II. Said party of the first part further agree to furnish Hedge Plants and set them in ground prepared according to instructions hereunto appended, in time for the growing year of 1874, to suitably cultivate the same during the Summer thereafter, to reset the vacant places in said hedge with plants, and further cultivate the row during the spring and summer of 1875; also, to train, trim and cultivate the same, so far as necessary, during the years of 1876 and 1877, and attend it thereafter until it shall become a complete Hedge as above specified.

III. If, after the said party of the first part have used all reasonable efforts, during two consecutive planting seasons, to grow plants in such hedge or parts thereof, the plants fail to grow, or if they be destroyed by anything beyond the control of the party of the first part, then said party of the first part are to be released from completing the number of rods so destroyed or failing to grow, and they hereby agree to refund one-half the money advanced by the party of the second part on as many rods as they so fail to complete: Provided, however, That if said hedge plants have been destroyed by stock, or by anything within the control of the party of the second part, then and thereafter said party of the first part shall be released from all obligations in these Articles of Agreement, so far as relates to the number of rods so destroyed.

IV. Said party of the second part hereby agrees to furnish good, dry and tillable ground, where water will not stand, on which to set said hedge, and to prepare the same for the reception of plants according to instructions furnished by said party of the first part, and hereunto appended; but if said party of the second part fail to prepare the ground as above specified by the 15 day of March 1874, then the party of the first part shall have the privilege of preparing the same, and shall be allowed 15 cents per rod therefor by said party of the second part.

V. Said party of the second part further agree to board men and teams while said hedge is being set, or in any way attended, to protect said hedge row from all damage by stock or other things within the control of said party of the second part, and pay to said party of the first part, for growing and completing said hedge as above specified, ONE DOLLAR (specie) per rod, in installments as follows, to-wit: Twenty-five cents per rod when the plants are set in hedge row; twenty-five cents per rod when the vacant places in said hedge have been reset with plants, and the row cultivated in the Spring of 1875; twenty-five cents per rod when the hedge has been further attended in the Spring of 1876; and the balance, twenty-five cents per rod when the hedge has been completed according to the terms of these Articles of Agreement.

VI. It is hereby expressly understood in these Articles of Agreement, that if, at any time, said party of the second part shall sell, grant, or in any manner convey the land or lands to which said hedge or hedges belong, then all payments specified in these Articles of Agreement being unpaid shall become at once due and payable to said party of the first part; but if the person or persons to whom said land or lands have been sold, granted or conveyed, shall assume said payment to the satisfaction of the party of first part, then and thereafter said party of the second part shall be released from all obligations in these Articles of Agreement.

In testimony whereof, the parties have hereunto set their respective hands and seal, this 12th day of November A. D. 1873.

E. S. Billings [Seal.]

Witness:

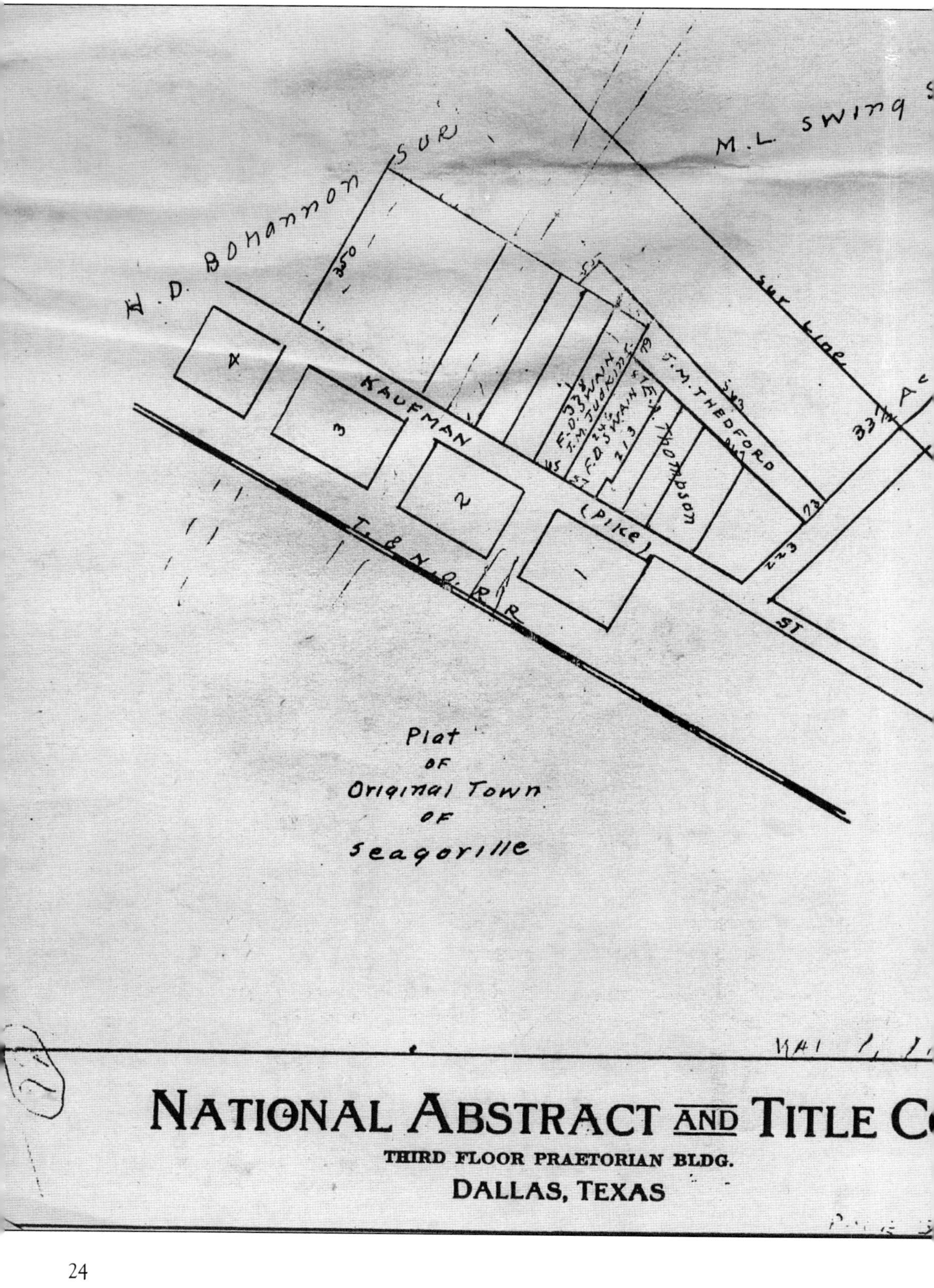
H. D. BOHANNON SUR
M. L. SWING
350
KAUFMAN
(PIKE)
ST
T. & N. O. R R
J. M. THEDFORD
sur line
F. D. SWAIN
J. M. JUDKINS
THOMPSON
223
73
4
3
2
1
Plat
of
Original Town
of
Seagoville
NATIONAL ABSTRACT AND TITLE Co
THIRD FLOOR PRAETORIAN BLDG.
DALLAS, TEXAS

This is a plat of the original town of Seagoville. Information is taken from an original copy of the abstract of title, state of Texas, county of Dallas, filed May 1, 1883, and recorded in volume 60, page 617. The deed was recorded in Dallas County, Texas, with the recording acknowledged by William. McHill, county clerk. The land Seagoville is situated on was originally deeded to Texan M. L. Swing as a Civil War veteran's benefit. It was a patent deed from the State of Texas, dated April 22, 1862. F. R. Lubbock was governor at that time. (Courtesy of the Phillips family.)

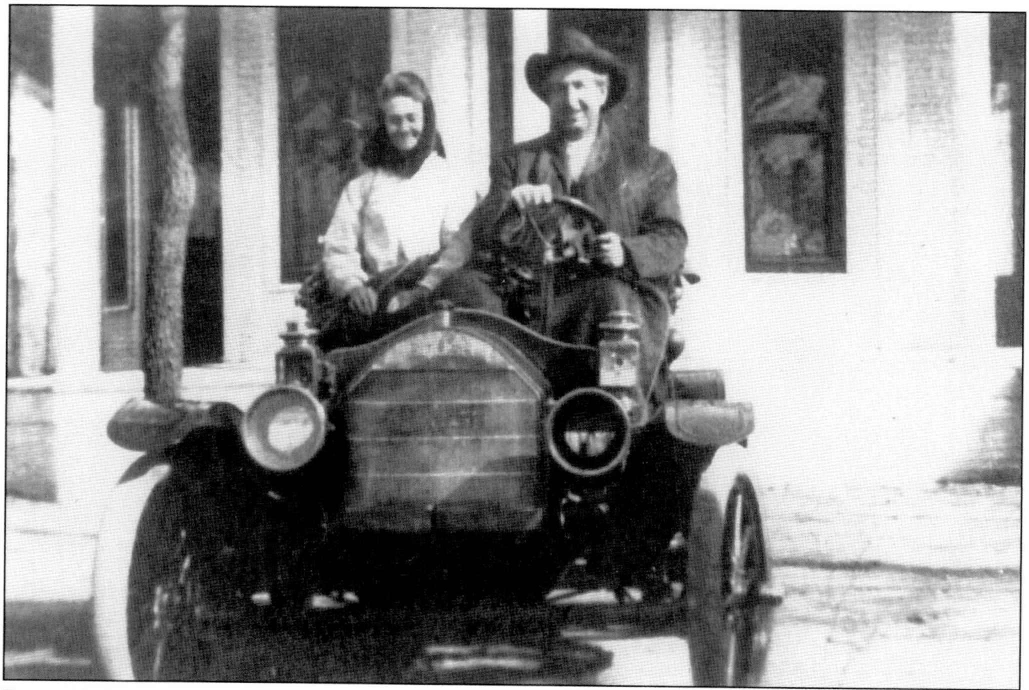

From 1910 to 1912, Martin Glenn and Alice L. Robertson Glenn owned this automobile. The first automobile in Seagoville was a buggy type purchased by Dr. C. E. McWhorter. As the car was going down Kaufman Street, J. M. Wilson's daughter hollered, "Mama, here comes a buggy without a horse." In 1901, A. H. McWhorter bought a used Buick and charged 10¢ for a round-trip ride. By 1911, there were seven automobiles in Seagoville. Pictured above are Alice and Martin Glenn. (Courtesy of R. L. Glenn.)

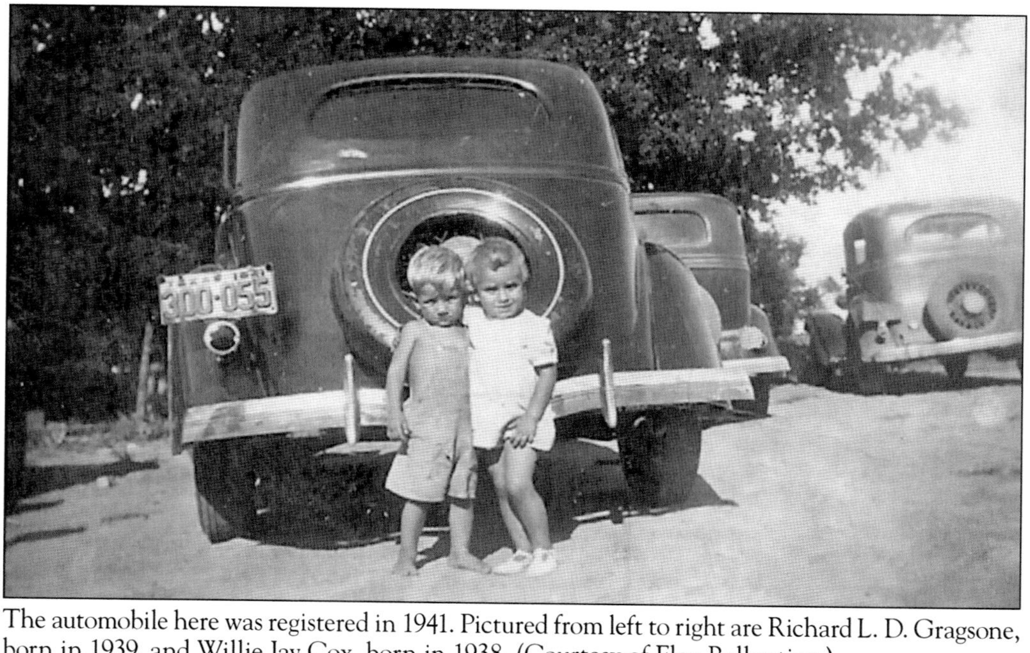

The automobile here was registered in 1941. Pictured from left to right are Richard L. D. Gragsone, born in 1939, and Willie Jay Cox, born in 1938. (Courtesy of Floy Ballantine.)

The Happy Hour Theater was the first motion picture house in Seagoville and was owned by A. H. McWhorter. The advertisement at right indicates that in August 1914 the theater showed film of Pres. Woodrow Wilson's inauguration. Besides the theater, McWhorter also owned a grocery store, a dry goods store, and one of the first automobiles in town. (Courtesy of Neal Wooley.)

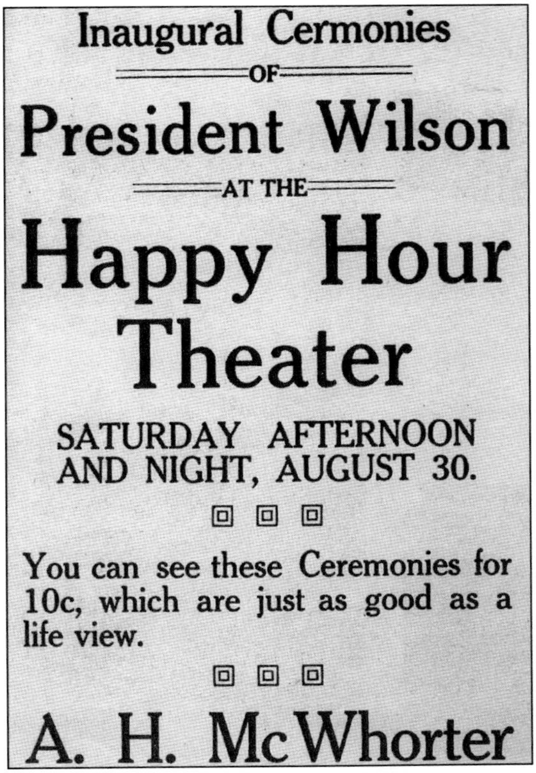

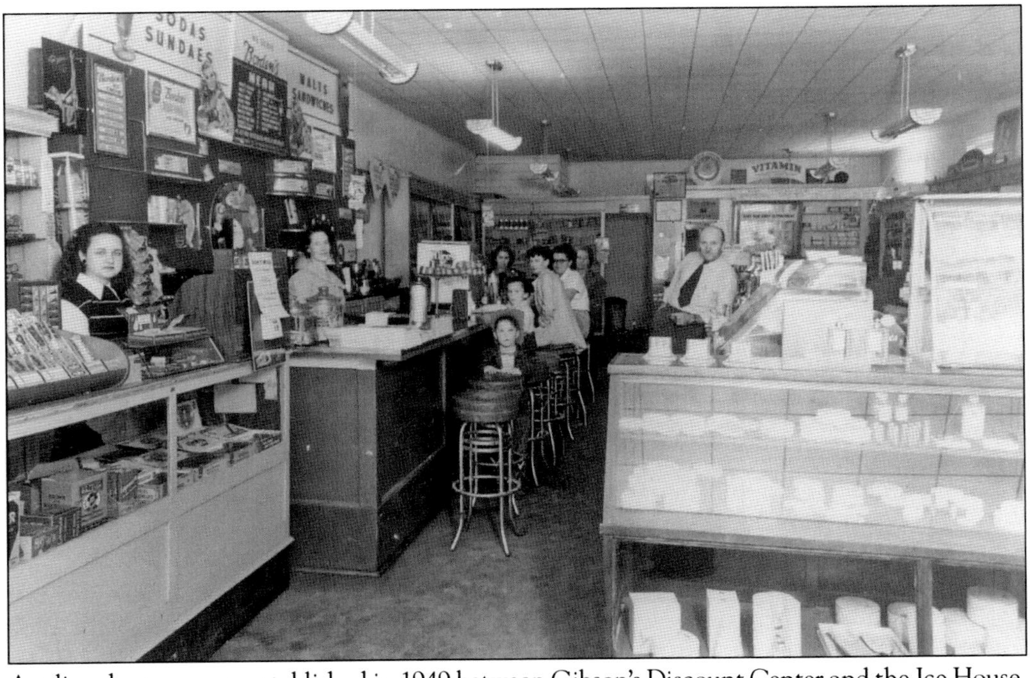

Appling drugstore was established in 1949 between Gibson's Discount Center and the Ice House. This drugstore served the public for many years. Pictured are, from left to right, Jeanine Noble, Iola Appling, Joel Morrison, Barbara Ogletree, Viola Ogletree, Billie Frances Ogletree, Estelle Cundiff, Jo Merle Morrison, and Harry Appling. (Courtesy of Neal Wooley.)

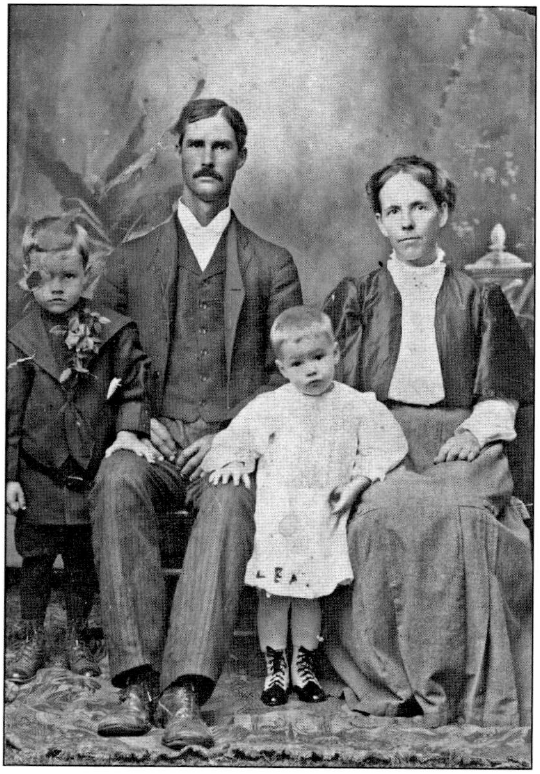

Edgar Alfonzo Robinson and his wife, Bertie Carmen, pose with two of their five children—Guy Lincoln, four, and Wilford Leonard, three. The Robinsons were early settlers and owned a construction company. They built many of the older homes in Seagoville, Crandall, and other nearby towns. Robinson built his own residence in 1906 and lived there until his death in 1953. The well he dug on his property is still there today. (Courtesy of Gwen Robinson Gaida.)

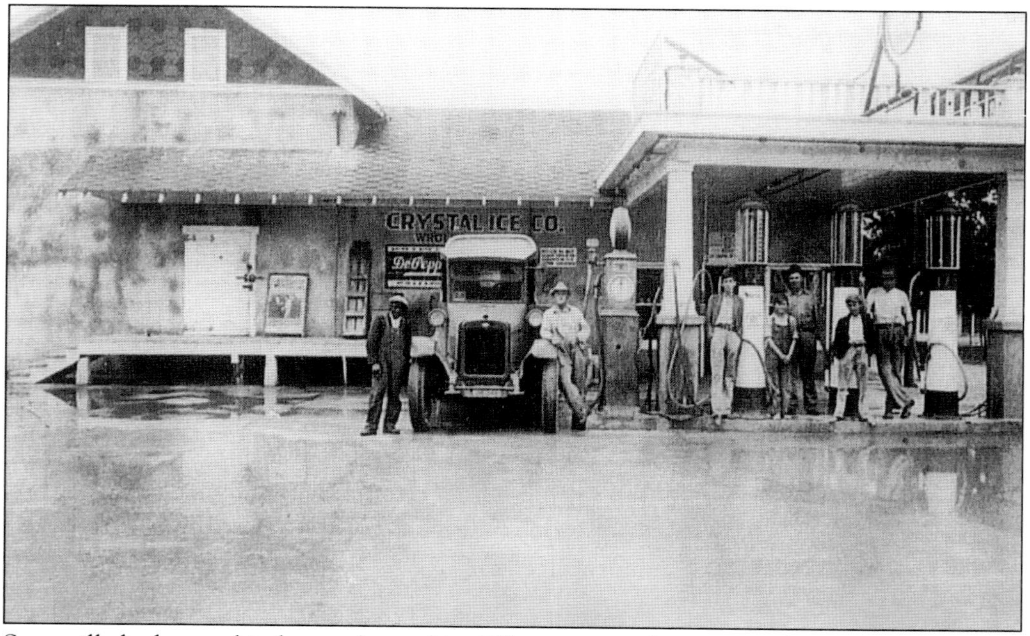

Seagoville had several icehouses located in different areas of town over the years. The first ice, though, was shipped in by train. Various known last names of owners/managers of icehouses are Garrett, Horton, Stark, Oliver, Whitworth, and Gibson. This icehouse was located on Malloy Bridge Road and Kaufman Street and remained in operation until 1982. Later part of it was demolished for the widening of Malloy Bridge Road. (Courtesy of Seagoville Library Archives.)

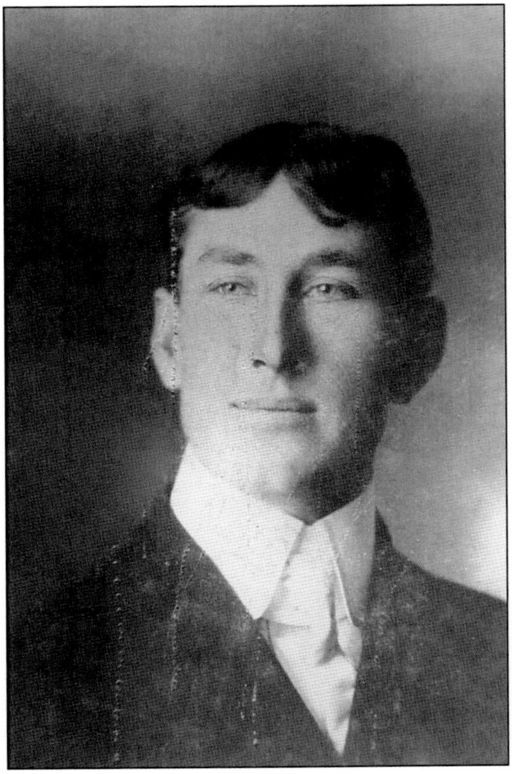

Dr. Oscar Glenn was known in the Seagoville area as the "whistling doctor." Doc Glenn was born on Stark Road to the family of Martin Glenn on October 12, 1880. He did his internship in Fort Worth, Texas, and then returned to Seagoville to practice medicine. Glenn drove a team of horses to make his house calls. In May 1907, he married Delia Cardwell. His patients sometimes paid him with eggs, chickens, and vegetables. The long hours and night calls took their toll, and he retired to farming in 1926. Glenn was also an avid hunter, stalking wolves in the Trinity bottoms with his hounds and his cronies. Dr. Glenn was a Mason for 55 years. An astute businessman, mayor, and director of Seagoville State Bank, he remained in Seagoville until his death on November 20, 1962. (Courtesy of R. L. Glenn.)

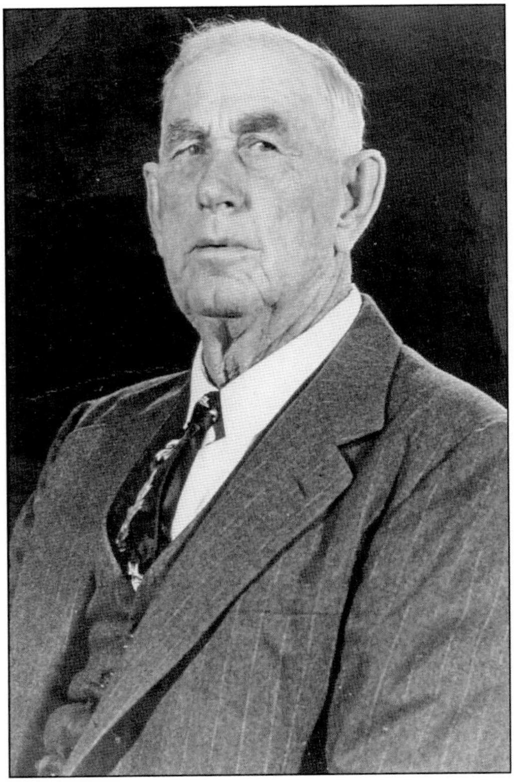

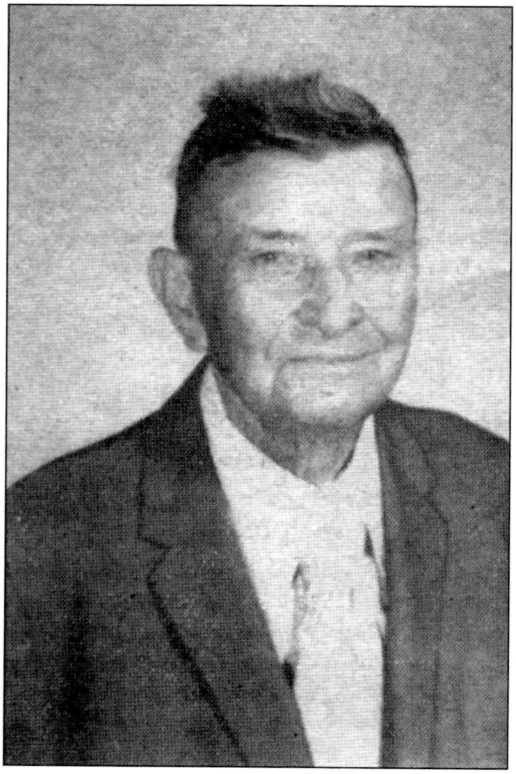

Dr. Albert Watkins was born on November 22, 1885, in Kemp. He received his bachelor of arts degree from Trinity University and his medical degree from Southwestern Medical College. Watkins married Kathleen Halbert in 1914 and moved to Seagoville in 1916. Often the only payment he received was vegetables, fruit, or meat. He served on the board of school trustees for five years and was a physician for 48 years. (Courtesy of Neal Wooley.)

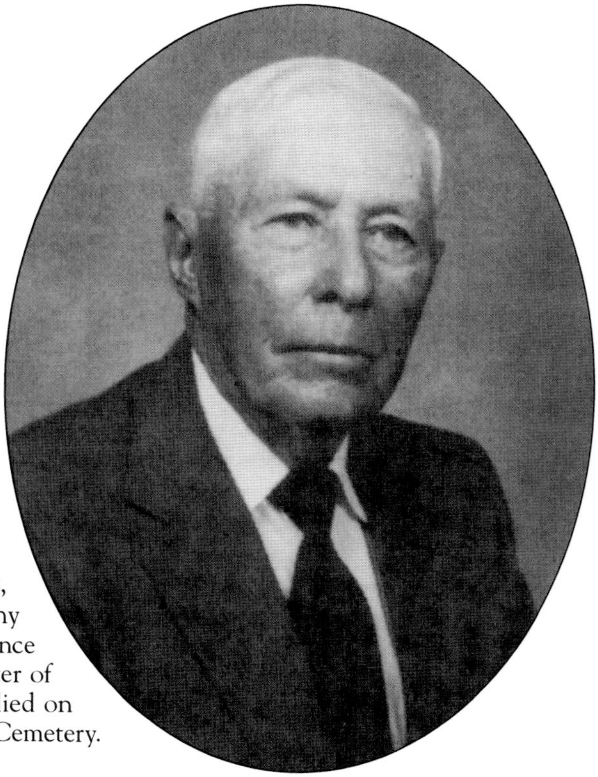

Clarence O. Bruce was born January 7, 1891, to W. C. and Edith Bruce. He had one brother and married Ethel Randerson Cardwell in 1923. She had two daughters, Ovis Cardwell (Ballard) and Dorothy Cardwell (Maroney). Bruce served in France during World War I and was postmaster of Seagoville from 1933 until 1958. He died on February 24, 1981, and is buried in Lee Cemetery. (Courtesy of Neal Wooley.)

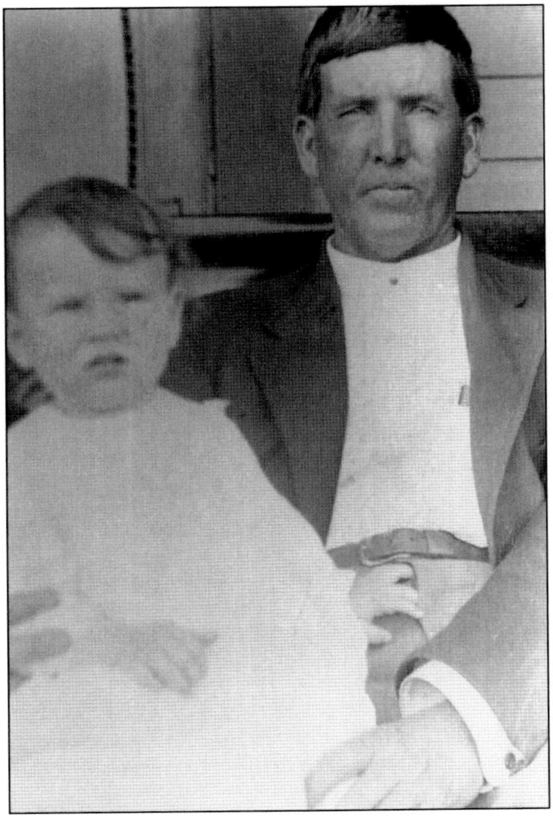

William M. Cardwell is pictured with his son Charles Wesley Cardwell in 1903. William owned the Cardwell Mercantile store that was located on Railroad Avenue between Elm Street and Malloy Bridge Road. The store faced the Texas and New Orleans Railroad tracks. (Courtesy of R. L. Glenn.)

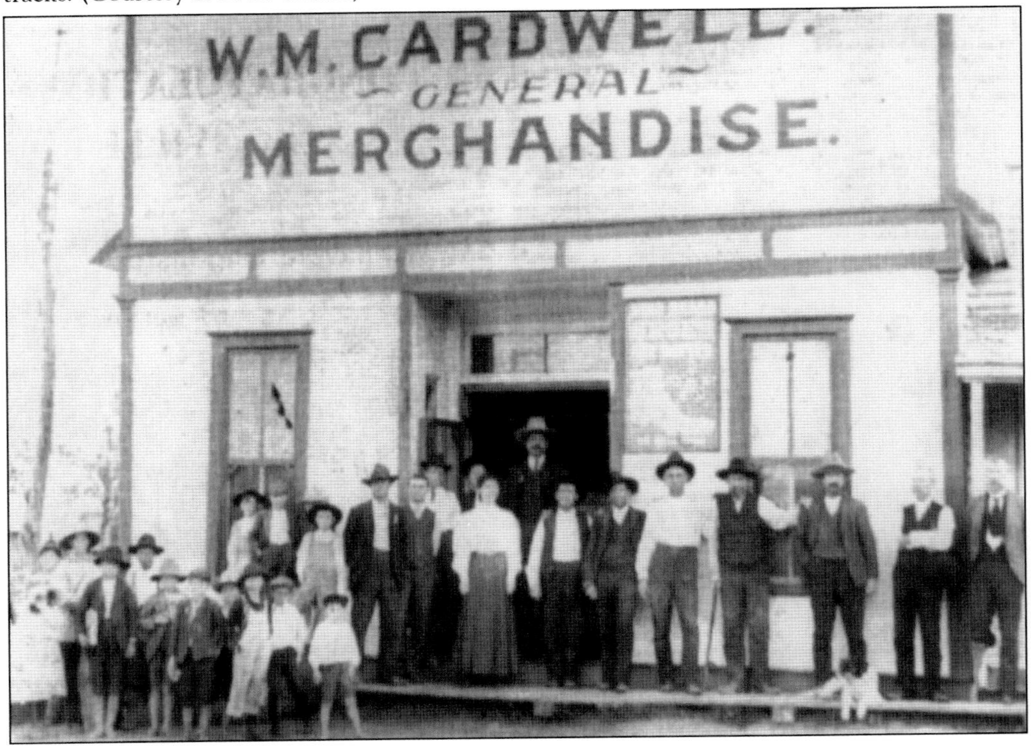

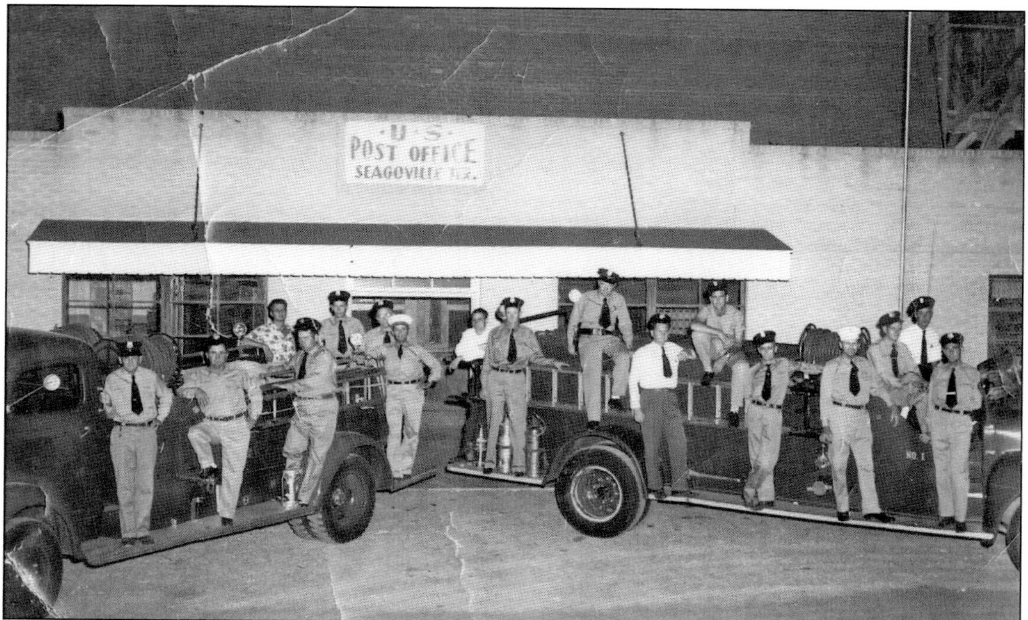

Richard N. Carder was appointed chief of the Seagoville Volunteer Fire Department in the 1940s and served until 1956. There were six volunteers—Weldon Dickey, Carl Thrasher, A. C. Tucker, Oscar Tucker, Fred Byrne, and Jack Ballard. In 1951, other volunteers were Richard Rucks, Lester Blackman, Homer Lee Rucks Sr., Roy Hitt, C. W. Rucks, Harold Altom, Rob Salters, Roy Lee Heard, Lewis Riley, William Rucks, I. W. Owens, and Grover Grose. (Courtesy of Carol Franks.)

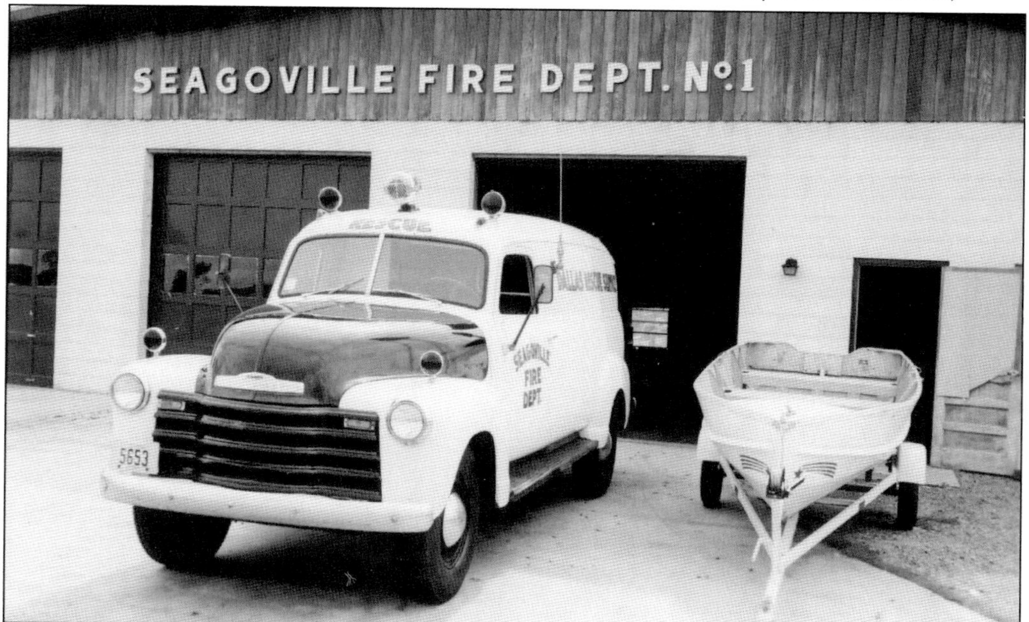

In 1957, the volunteer fire department moved to a new location on Watson Street. Firemen did the framing on the facility. In 1964, the first salaried firefighter was George Melaun. He later became chief, and three other men were hired. In 1979, there were six hired firemen, a chief, and nine volunteers. Their equipment has been frequently upgraded and modernized. (Courtesy of Neal Wooley.)

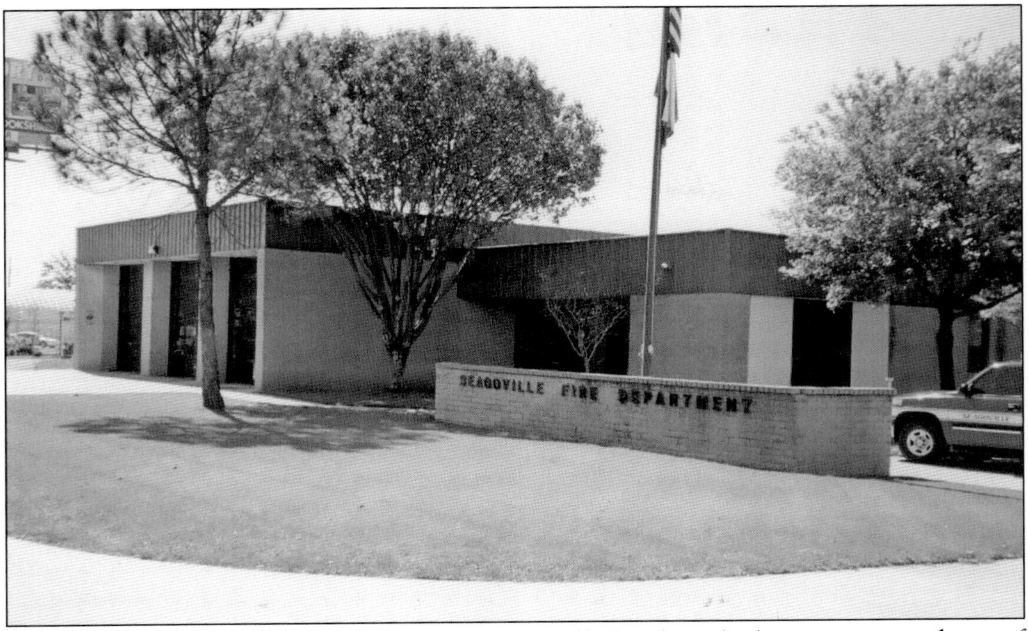

The present fire station at Highway 175 and Seagoville Road was built at an estimated cost of $20,000 and dedicated in 1980. It has a three-bay apparatus room, living quarters, day room, radio room, and an office. From working with a Model T Ford in years past to present-day modern equipment, dedicated employees and volunteers have made the Seagoville Fire Department one of the best. (Courtesy of Carol Franks.)

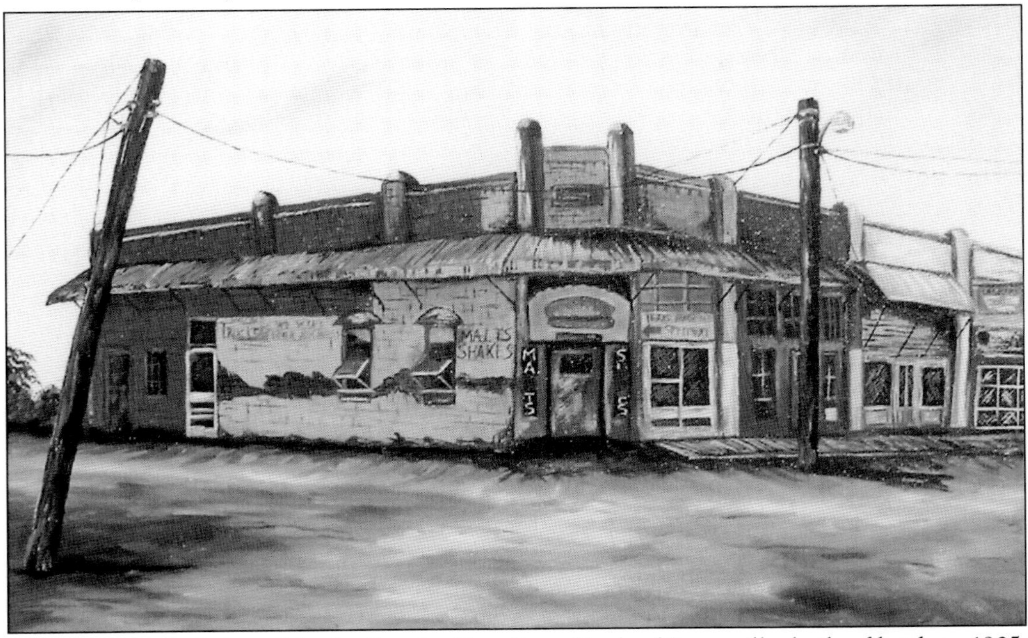

This painting by JoAnn Woodruff is the First State Bank of Seagoville, built of brick in 1905. Seagoville had another bank in that era—Farmers Guaranty Bank, established by M. B. Hawthorne in 1912. The two banks merged later as First State Bank, which closed in 1932 due to the Depression. After the bank closed, the building was used as the post office until the late 1940s or early 1950s. (Courtesy of the Phillips family.)

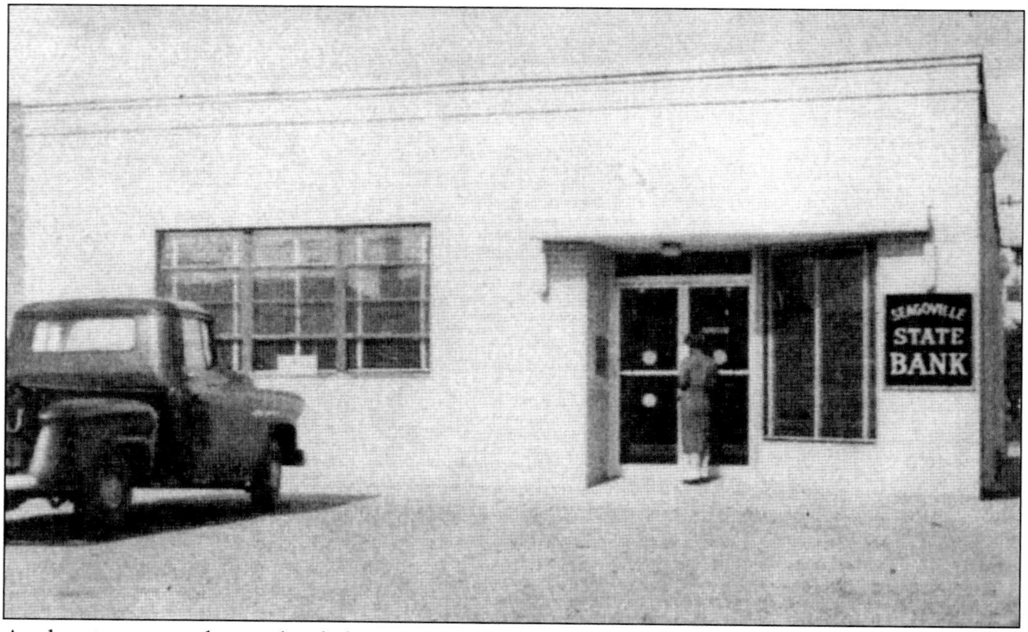

As the city was without a bank from 1932 until 1952, five prominent Seagoville citizens took an application for a bank charter to the Texas Bank Board in Austin. F. B. Fowler was added to this group and formed the first board of directors. The Seagoville State Bank opened for business on April 7 on North Kaufman Street. In 1953, M. D. Reeves purchased 51 percent of its shares and shortly after hired David King. (Courtesy of Carol Franks.)

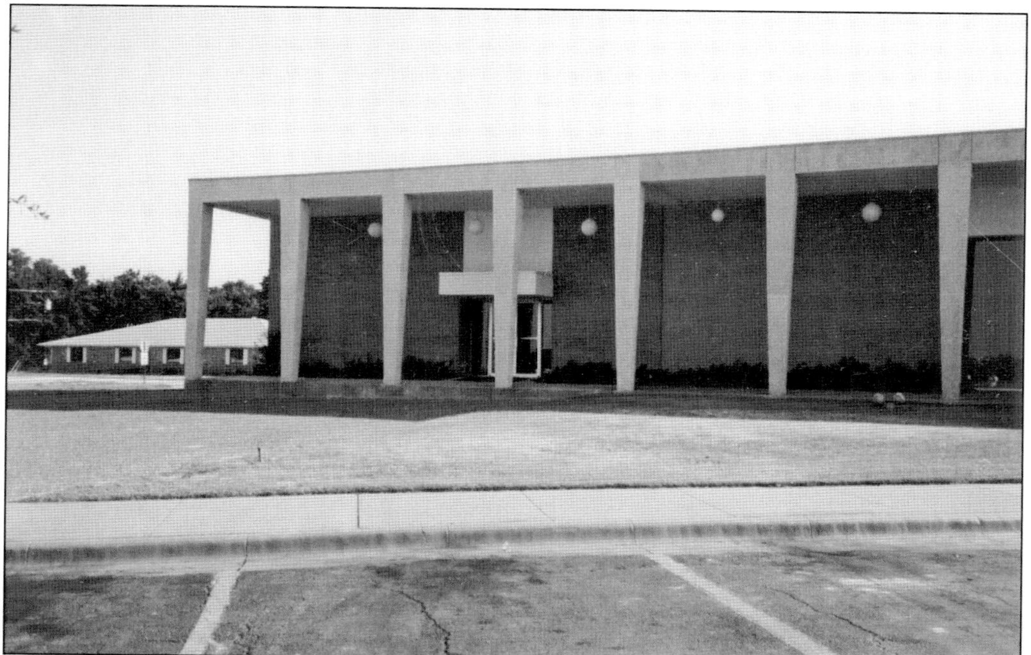

After planning and constructing a larger building because of growth, the bank moved to Highway 175 in January 1967. Since its opening, the bank has expanded twice and added a multilane drive-through facility. M. D. Reeves served as chief executive officer until his death in January 1979. (Courtesy of Carol Franks.)

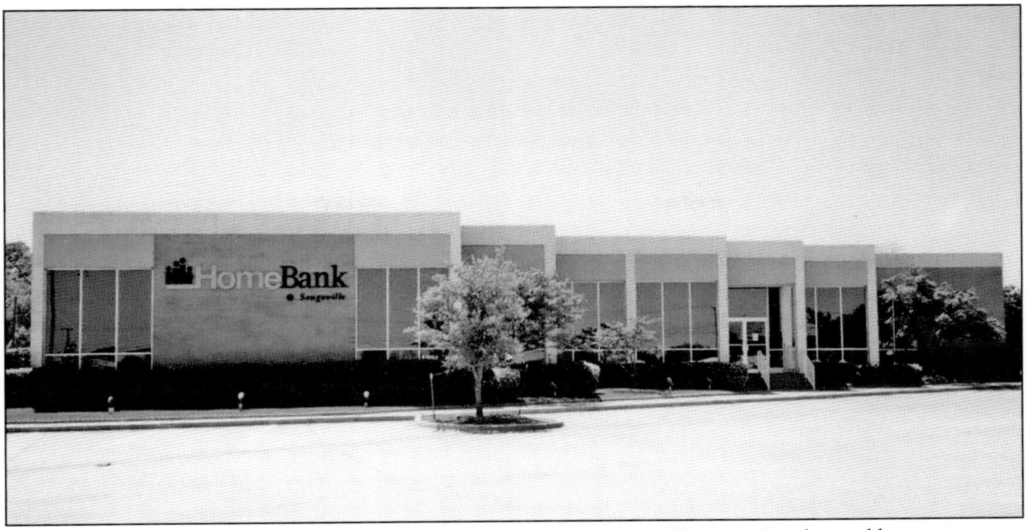

David King held different leadership roles for 35 years at Seagoville State Bank until his retirement in the spring 1989. In October 1995, Seagoville State Bank purchased Buckner State Bank, located on North Buckner and I-30. HomeBank became the new name of the combined institution in 1998. As of June 2008, HomeBank has a full-service branch in Rockwall, Texas. (Courtesy of Carol Franks.)

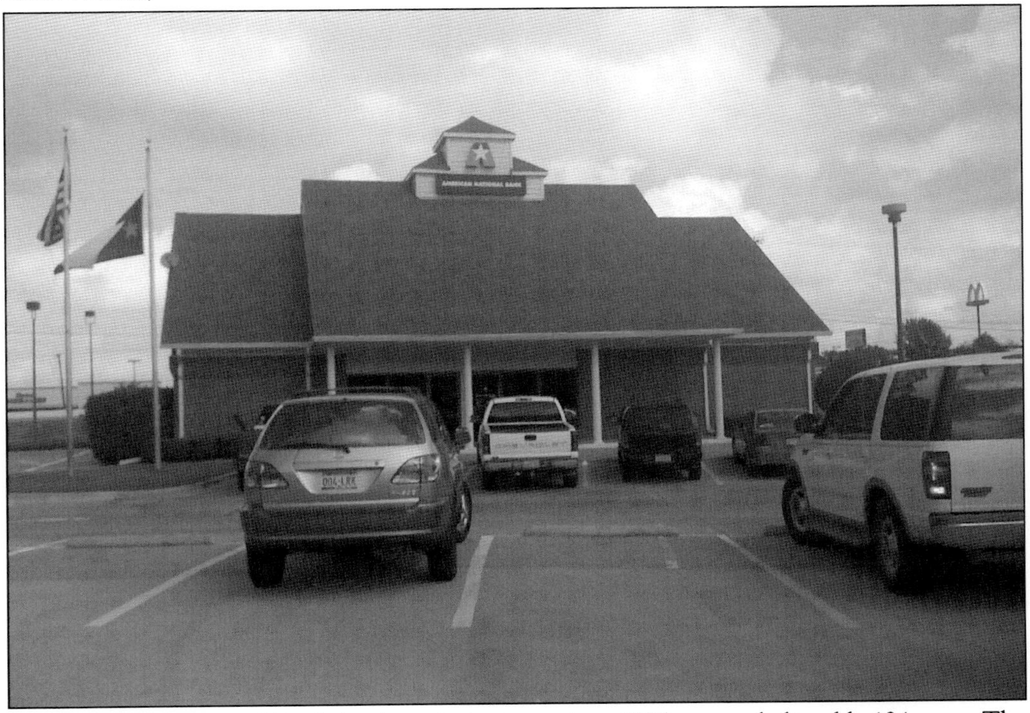

The American National Bank has been in business since 1875—an unbelievable 134 years. The original home office is in Terrell. Robert A. Hulsey is the president and chief executive officer and is a descendant of the founder. There are about 40 branches throughout North Texas. Debra McClellan is president of the Seagoville, pictured above, and Crandall branches. Guinn Godwin is the senior vice president of Kaufman and has been with the bank since 1952. (Courtesy of the Phillips family.)

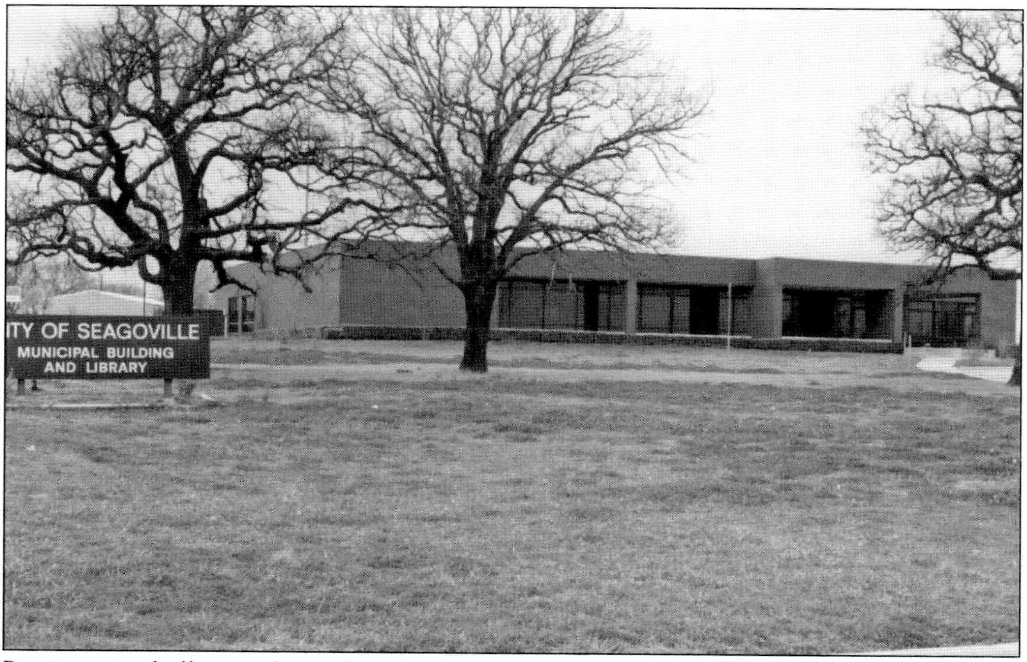

Previous city halls were located in the downtown area of Seagoville on West Elm Street for many years. A new municipal building was erected and dedicated in March 1975 at Highway 175 and Farmers Road. The building housed the city hall, police substation, and the present library. (Courtesy of Carol Franks.)

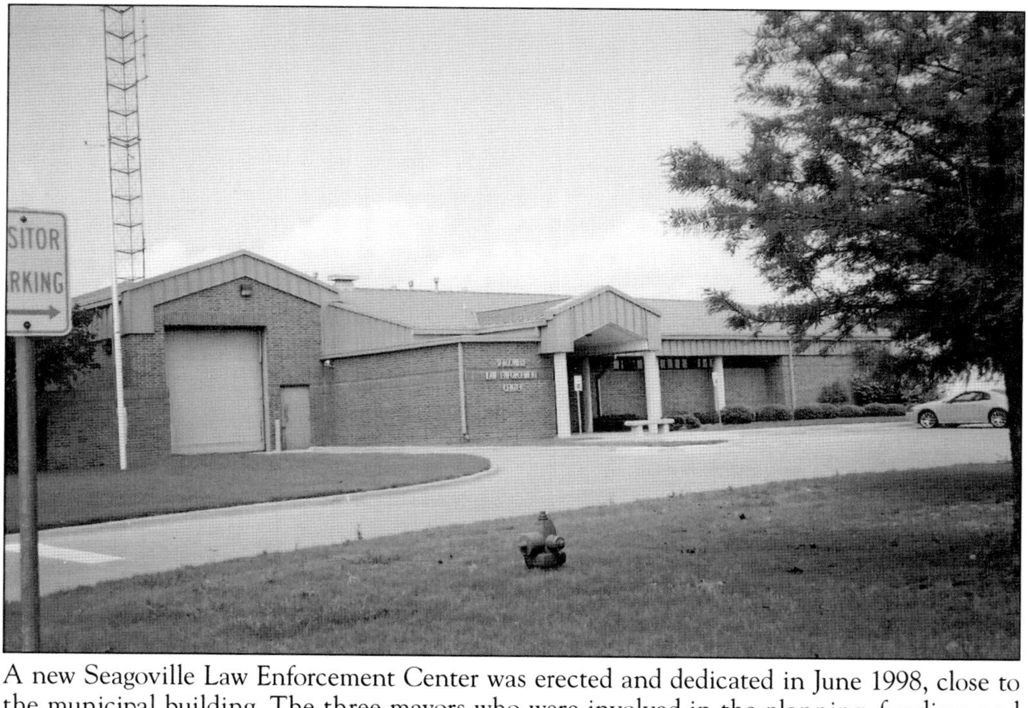

A new Seagoville Law Enforcement Center was erected and dedicated in June 1998, close to the municipal building. The three mayors who were involved in the planning, funding, and constructing of the center were Neal Wooley, Lonnie Hopkins, and Calvin Travers. (Courtesy of Carol Franks.)

Four

Farming

The Seagoville area has been an excellent area for agriculturists for centuries. Early settlers found the upland area very suitable for farms. They first settled in the Cross Timbers as they could cut the trees for their homes, clearing land for cultivation in the process. There were also areas of the Blackland Prairies and the Grand Prairies but pioneers found the sandy land of the Cross Timbers more to their liking as it was easier to till. The flood plains of the East Fork and Trinity Rivers were very fertile, heavily covered by timber and subject to floods; they became more important as farm land after levees were built. It is reported that in 1908, on one occasion, not a drop of rain fell in Seagoville, but residents awoke to a flood of the Trinity that came up halfway to the top of Cobb Hill on present-day Malloy Bridge Road. At this time, only a small levee on Parson's Slough was in existence. This had been constructed using horses, mules, and slip scrapers under the supervision of C. C. Cobb to protect his 1,000 acres of alfalfa plus 1,000 acres devoted to cotton, corn, and other crops and hundreds of acres in timberland range for cattle. This farm, at the time, was the largest in Texas. Cobb, a Dallas lawyer, assisted many in the farming business. There are numerous surnames of present residents included in some of Cobb's ledgers, including Hawthorne, Miller, Hurt, Jones, Lawson, and Ballard. It is said Cobb had several barns scattered over his fields. When the water started to recede and the barns opened, thousands of bales started downriver. It was reported that snakes, coons, opossums, and skunks were on top of the bales.

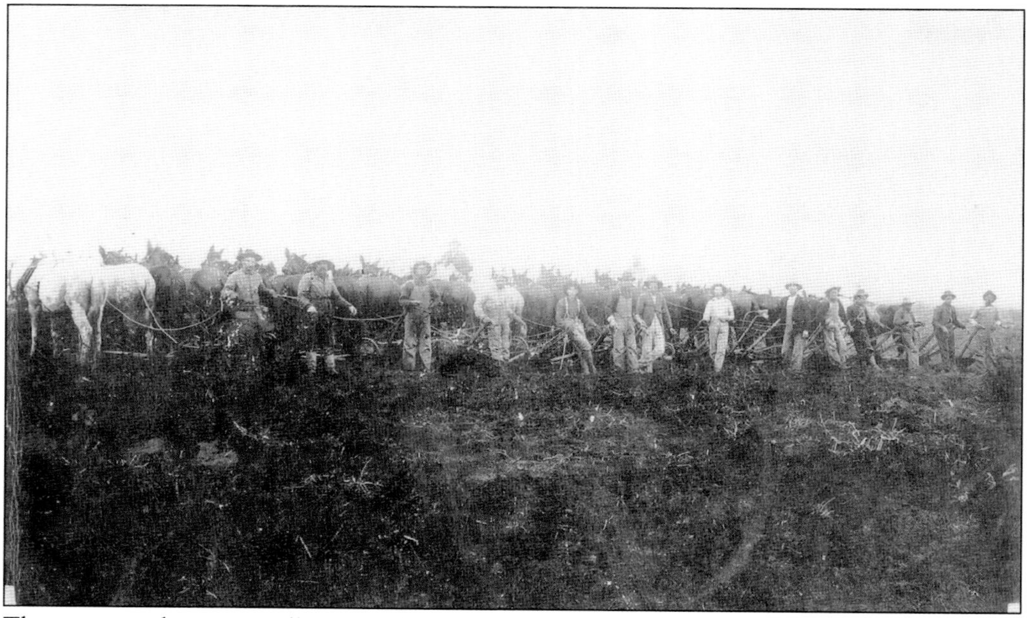

The teams in this picture illustrates the increase in the size of farming operations after the land was cleared in 1910. Frank Crouch was in charge of the alfalfa mowing crew. C. C. Cobb utilized county prisoners for some of his labor. They cut and hauled wood, made ax handles, plowed, hauled hay, and performed many other tasks. They transported cordwood to boxcars for shipping and camped on the farm. (Courtesy of Delta Mathis.)

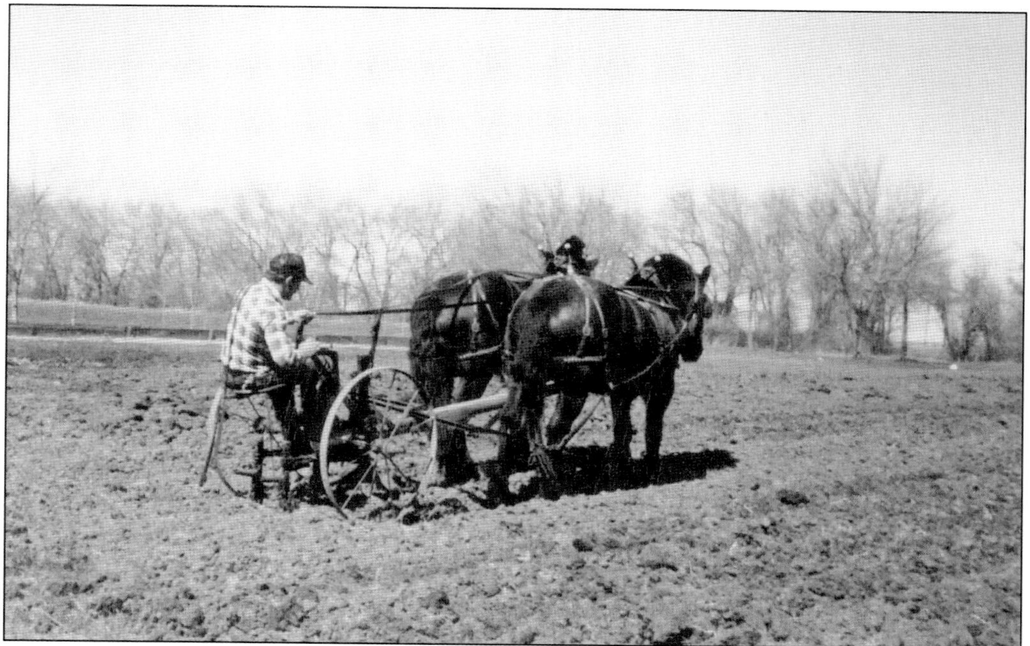

Delta Mathis illustrates the type of farming done in the early days of Seagoville, when subsistence farmers tilled small acreages devoted to cotton, corn, and oats. There were chickens, milk cows, and hogs. With the construction of a levee by L. A. Price in the 1920s, larger, more commercial farms evolved. Price brought many workers with names familiar today—Maroney, Orrell, Ballantine, Pollan, Smith, Taylor, Waldrum, and Les Pharr. (Courtesy of Delta Mathis.)

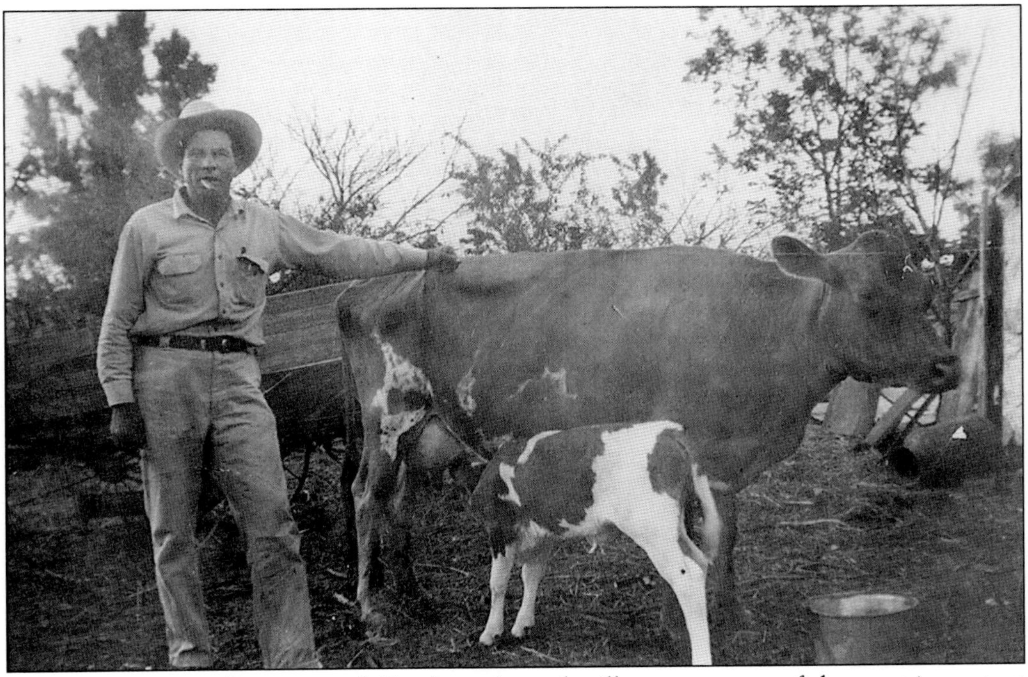

L. D. Gragsone's milk cow raised 17 calves. A good milk cow was one of the most important possessions of a subsistence farmer, as well as most of the small-town homesteads. It has been said that many of the early Seagoville families would run their milk cow on the free-range area in the Seagoville bottoms. They were trained to come up at morning and at night to be milked. (Courtesy of Floy Ballantine.)

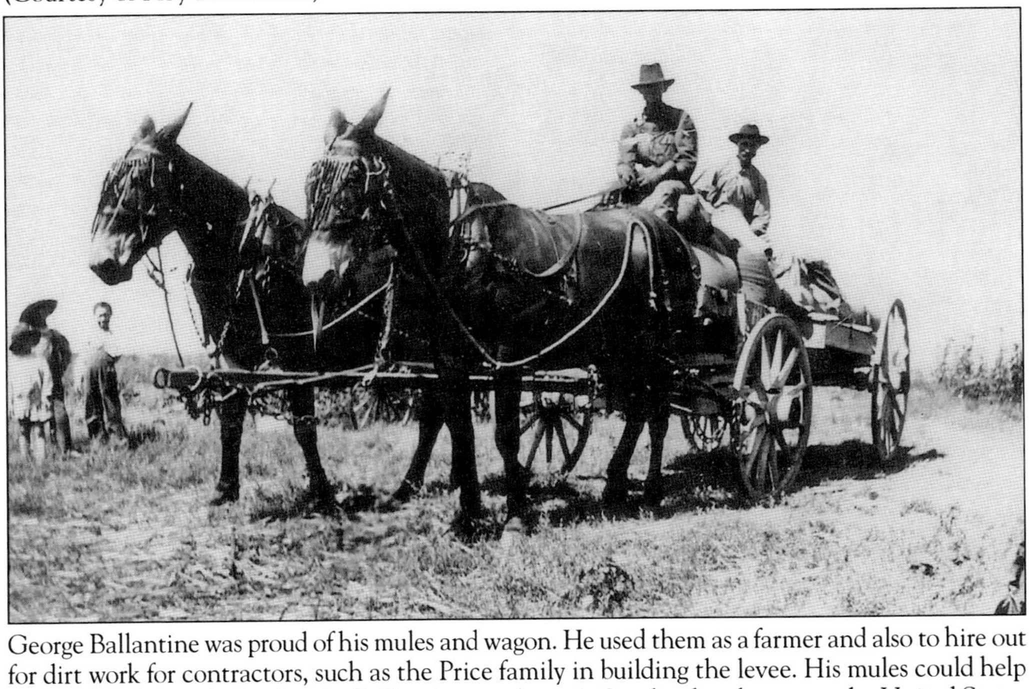

George Ballantine was proud of his mules and wagon. He used them as a farmer and also to hire out for dirt work for contractors, such as the Price family in building the levee. His mules could help him make a living for his family. Ballantine was born in Scotland and came to the United States in 1883 when he was 19. His work on the levee was in the 1920s. (Courtesy of Floy Ballantine.)

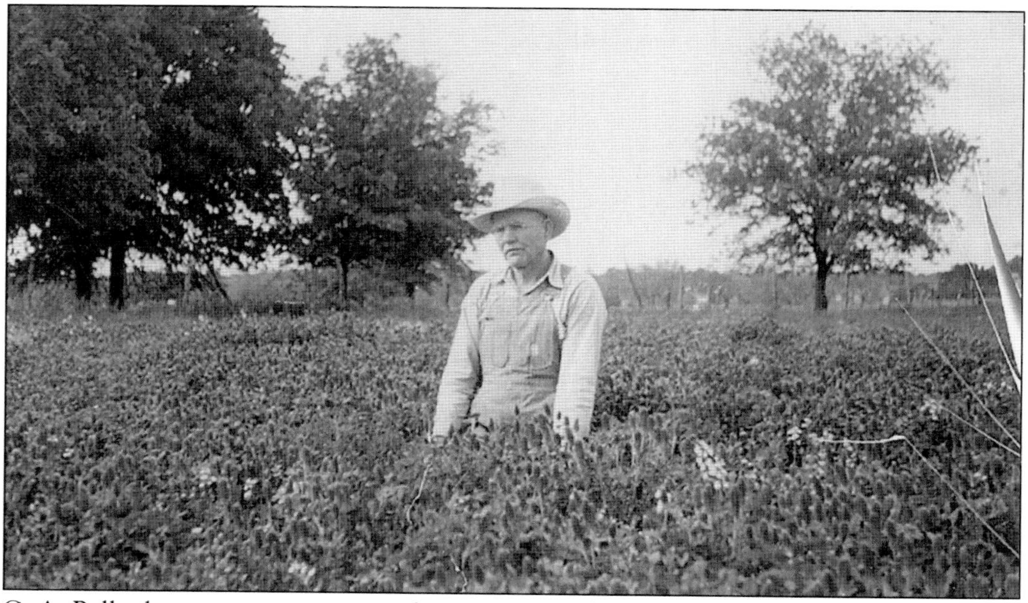

C. A. Ballard was a very progressive farmer. A rugged individual, he was born in a house on Malloy Bridge Road owned by his father and known more recently as the Cobb home. As a two year old, he fell out of a second-story window and broke his arm. Ballard and his descendants are agriculturists. He is shown here with his excellent stand of red clover that was planted as an experiment conducted by the Farm Bureau. (Courtesy of Kathryn Ballard.)

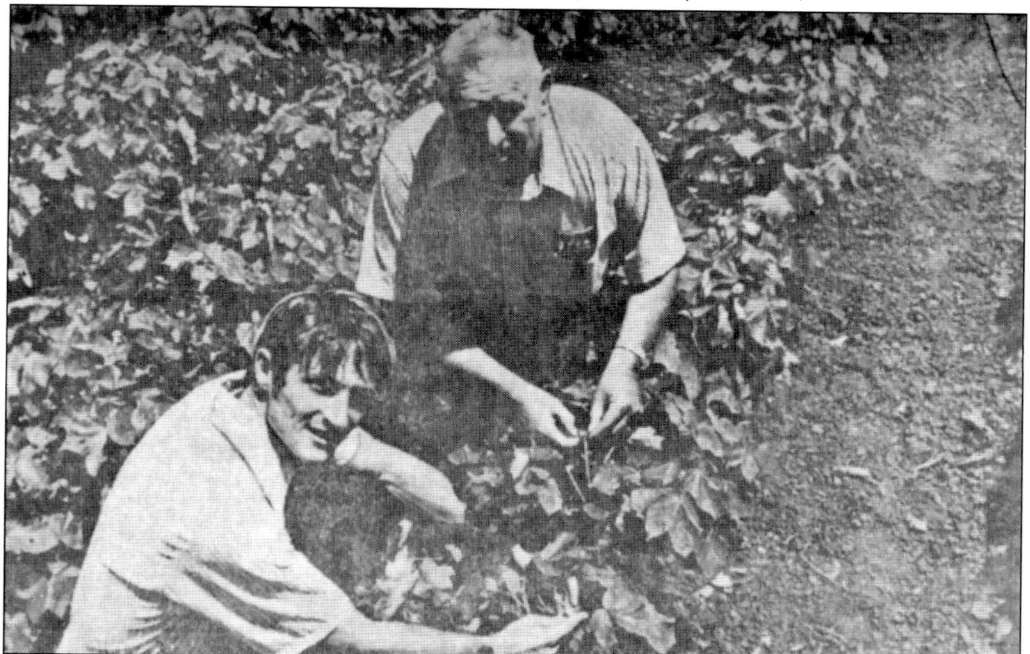

Reagan Glenn is one of a group of many outstanding farmers from this area. Familiar names are the Hawthorns in the East Fork bottoms, Floyd Pollan, Fran Mathis, Ollie Waldrum, Howard and Ted Price, Perry Tabor, George Willis, Dr. O. Glenn, and C. A. Ballard. Cotton was king, with alfalfa and milo coming on strong later. Cantaloupes were important from 1958 to 1968. (Courtesy of the Wooley family.)

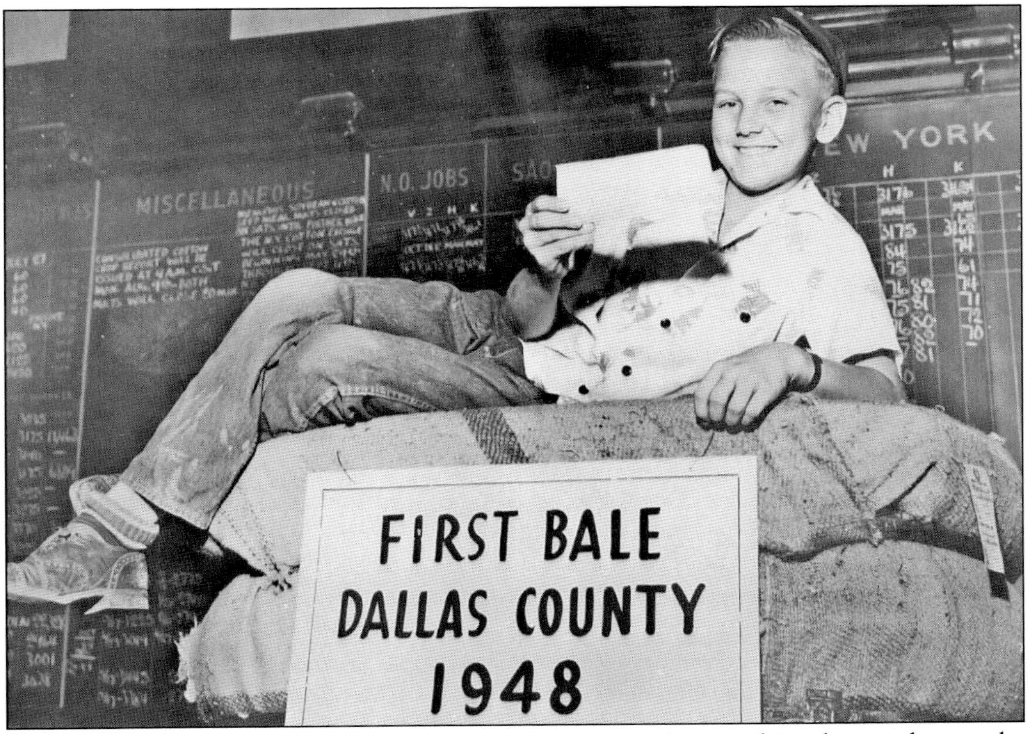

It takes outstanding farmers to develop outstanding farmers. John David Smith started out in the drought of the 1950s. He was recognized by the Dallas Junior Chamber of Commerce in 1963 as the outstanding young farmer of Dallas County. Speer Waldrum won the same honor the next year. In 1948, Waldrum, at age nine, won the award for having the first bale of cotton that year. Waldrum's son continues to farm. (Courtesy of Jerry Waldrum.)

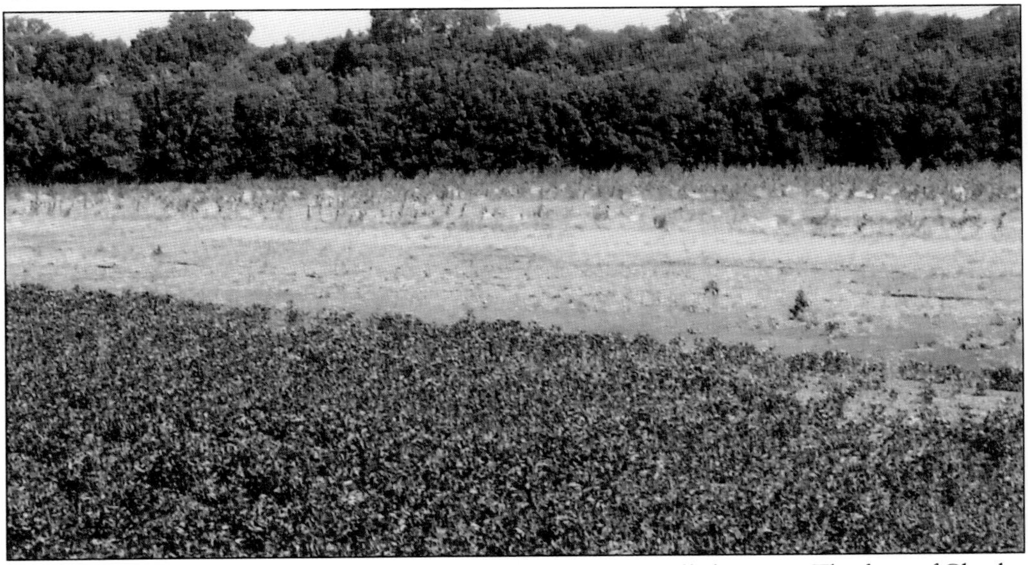

This picture illustrates a common problem in the fertile Seagoville bottoms. The farm of Charles and Brock Beach shows an area of their soybean field that has been under water. The Beaches are assisted by Keith Davis, who grew up with the family. The Beaches are top-of-the-line farmers as were their predecessors. (Courtesy of Wayne Phillips.)

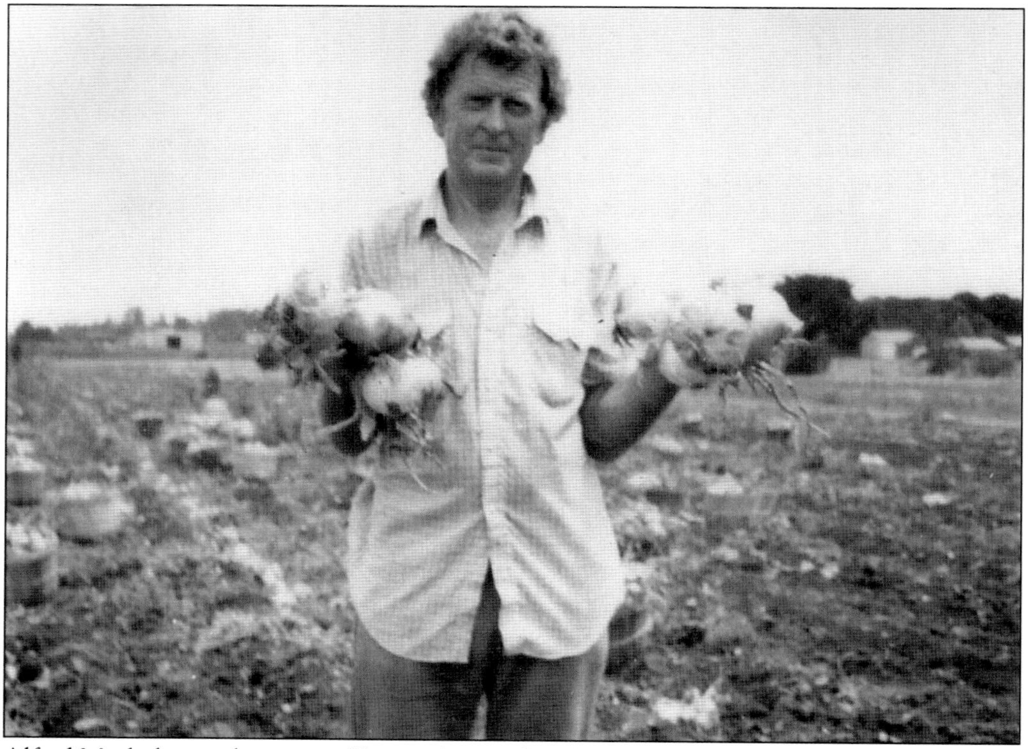

Alfred Machala stands in one of his gardens with a display of onions. It appears he is pleading for rain although his furrows indicate they are being irrigated. The Machalas were one of several families engaged in raising vegetables largely for the Dallas market. In this group were Ernest Walton, Tommy Hoops, the Ryer family, Jack Hall, the Kollers, and the Landwermeyers. The Kollers, after gardening in the White Rock bottoms, moved to Seagoville where they produced many fine vegetables. Vegetable farming was a very competitive business. Grocery chains, wholesalers, and farmers' markets were customers. The Hoops only sold at farmers' markets. (Courtesy of Wayne Phillips.)

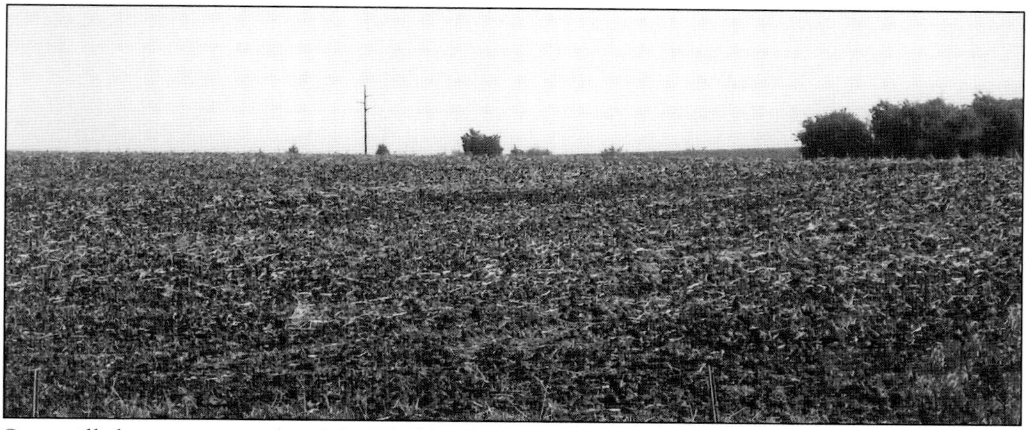

Seagoville has areas considered the Blackland Prairies. These are upland soils and have much more clay than the bottomlands. The more common soil series are the Houston and Crockett. When the first settlers arrived, these prairies were covered with grasses so tall that a horseman could barely be seen. These grasses were big and little bluestem, Indian grass, and switch. (Courtesy of Wayne Phillips.)

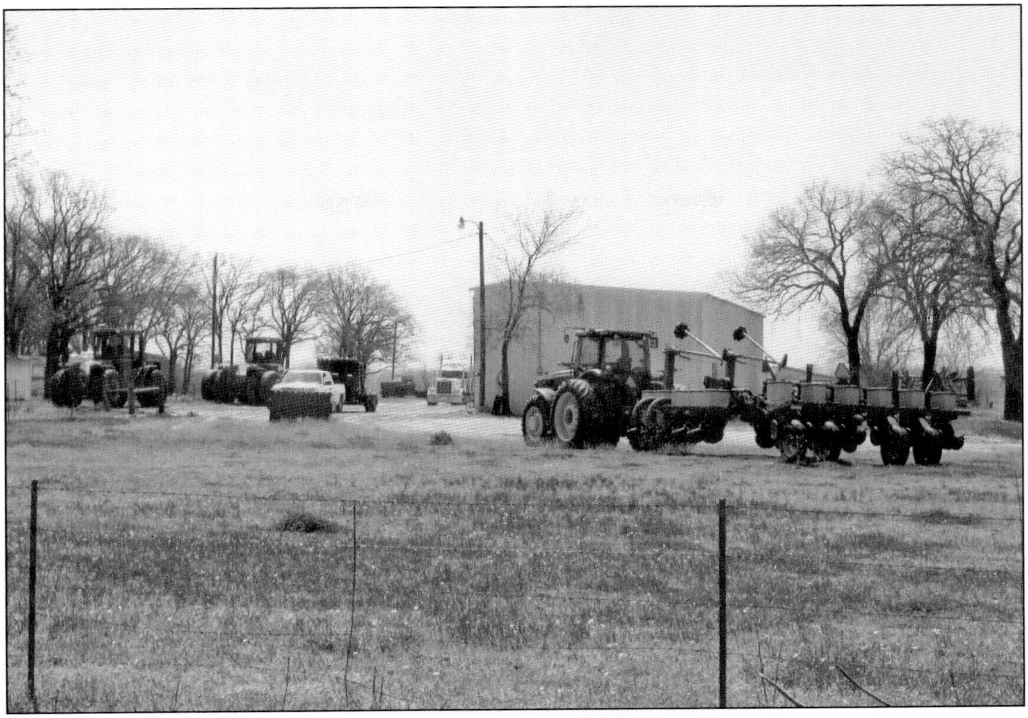

This photograph shows some of Greg Waldrum's farm equipment and illustrates the great expense of farming. Waldrum is a third-generation farmer. (Courtesy of Wayne Phillips.)

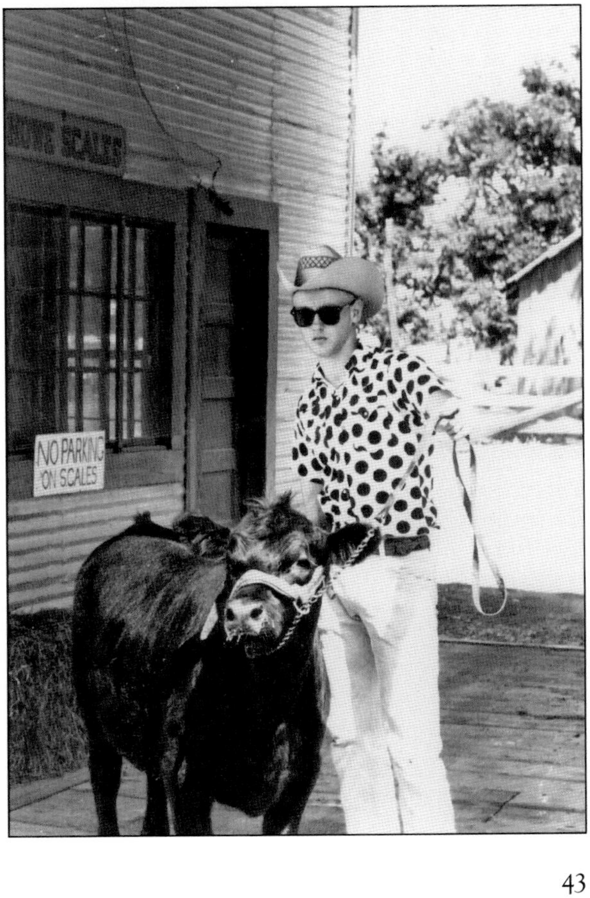

Mike Thomas was a city boy who made a greater impact on the agriculture industry than most. He raised sheep as a vocational agricultural student and caught a scramble calf at Houston. He studied feedlot management at Texas A&M University. Thomas became manager of several feedlots, buying and selling more cattle in one day than anyone in national history. (Courtesy of Wayne Phillips.)

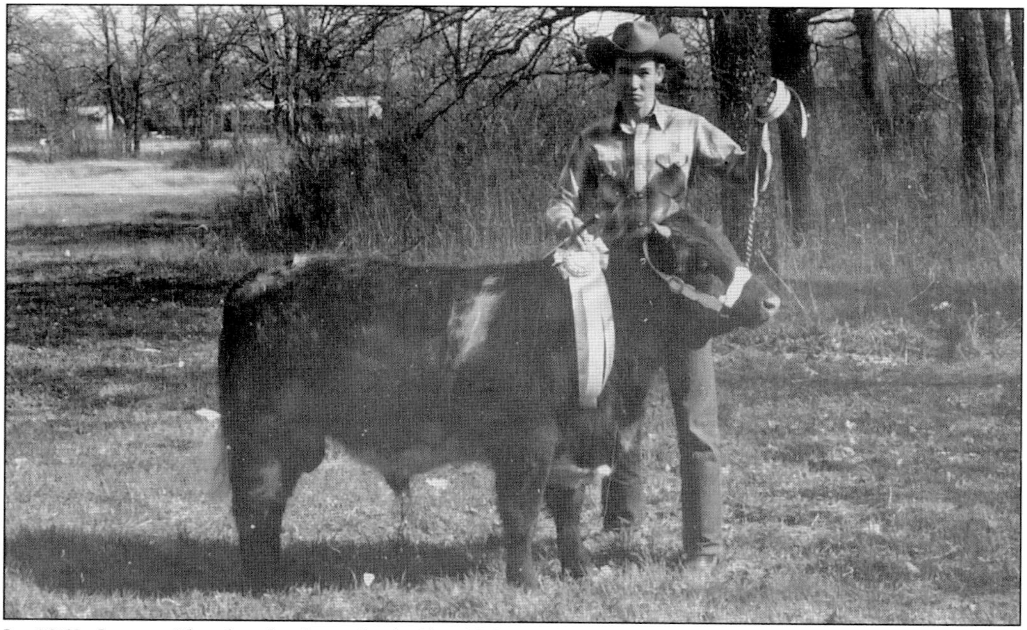

In 1962, Jimmy Shepherd selected a bull calf from the family herd of Shorthorns. He exhibited this calf successfully at the local show. The next year he decided to take his yearling bull to the Central Texas Shorthorn show and sale. On account of Jimmy's age, Michael Martin, a cousin, accompanied Jimmy to the show. Jimmy won the show and had the top selling bull. (Courtesy of Wayne Phillips.)

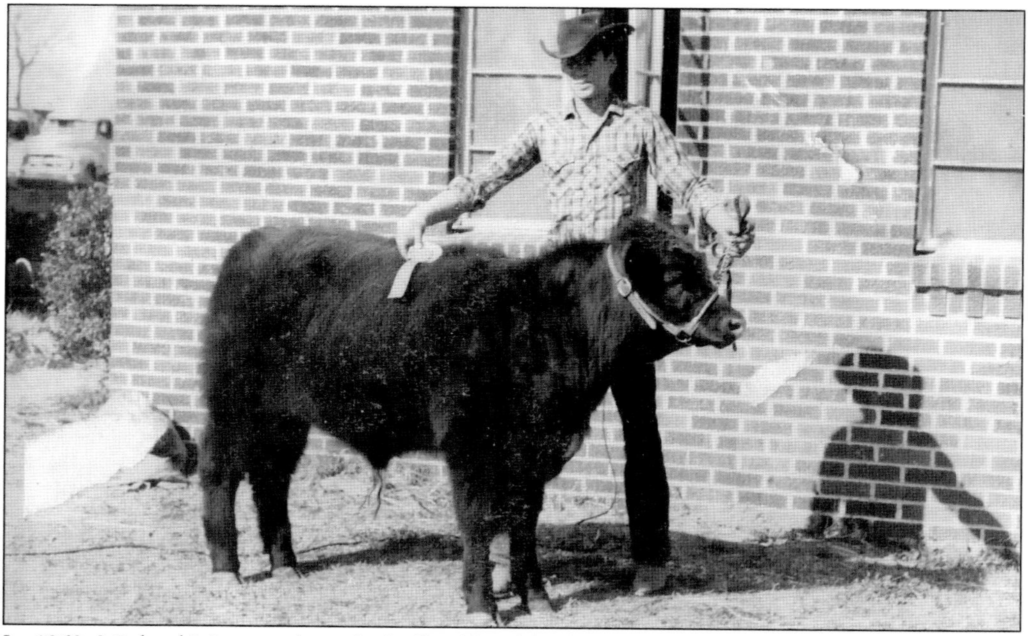

In 1962, Michael Martin selected a bull calf and heifer from the Leo McGuiness herd. He won his class at the state fair with the heifer and exhibited his bull calf successfully at the local show in 1963. He decided in 1964 to take his yearling bull to the Central Texas Shorthorn show and sale. Jimmy Shepherd went with Michael to the show, where Michael won and had the top seller. (Courtesy of Wayne Phillips.)

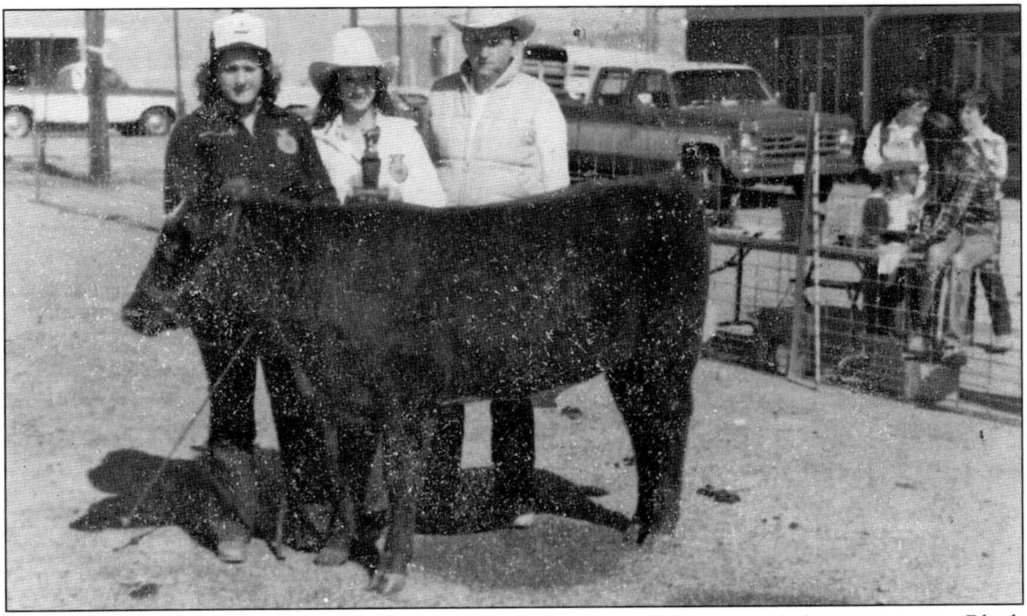

In 1980, Melanie Smith is showing a heifer from the Smith farm. The Smith farm now raises Black Baldy cows. Herds of beef cattle within the city limits include those of R. A. Hall, the Shepards, the Kirbys, the Phillips, and the Kollers. Jack Glenn has cattle from Seagoville to Clarksville. The East Fork bottoms have large herds, including those of Bob Mitchell, the Hunt Trust with Richard Broddock, the Binghams 7L, and the Risingers 3C. (Courtesy of Wayne Phillips.)

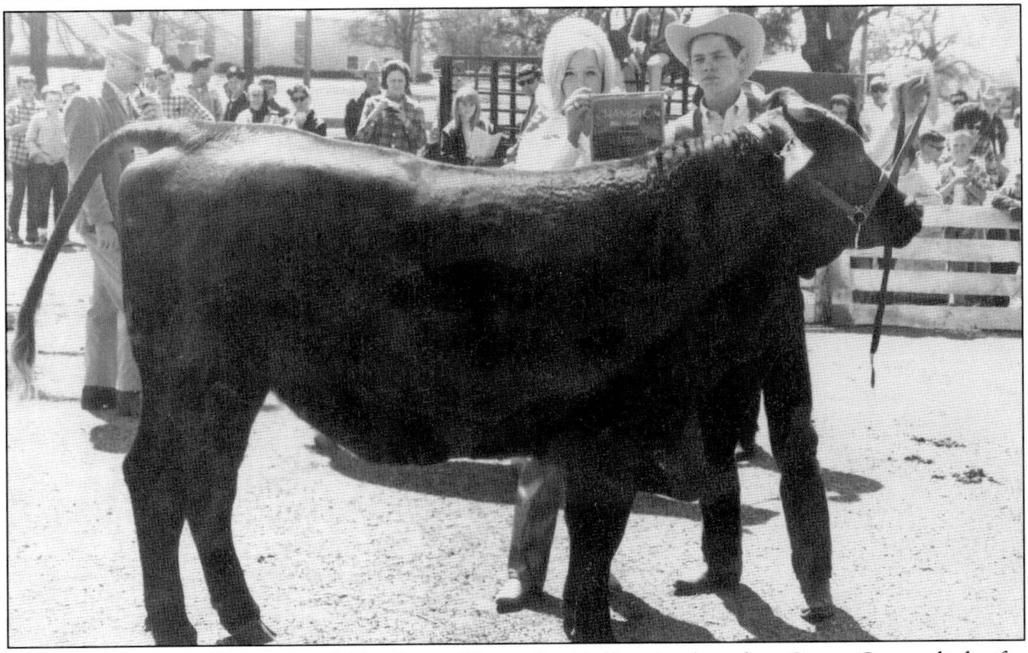

Pictured are Jim Ballantine and Charlotte Glenn. Jim Ballantine bought a Santa Gertrudis heifer in 1959. He showed her successfully and later acquired more Santa Gertrudis and increased his herd. Ballentine went to East Texas State University, graduated, and took a job teaching vocational agriculture in Dell City, where he leased a ranch over the state line in New Mexico. He later moved to Clarksville and is now in the car business. (Courtesy of Wayne Phillips.)

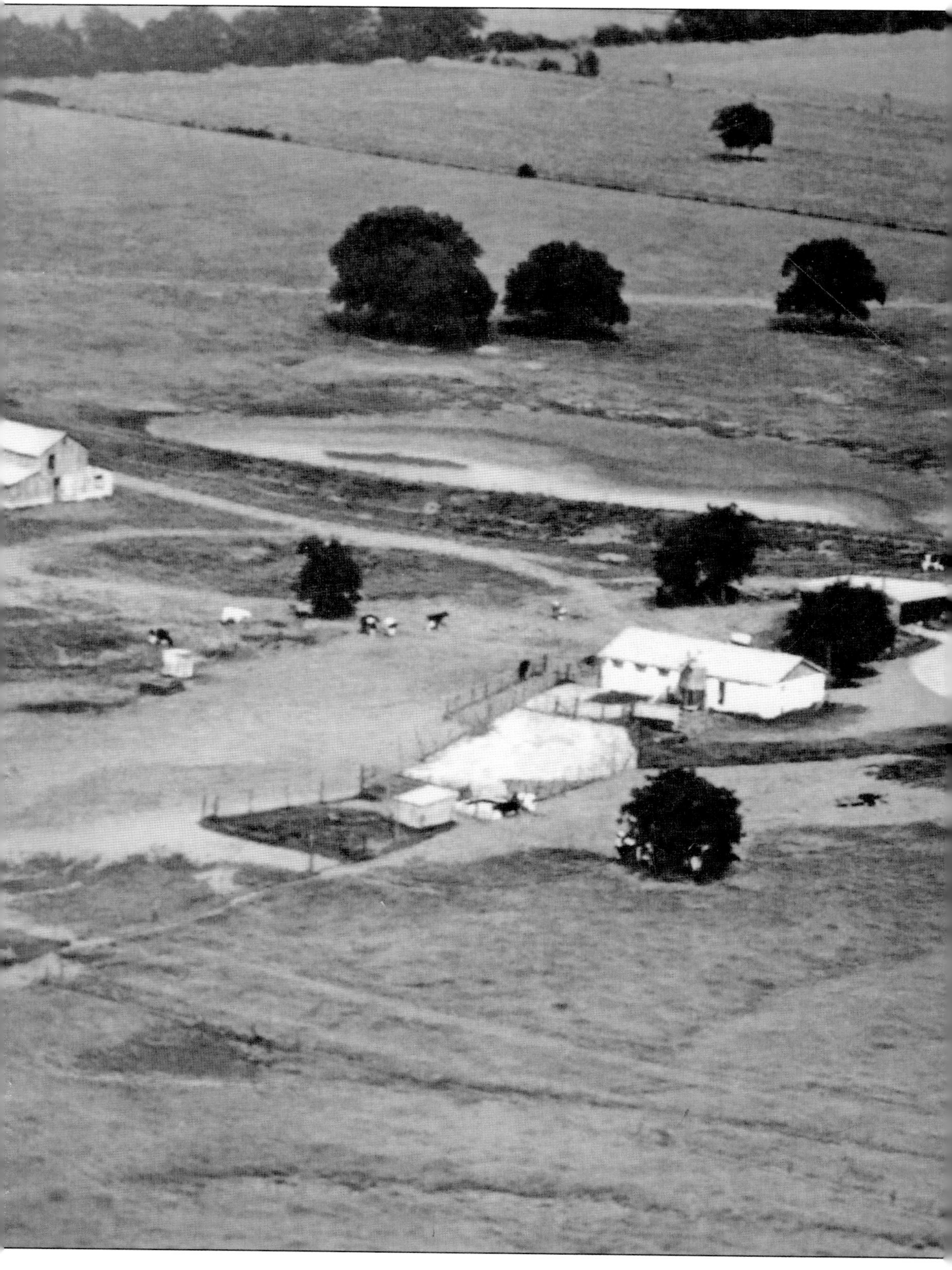

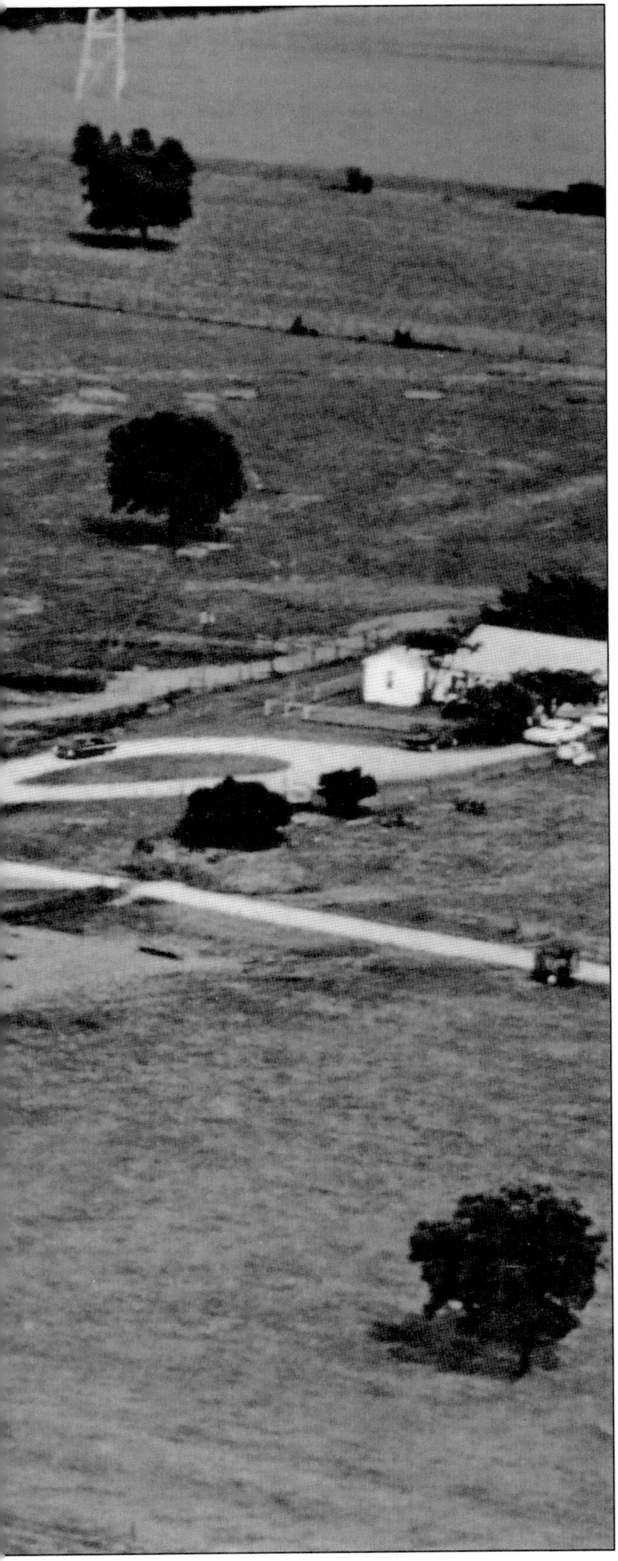

This photograph was taken in 1955 and shows the Gene Miller and C. L. Wilson dairies. They were across Hanes Road from one another. Wilson had partnered with John W. Carpenter. It was said that Wilson was the only person to ever get ahead of Carpenter in a trade. Both were Grade A dairies. Jack Wilson says everyone dreaded electricity outages since they had to hand milk. Some folks dread hand milking one or two head. (Courtesy of Wayne Phillips.)

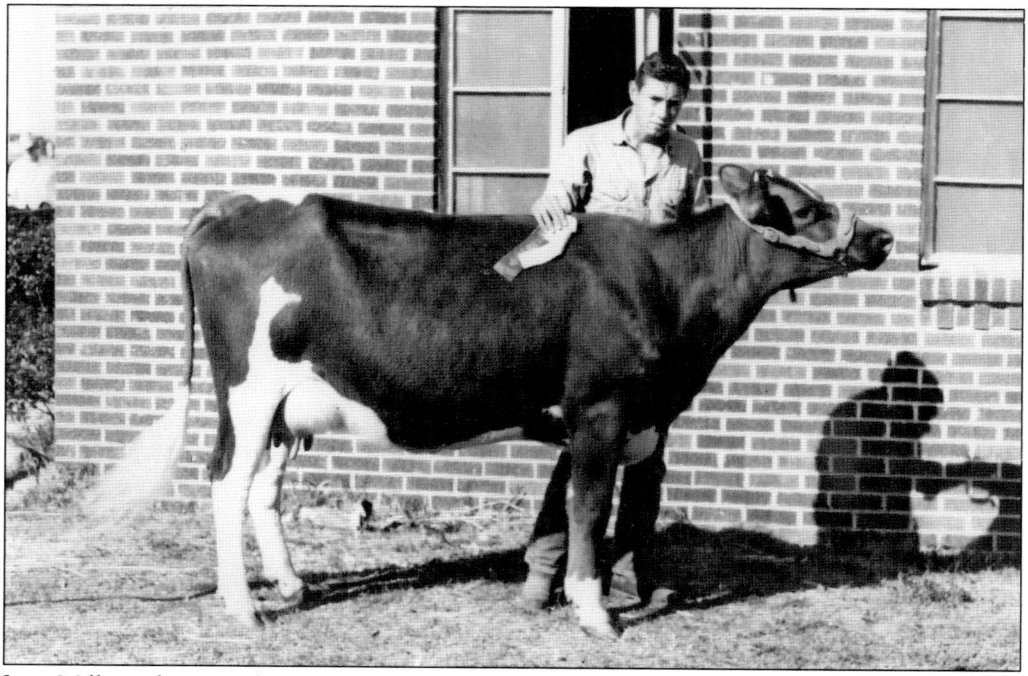

Jerry Miller is shown with one of the many good cows the Millers had. Jerry continued running the dairy for a time after his father, Gene, retired. Jerry is still interested in the cows. Other area dairies included one across from the Landesses on Bois D'arc Road that was established by Granville Rives's father. It was operated for a time by Buddy Jenkins and his father. (Courtesy of Wayne Phillips.)

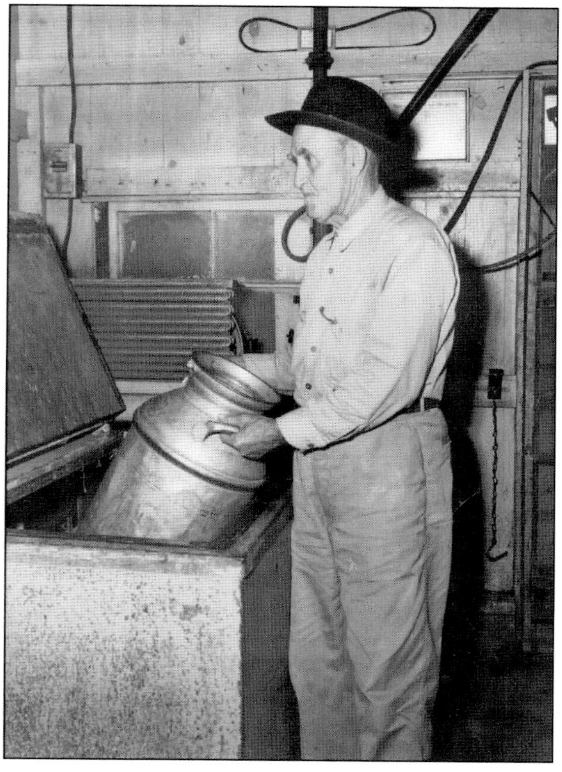

Monroe "Mun" Thedford's dairy was on Water Street. Kalton Burt, his grandson, said that, at one time, they had to build a pit-type outhouse to upgrade the dairy. They sold some milk (bottled to local businesses but not to individuals). Thedford sold milk primarily to Metzgers dairy. (Courtesy of Kalton Burt.)

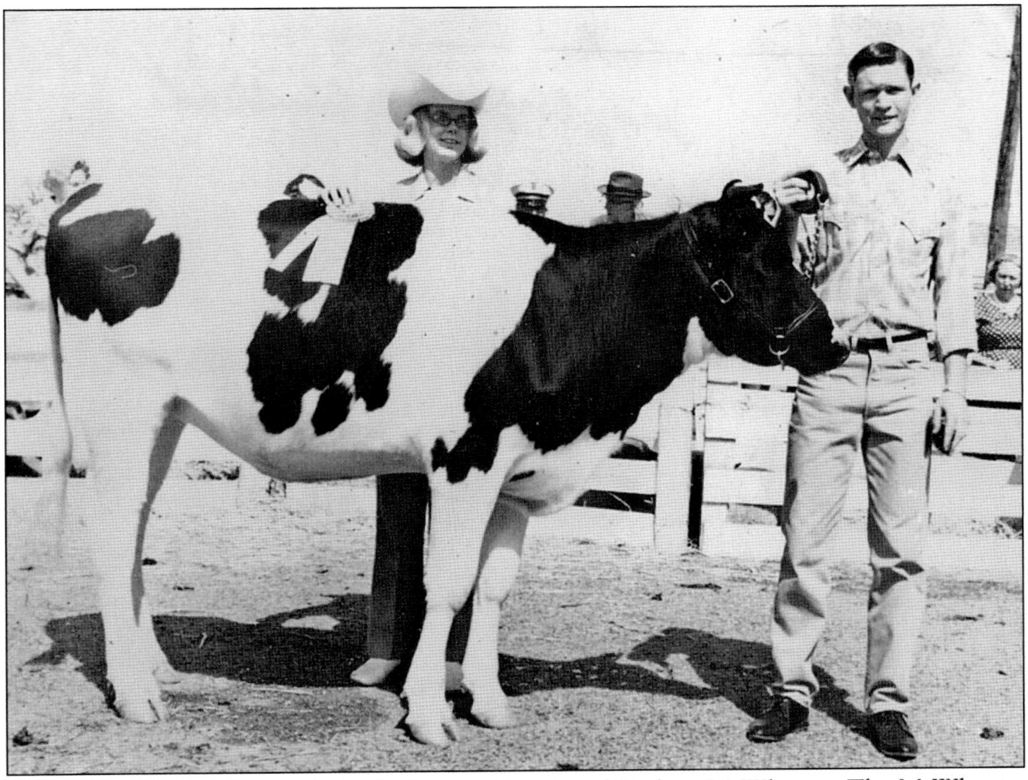

Pictured are, from left to right, Jody Cooper (Crow) and Rodney McWhorter. The McWhorter name has been around Seagoville for a long time. A. H. McWhorter constructed three of the first buildings in Seagoville, one of which was his prominent mercantile store. Rodney McWhorter, son of Felton, can be proud of his heritage. His ancestors would also be proud of him and his accomplishments. (Courtesy of Wayne Phillips.)

In 1966, Larry Dailey's cow represents the quality of the Cobb and Durham Jerseys. The Cobb herd, managed by Ross Durham, was one of the largest in the state. Ross sold the cow to J. B. Kunkel. The cow won five straight state fairs titles and was later sold for $15,000. The Cobb, Bennett, and Thedford dairies were in the Seagoville city limits. (Courtesy of Wayne Phillips.)

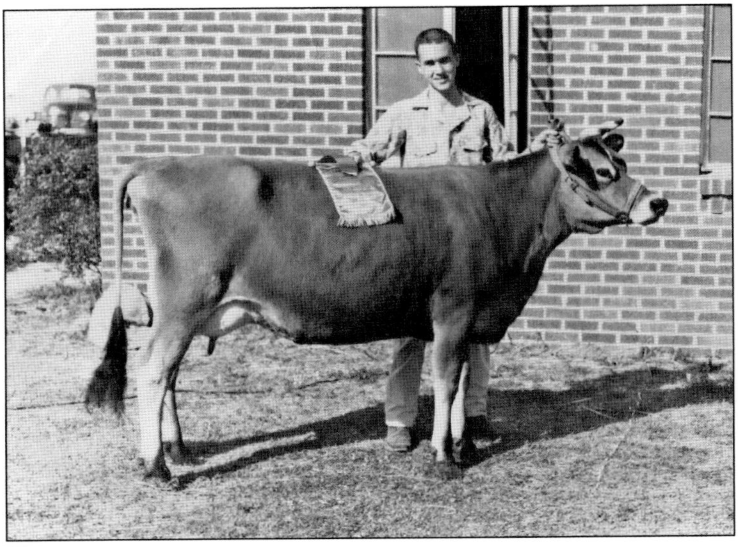

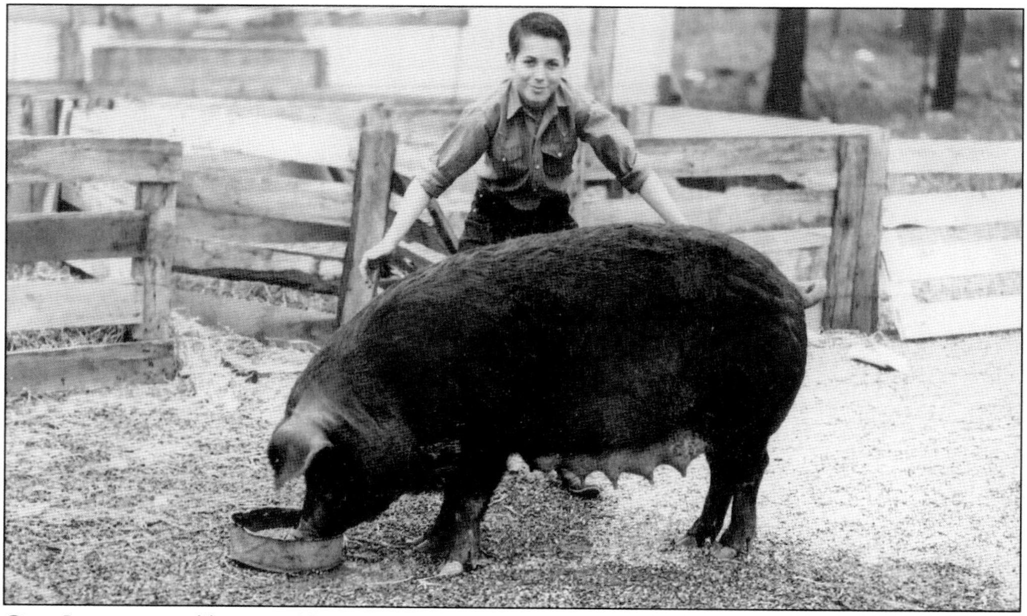

Gary Lanier raised hogs and Jersey cattle. Others local hog farmers included Phil Prestridge and David Rucks, who still has some hogs in the area as well as in Oklahoma. The Waltons, according to Newell Ballard, had a standing order for 55 feeders a week from a dealer in Greenville. They would take 55 finished hogs to sell and bring back the feeders. This lasted until garbage had to be cooked. (Courtesy of Wayne Phillips.)

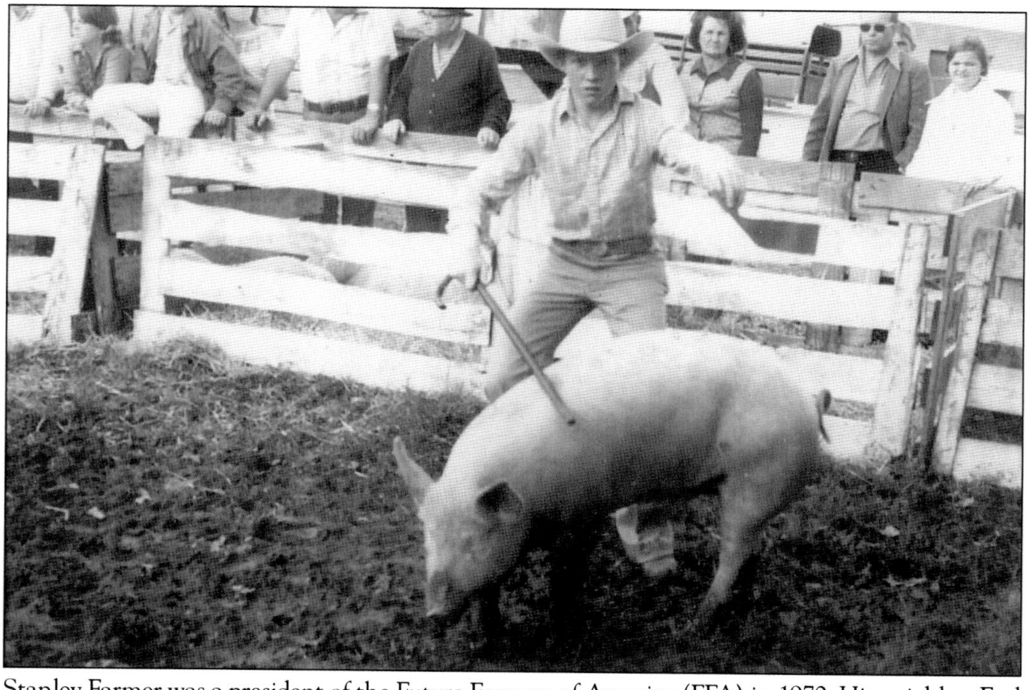

Stanley Farmer was a president of the Future Farmers of America (FFA) in 1970. His neighbor Earl Woody was a major pork producer who bought and raised hogs. He fed the hogs garbage, which had to be picked up in town. Newell Ballard recalls it being very exciting to go into town with Uncle Tommy and Charley Walton at 2:00 a.m. to bring garbage back to feed. (Courtesy of Wayne Phillips.)

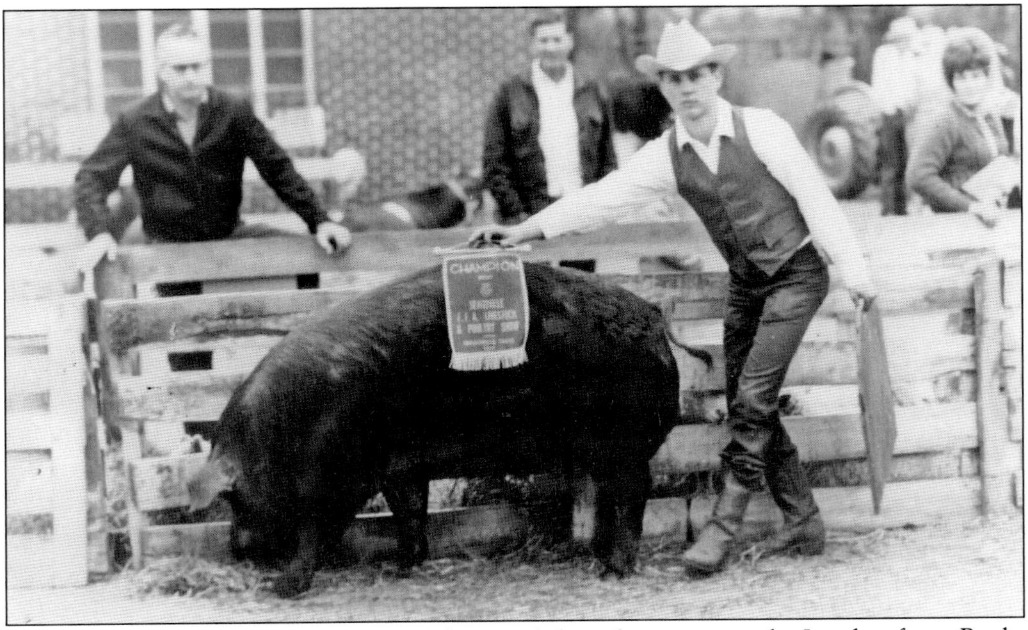

David Rucks liked Duroc hogs. In 1966, he raised them for a time on the Landess farm. Rucks continued to raise Durocs on Bonnie View and exhibited at some national shows and still raises hogs on Bonnie View and in Oklahoma. In the 1950s, Seagoville had certified meat sire number 6, the premier sire of the State Fair of Texas and the grand champion boar at the state fair and at Houston. (Courtesy of Wayne Phillips.)

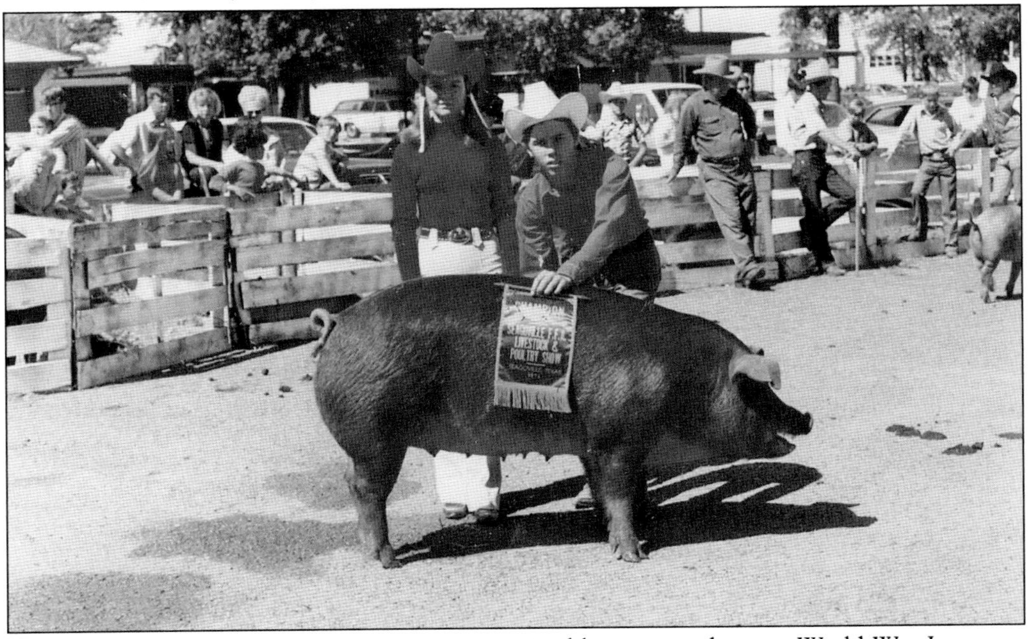

Phil Prestridge raised good hogs. He was supervised by two good men—World War I veteran and his grandfather, Rowe Lanier, and his daddy, Kenneth Prestridge. His hogs were recognized at shows in a wide area. Here Phil and Becky Harrell, FFA Sweetheart and daughter of Hattie Mae Harrell, pose with his Seagoville FFA Livestock and Poultry Show champion hog in 1972. (Courtesy of Wayne Phillips.)

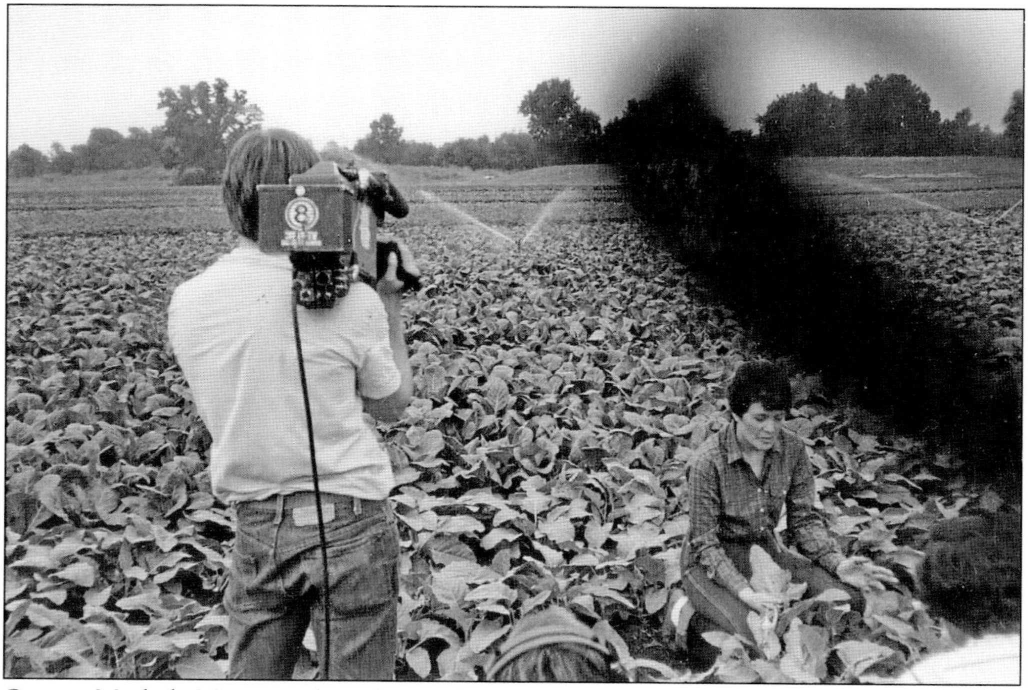

Georgia Machala Massie works in her garden while being photographed by a WFAA Channel 8 photographer for a feature story. Georgia had the farmers' market in Plano and published a cookbook. Brothers Louis and Edward Machala were also active in the vegetable business. (Courtesy of Wayne Phillips and Alfred Machala.)

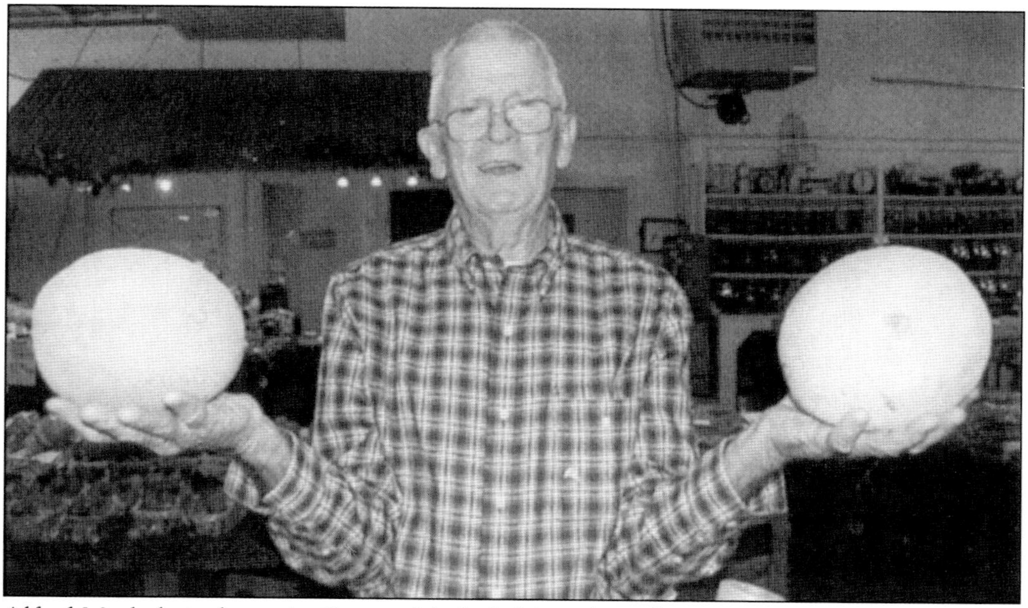

Alfred Machala is shown in Georgia Machala Massie's market in Plano. His smile is not the same expression he had one very early morning when he grabbed a rattler instead of a head of broccoli. Albert Machala says he and Alfred were working for Ernest Walton when they were 10 and 12. He says he would be planting at 2:00 a.m. when others were sleeping. (Courtesy of Alfred Machala.)

Georgia Machala Massie is shown with dishes taken from recipes from her cookbook; she published an excellent cookbook featuring vegetables grown on their farm. Vegetable farming was very demanding of labor and time. Producers would often harvest by 2:00 a.m. or 3:00 a.m. in order to be on the market by 8:00 a.m. (Courtesy of Alfred Machala.)

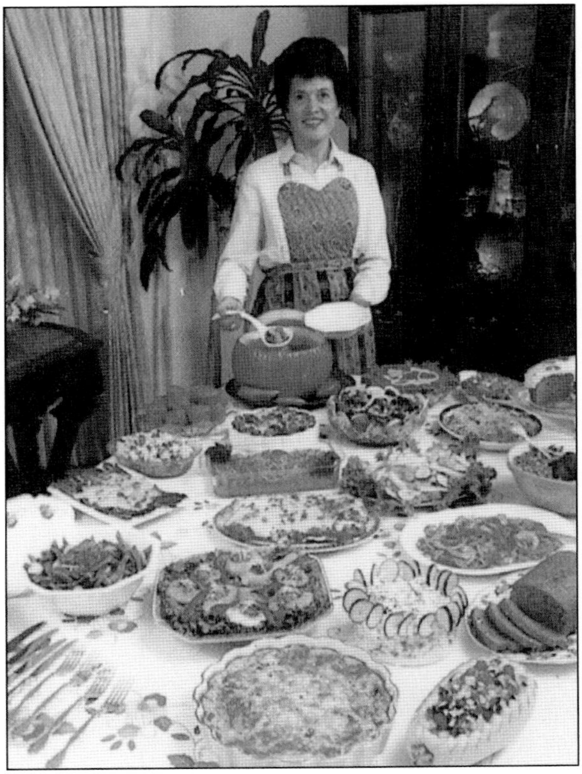

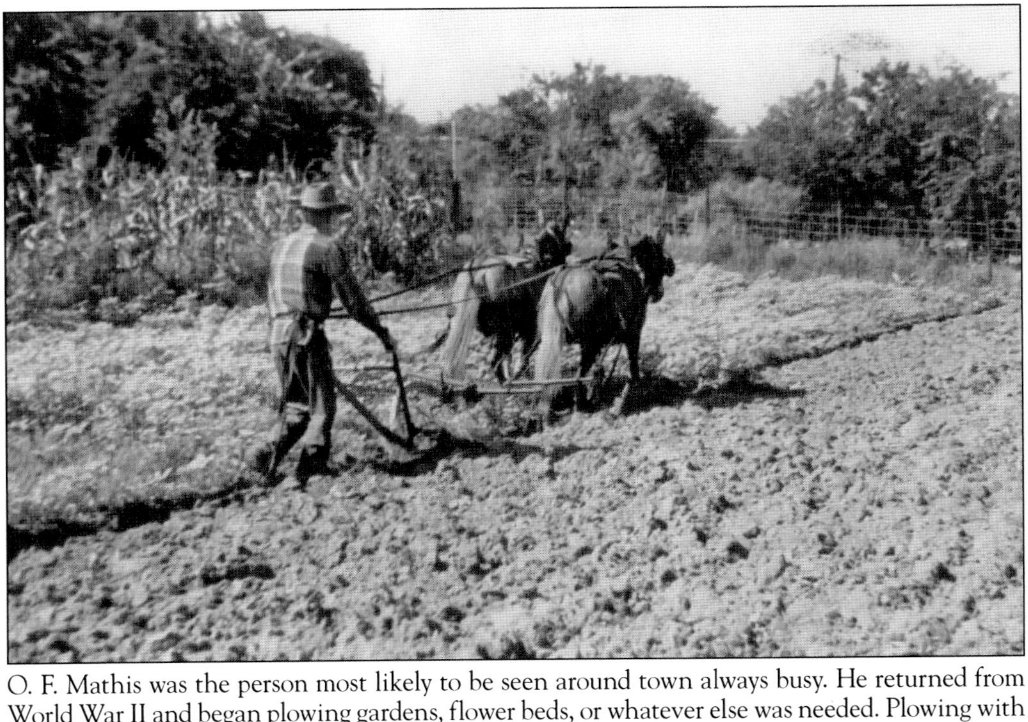

O. F. Mathis was the person most likely to be seen around town always busy. He returned from World War II and began plowing gardens, flower beds, or whatever else was needed. Plowing with a team of horses among a ladies prize flowers or garden was not an easy task. Mathis trained his team to never misstep. For many years, he also drove a school bus. (Courtesy of Delta Mathis.)

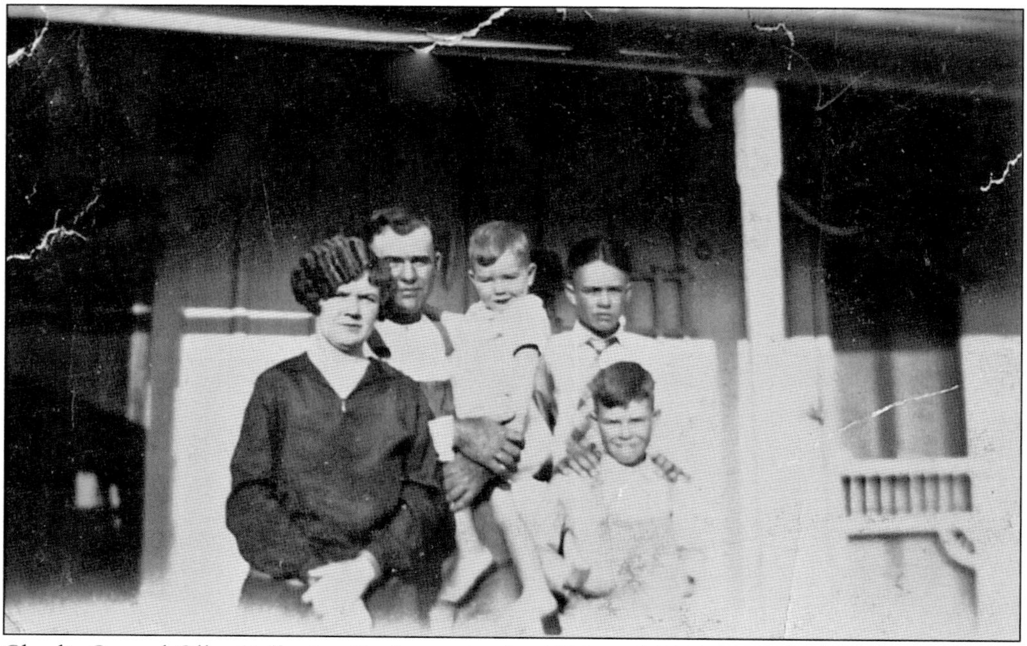

Charlie Sr. and Ollye Ballard milked cows in the 1930s and 1940s. Jack Ballard delivered milk or cream in the mornings before school, and Charles Jr. helped him when he turned 10. One morning, Charles Jr. decided to drive, and he turned the pickup over. Charles Jr. would take his friends home after school to milk at the rate of 1¢ per cow. The operation stopped when Charles joined the army. The Ballard family pictured from left to right are Ollye, Charles Sr. holding Charles Jr., Lloyd, and Jack. (Courtesy of Kathryn Ballard.)

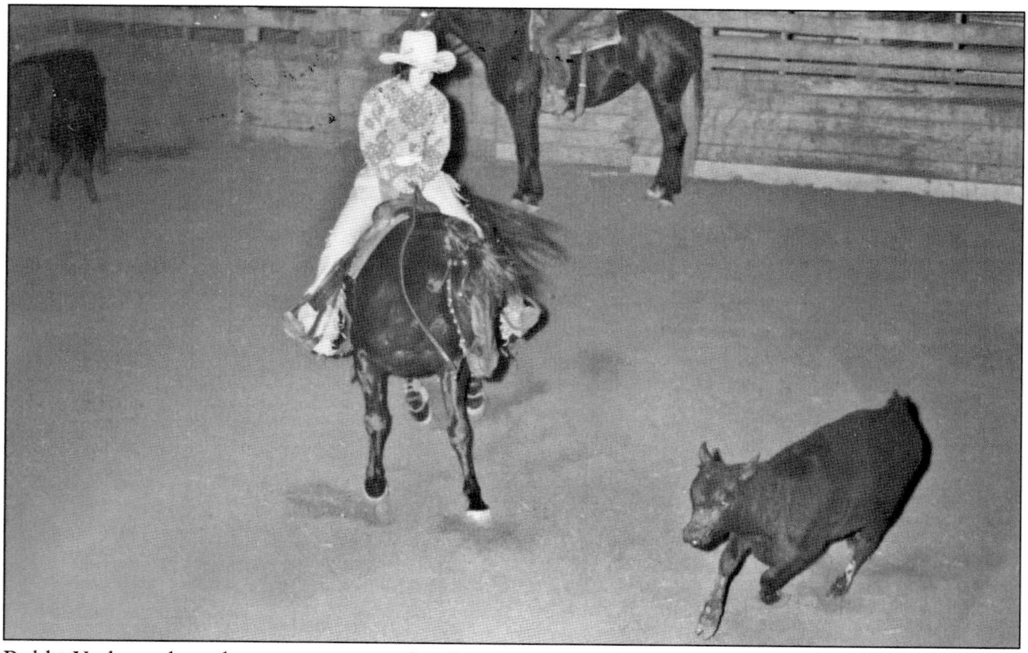

Bobbi Yarbrough is shown cutting on her horse, Sports Edition, at the state junior rodeo finals. This is an illustration of Cotton Marriott's generosity in helping others. Sports Edition was a half brother to Mito Commander, the $2-million horse. (Courtesy of Barbara Yarbrough.)

Playboy Tom won a Buick for accumulating the most performance points in quarter horse competition. He is shown heading for Guy Yarbrough at the state high school finals rodeo with Johnny Emmons heeling. Cotton Marriott was generous in letting other people use his horses. After his passing, the ranch was sold to Joe Huerta, who continues to raise horses, including some daughters of Secretariat. (Courtesy of Rodney Yarbrough.)

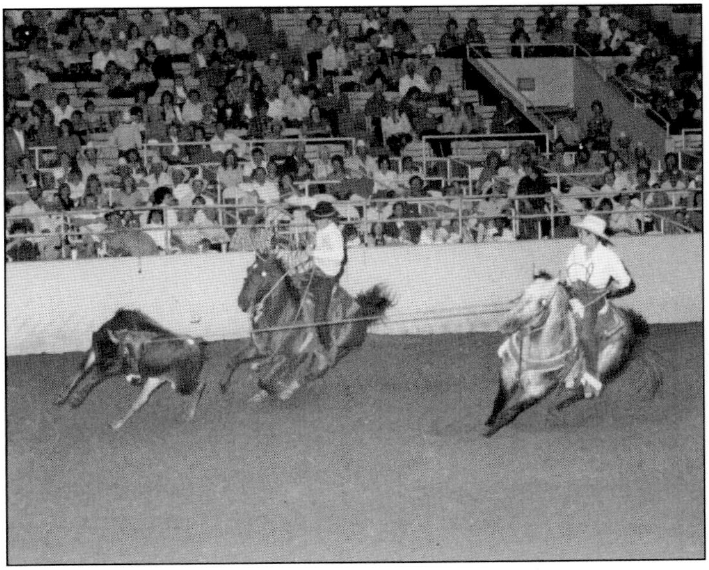

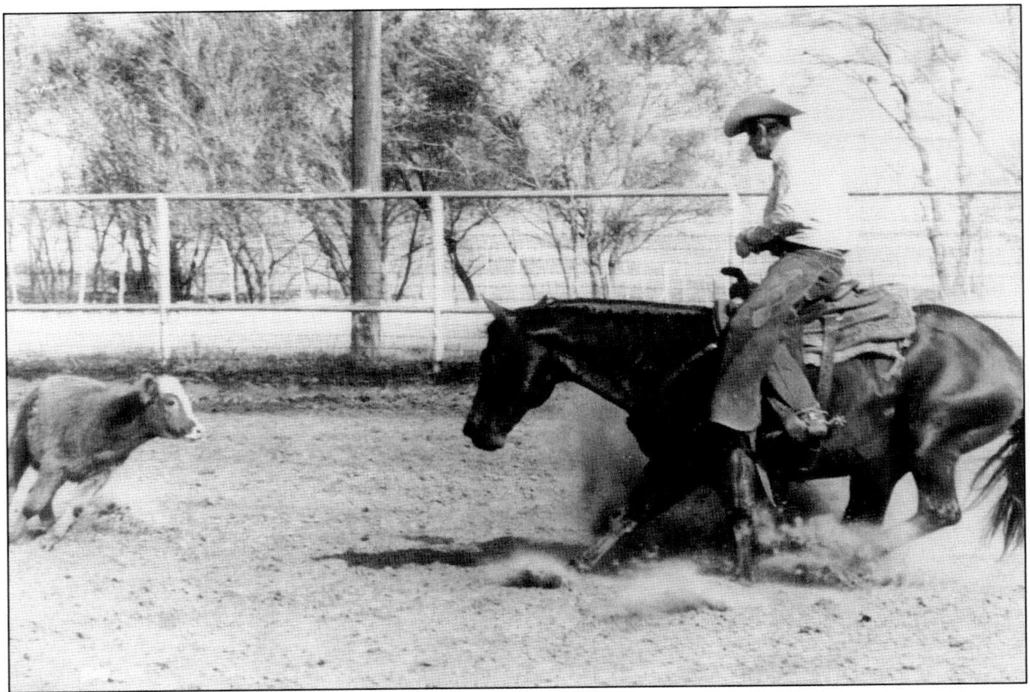

What place would produce a $2-million Halter horse, two full brothers that became world champion cutting horses, and one that claimed a new Buick for winning the all-around performance award? The answer is the former Wilber Ard farm, 18 miles from downtown Dallas, in Seagoville. Three men are responsible for these accomplishments—Matlock Rose, G. B. Howell, and Cotton Marriott. G. B. Howell of Dallas and New Mexico bought the Ard property with the plan to develop the best possible all-around horse. They had the top Halter horses in 1960, 1961, and 1962 and disbursed in 1963 with buyers coming from a great many places, including Canada. The local buyers were Rayburn Patterson and Reagan Glenn. G. B. Howell offered the ranch for sale, and only Cotton Marriott came up with an offer. He began producing some outstanding horses. Pictured is Matlock Rose riding his horse, Peppy San. (Courtesy of Laverne Rose.)

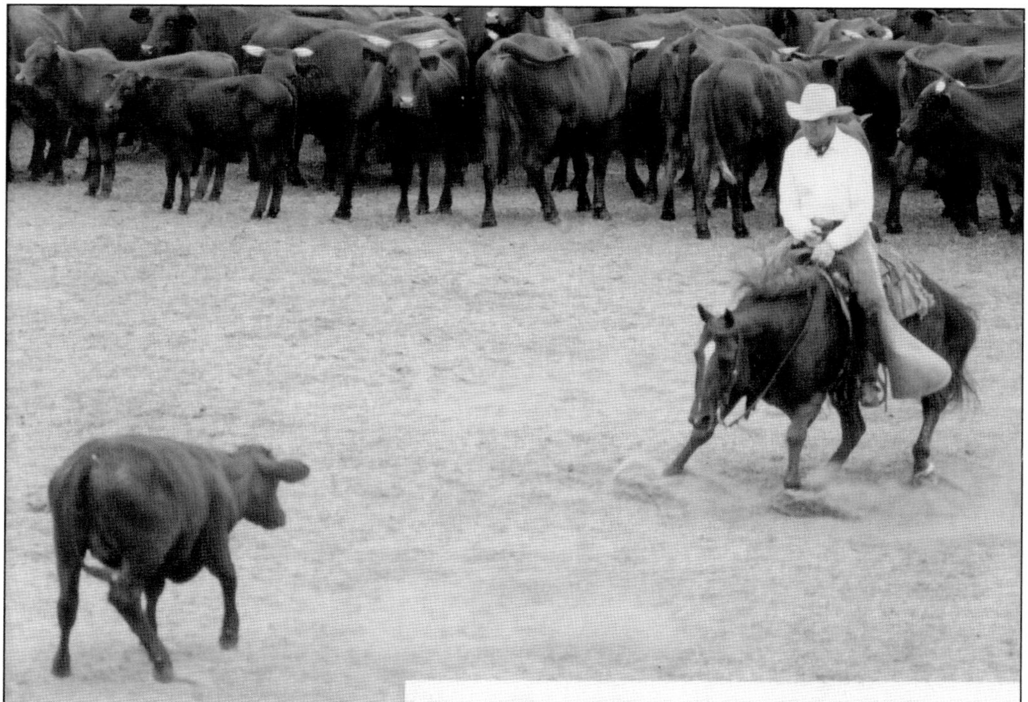

KING RANCH, KINGSVILLE, TX.: BUSTER WELCH RIDES

G. B. Howell gave his prize horse, Peppy Belle, to Cotton Marriott to foal out Mr. San Peppy. Among the many fine horses raised by Cotton Marriott was the $2-million stallion, Mito Commander. Buster Welch bought Mr. San Peppy from G. B. Howell and trained him to win the National Cutting Horse Futurity and later the year-end championship. He sold Mr. San Peppy to the King Ranch, and Buster went with the horse. Mr. San Peppy sired Peppy San Badger, who also became a futurity and year-end champion. (Courtesy of Buster Welch.)

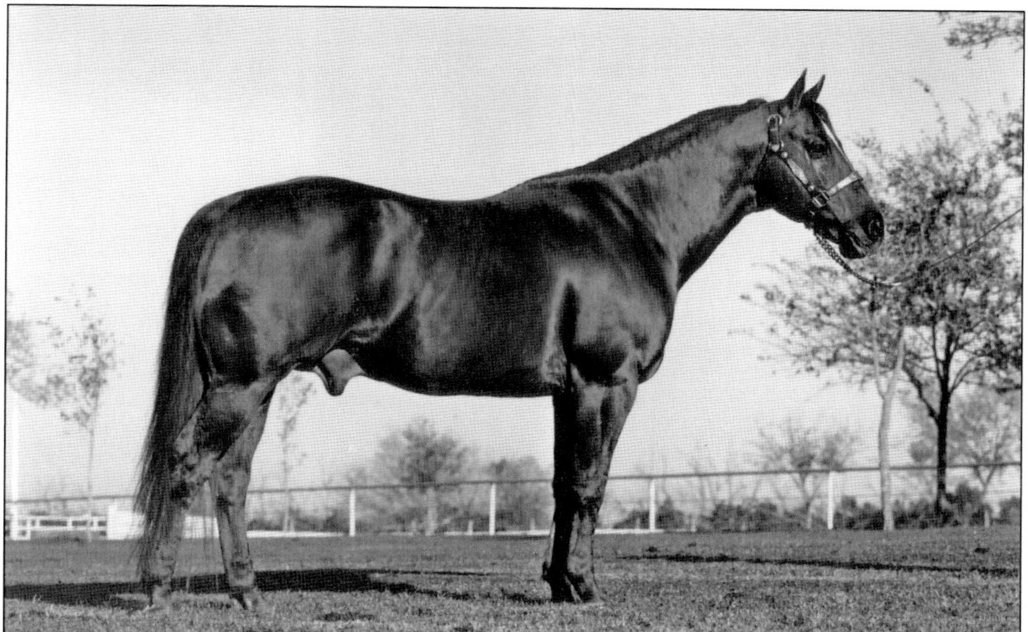

Five

Churches

The first known church was Friendship Baptist, organized in the spring of 1872. In 1877, an organ was purchased for the services. At this time, the church was being used as a school, so the Sewell family kept the organ in their home. Each Sunday, they would load it in their wagon and take it to church. After the evening service, they would take it home until the next meeting time. Later they purchased a large black bell for $1 and mounted it outside the church. At meeting time, the bell was rung to remind the people of the services. The bell could be heard for some distance.

The first Methodist church was organized in November 1882 and met in the Woodside School for a few years until they built their first church in 1895. The Church of Christ, at the urging of some local ladies, began meeting in various homes and was organized in January 1935. The Assembly of God was organized in the 1930s and met in one of the local stores until they constructed their first building. Other churches have been built since these. Today there are several different denominations within the city limits. The denominations represented are Baptist, Methodist, Church of Christ, Assembly of God, Episcopal, Christian, Spanish Baptist, and nondenominational. Each group ministers to the city on a weekly basis.

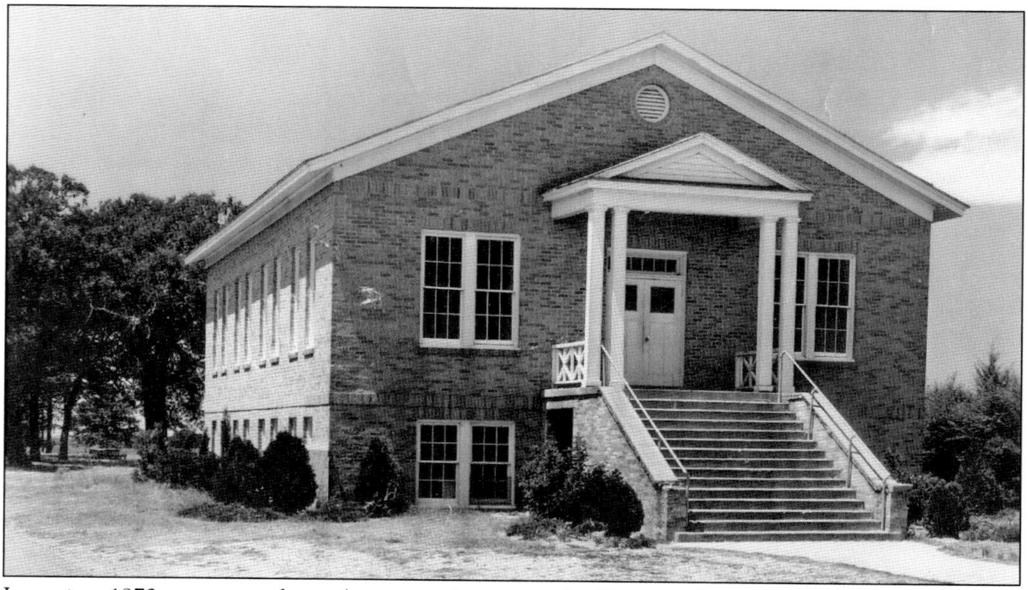

In spring 1872, a group of people met and organized a Baptist church. Eight charter members purchased an acre of land for $13 and constructed a one-room frame building. They named it the Friendship Baptist Church. Brother A. E. Baten was called as first pastor, with preaching once a month. In 1894, they replaced the building with another frame structure. A music school was held there in 1906 and services were held twice a month in 1913. In 1929, the name was changed to First Baptist Church of Seagoville. A two-story brick structure was erected in 1930 on the same site on North Kaufman Street as the previous two buildings. In 1945, a brick educational building was constructed beside the church. (Courtesy of Carol Franks.)

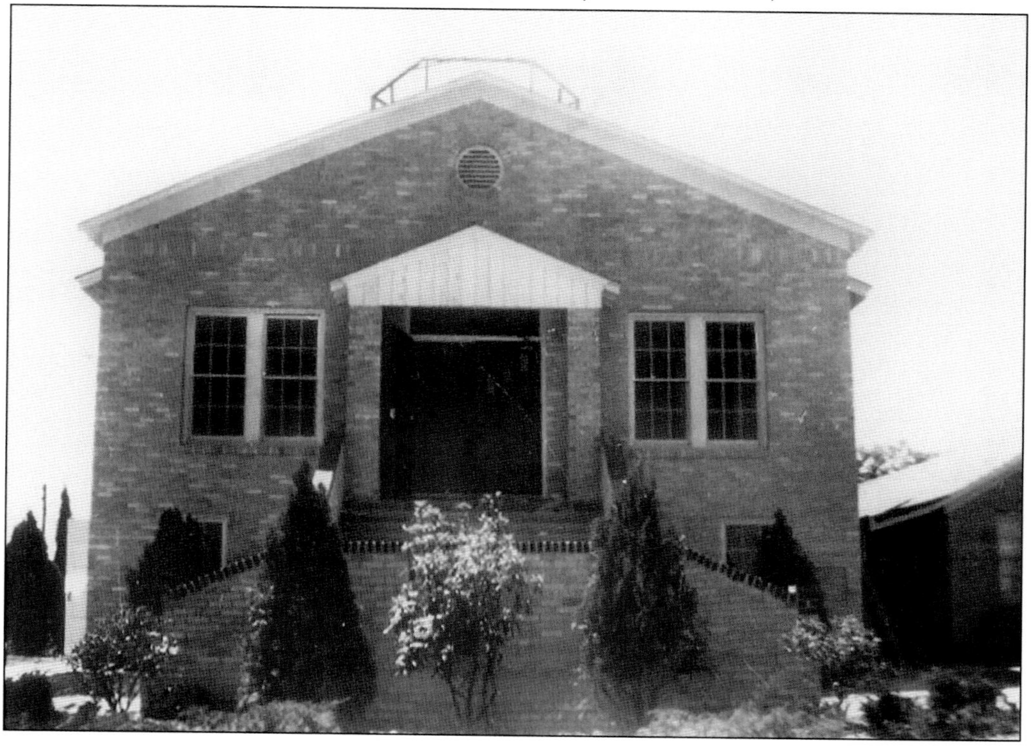

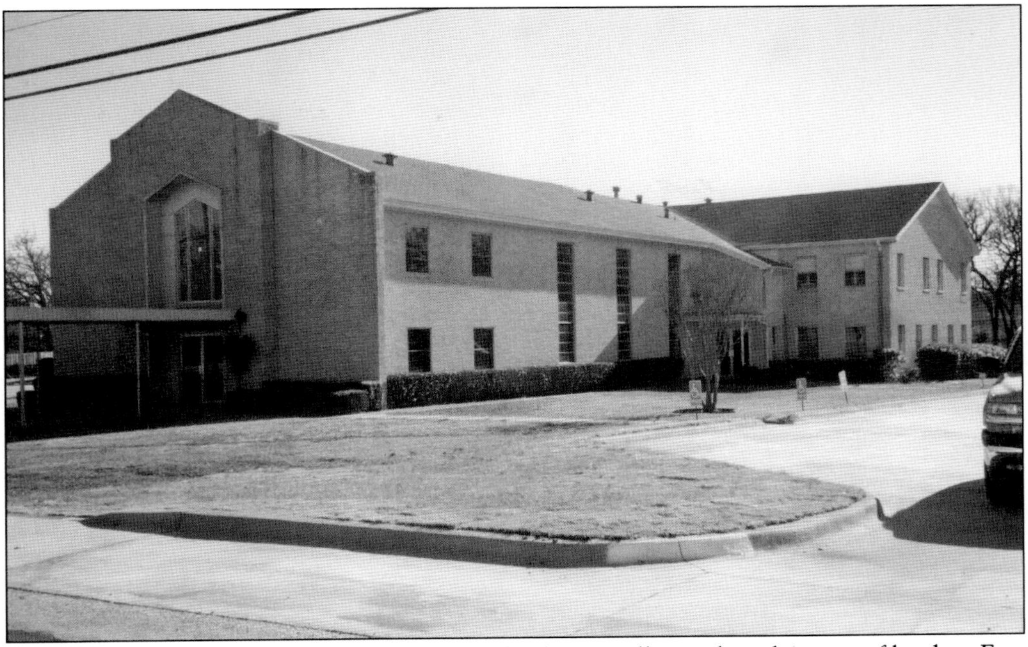

Because of growth in 1956, First Baptist Church of Seagoville purchased 4 acres of land on East Farmers Road from the Andrews family. A T-shaped, two-story brick building was erected and dedicated in June 1958 with an actual move-in date of August 1958. The brick Mary Percival Educational Building was dedicated in November 1974. This structure provided more classroom space, a larger fellowship hall, more restrooms, and a large kitchen area. The two buildings stand today as a lighthouse set on a hill, inviting the saved and unsaved to pass through its doors. (Courtesy of Carol Franks.)

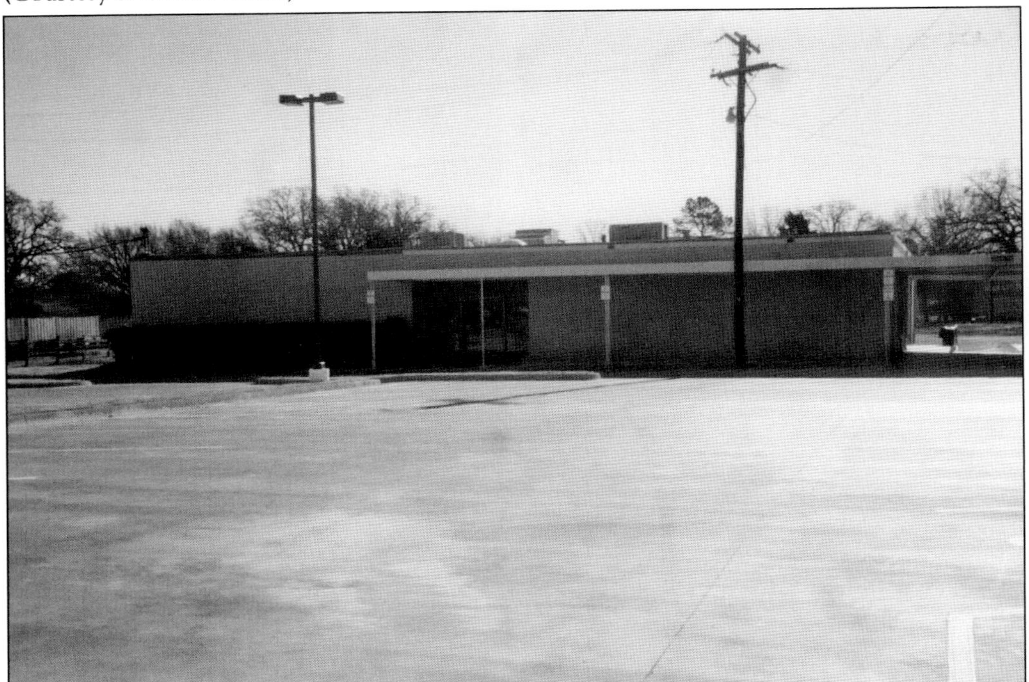

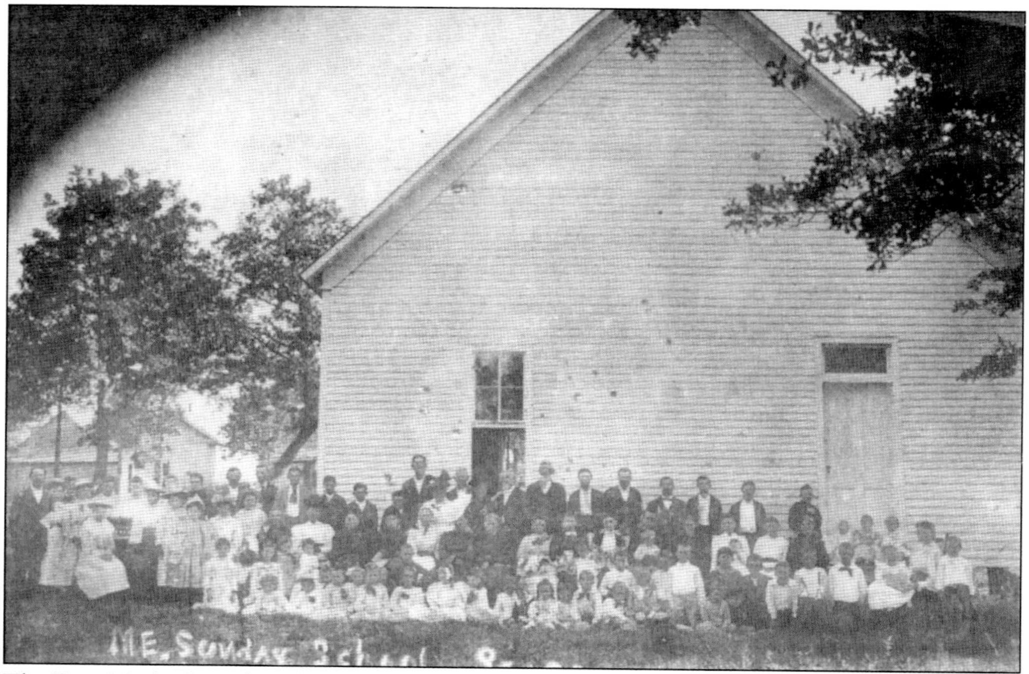

The First Methodist Church was organized in 1882 and met in the Woodside School. Members constructed their first frame building in 1894 on land donated by the E. A. Thompson family at Malloy Bridge Road and Kaufman Street. A Sunday school was organized with E. A. Thompson serving as the first superintendent until 1906. That year, a missionary society was organized that was known as the United Methodist Women. (Courtesy of United Methodist Church.)

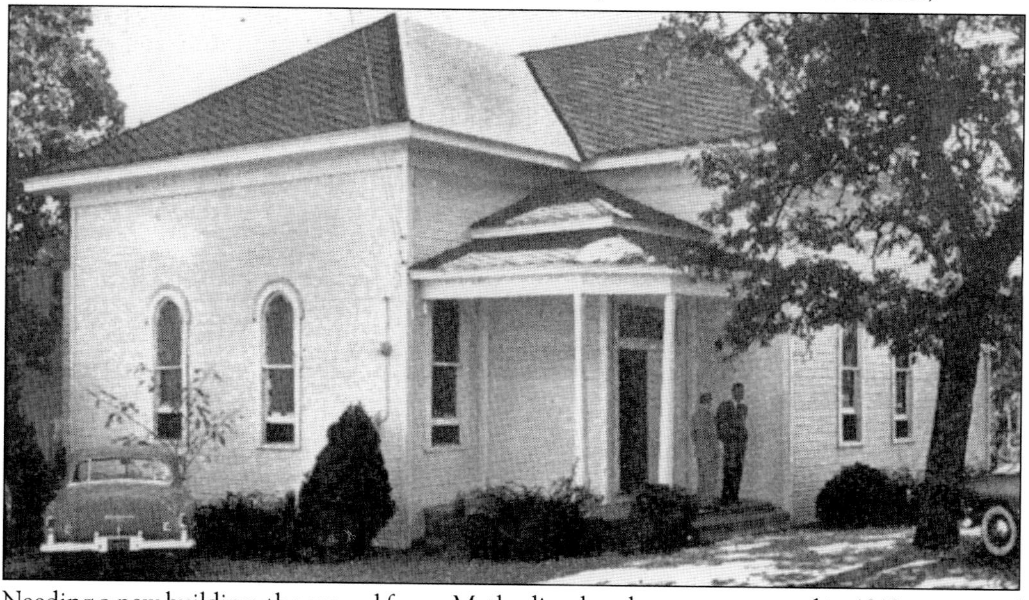

Needing a new building, the second frame Methodist church was constructed in 1912 at a cost of $4,000 on the same site as the previous church. Rev. O. E. Moreland was the first pastor in this building. The structure served its purpose for 40 years. In 1945, the church was taken from the Crandall Circuit and made a station church with Rev. William Greenhill as pastor. (Courtesy of United Methodist Church.)

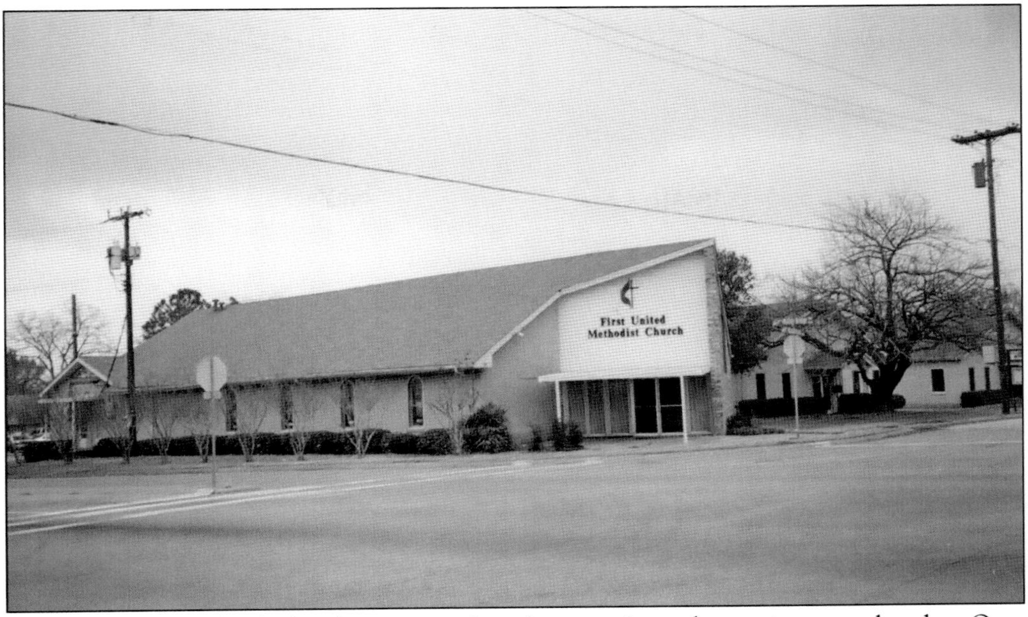

In 1955, the present brick church was erected on the same site as the previous two churches. Over the years, this church has provided the Teen Towne House as a community youth gathering place and the Senior Citizens Nutritional Program. The Methodist Episcopal Church South united with the United Brethren Church in 1968 and became the First United Methodist, the name the church is known by today. (Courtesy of Carol Franks.)

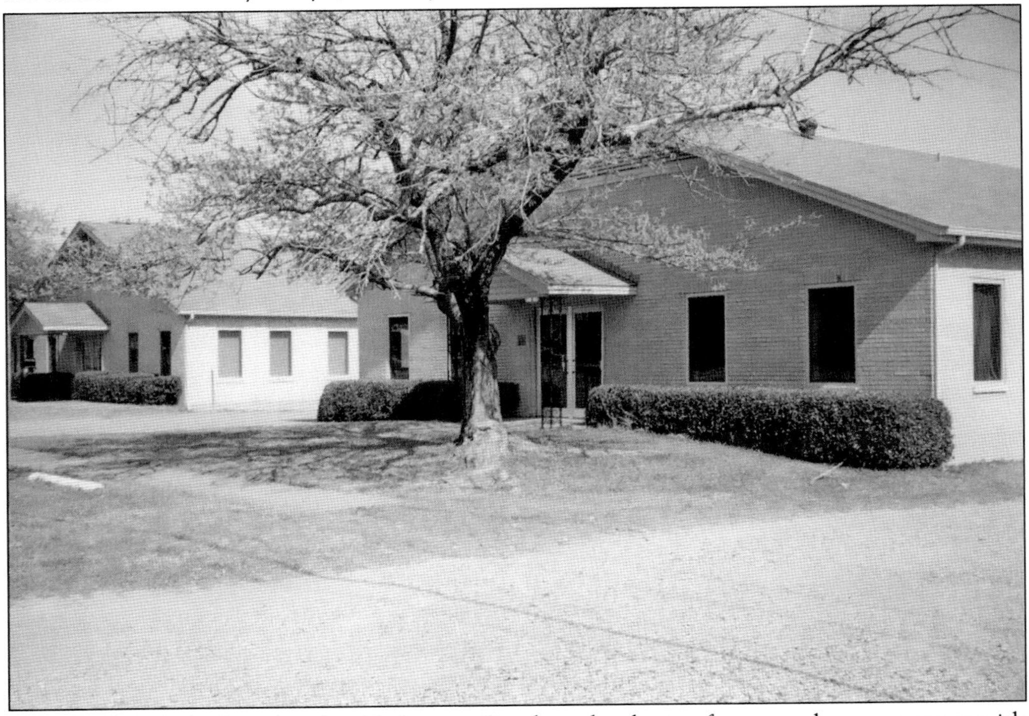

In 1952, the Methodist church added a new Sunday school wing for more classroom space with a fellowship hall and kitchen. The Children's Education Wing was built in 1965, for additional classroom space, beside the Sunday school wing. (Courtesy of Carol Franks.)

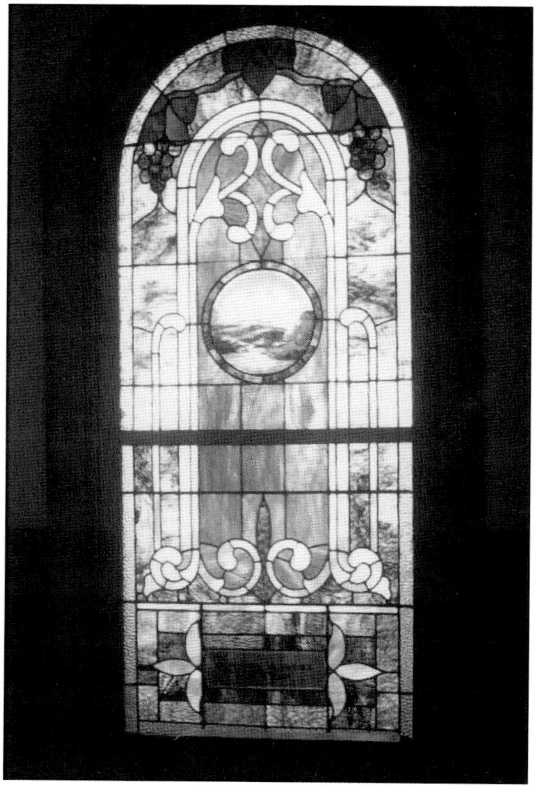

This window was given by J. L. Ballard in memory of his mother who was a longtime Methodist. J. L. Ballard was the father of Charley Ballard Sr. and Nora Webber. (Courtesy of Billie Frank Phillips.)

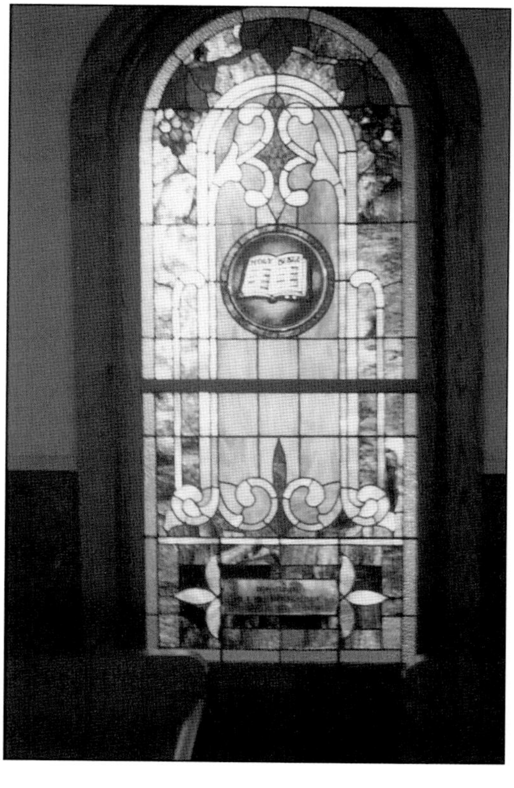

This window was donated by Sam Sullivan and his family. Sam Sullivan is the father of Dudley Sullivan and father-in-law of Gladys Sullivan. The Sullivans were some of the early settlers in Seagoville. (Courtesy of Billie Frank Phillips.)

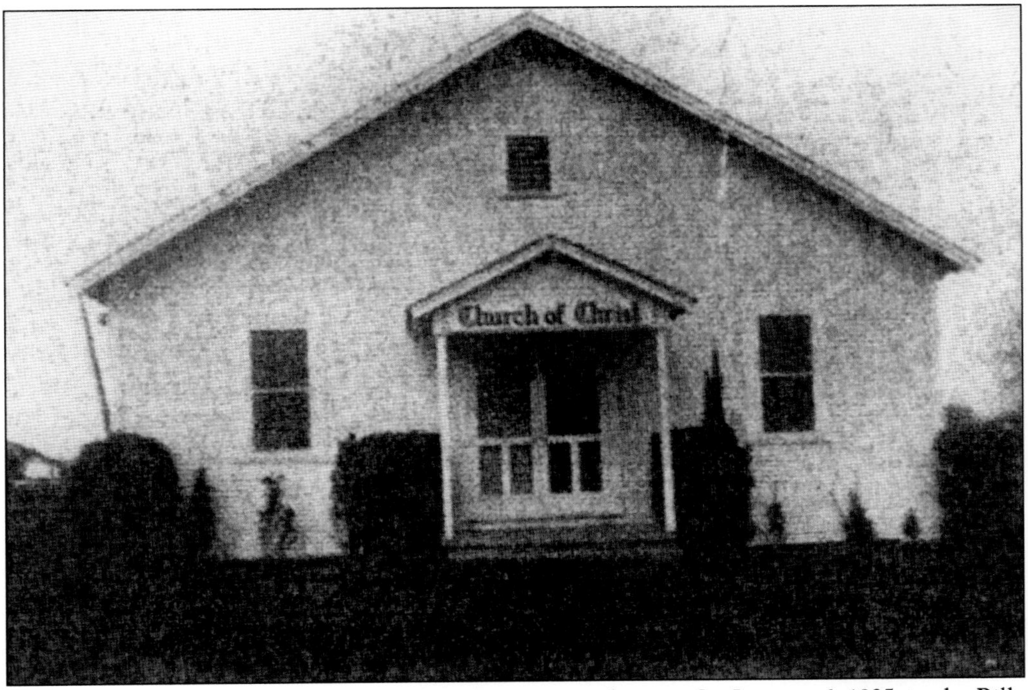

Desiring a local church, several people began meeting in homes. On January 6, 1935, in the Billy Cawthorn home, the Seagoville Church of Christ was organized. Later the congregation met in the schools until they bought a lot on North Kaufman Street for $137 in October 1936. They obtained a $500 loan and built a frame church. Homer Mathis was the first preacher. (Courtesy of Nobie Patterson.)

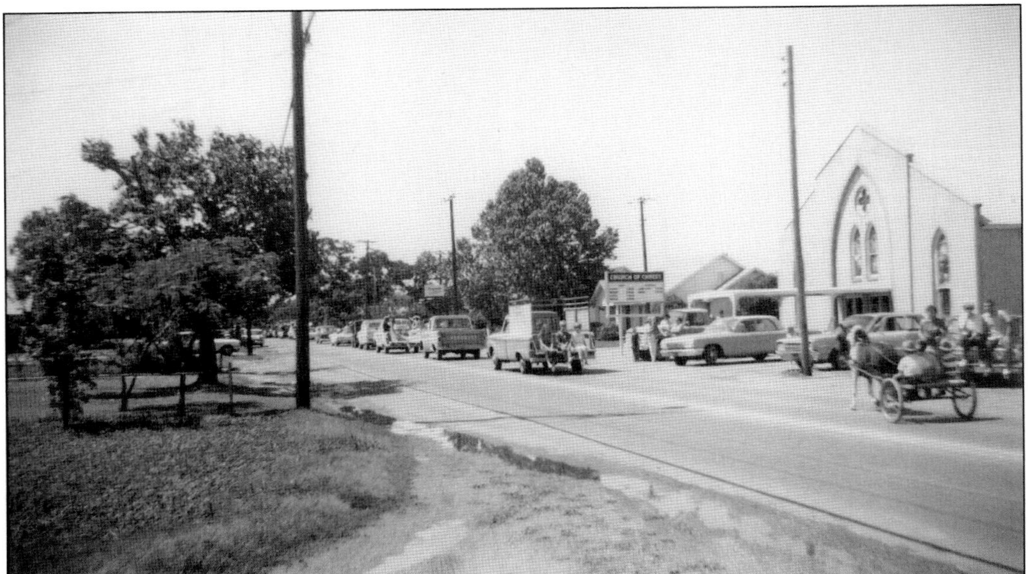

In 1950, the second Church of Christ building was constructed of brick and incorporated into the first frame structure. The new building had an auditorium capacity for 450 people, 17 classrooms, 4 restrooms, a large nursery, and a study for the pastor. (Courtesy of Carol Franks.)

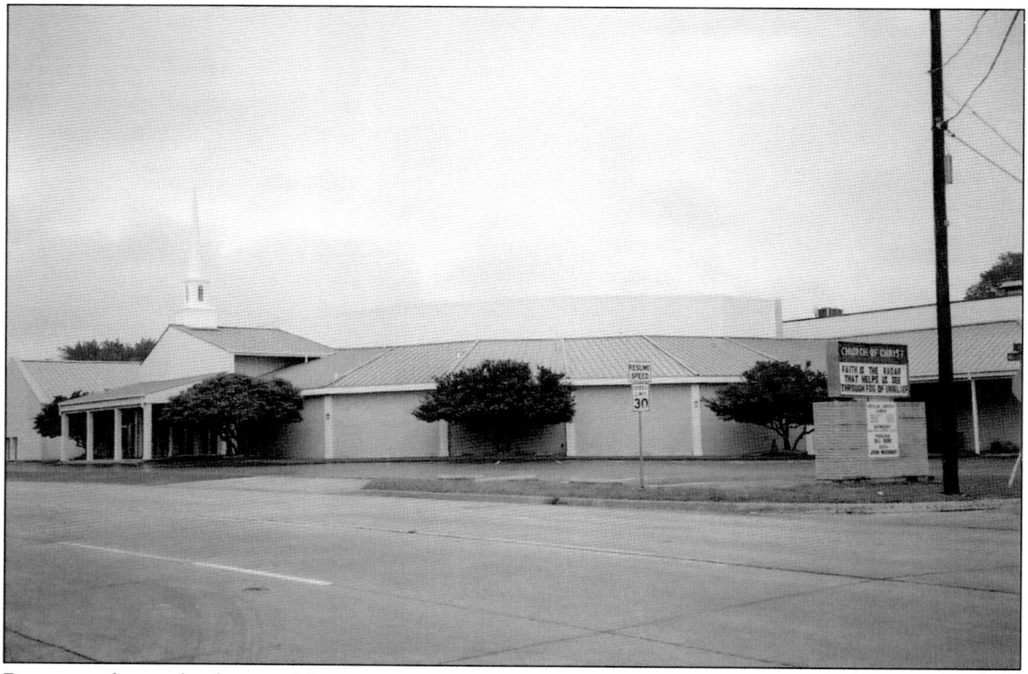

Because of growth, the need for even more space led to plans and construction that began in 1968 on the present Church of Christ building. The auditorium was to seat 1,200 people. Members sold bonds in the amount of $300,000 for construction and moved into the new building in 1970. In 1985, ground was broken for a new multipurpose building (the annex) behind the sanctuary. (Courtesy of Carol Franks.)

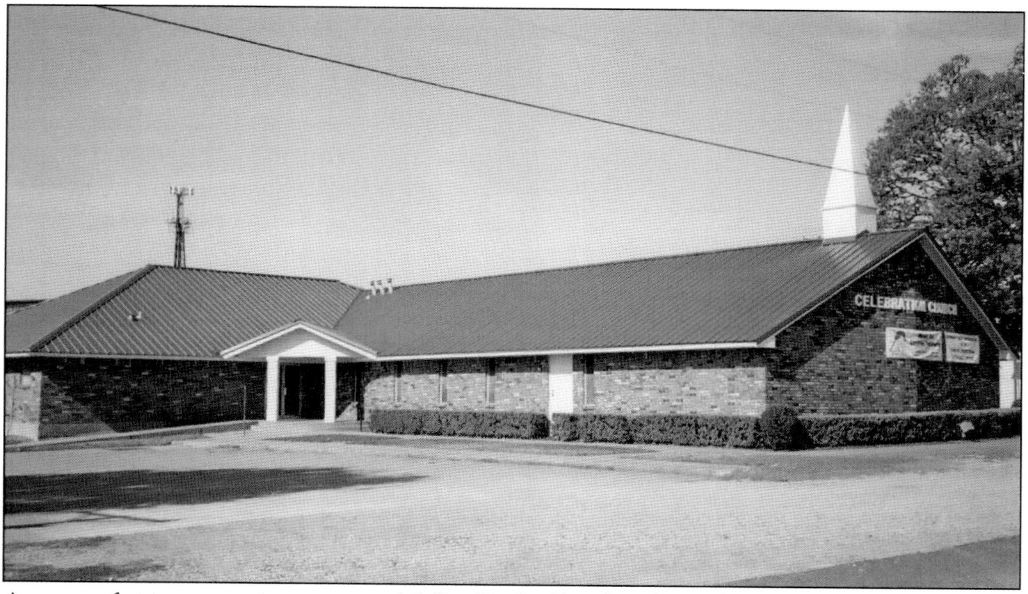

A group of citizens met in a store on Malloy Bridge Road in the early 1930s and became known as the Assembly of God church. Later they constructed a church building on Johnson Street. In September 1946, they held a dedication service for their new church on South Kaufman Street. In the mid-1970s, they moved into a new brick building on Highway 175 that is now called Celebration Church. (Courtesy of Carol Franks.)

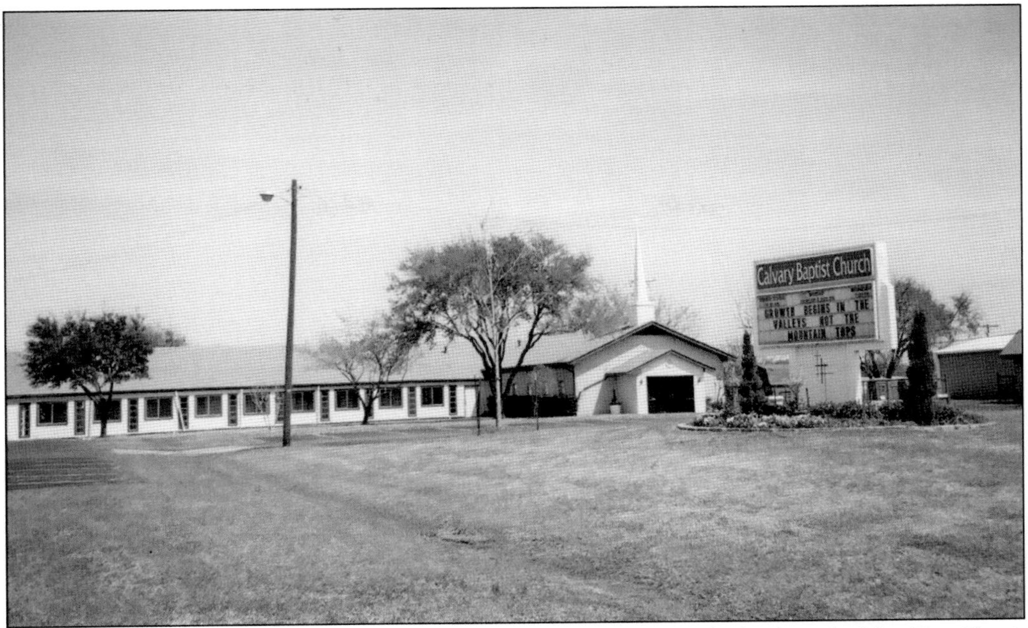

Calvary Baptist Church was organized on September 12, 1955, in the backyard of the Tom Davis home. Rev. S. C. Crumley was called as pastor, and the name Calvary was chosen. Services were held in an office building owned by the Paul Tiner family on the corner of May Road and Highway 175. They started making plans for their church by purchasing 3 acres from the W. A. Ballard family for $4,000 and obtaining a $20,000 loan for construction. On February 26, 1956, the congregation met in the new church located between Highland Drive and May Road. In 1960, they added additional classrooms, and in 1975, also added a library and Family Life Center, which became a worship center in 1993. (Courtesy of Carol Franks.)

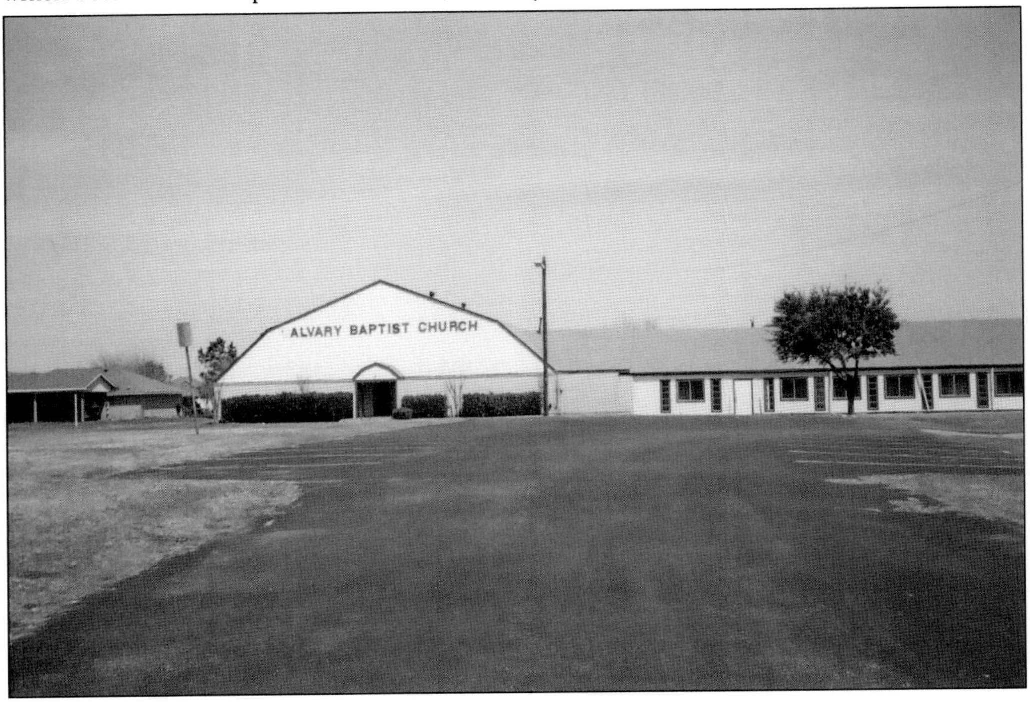

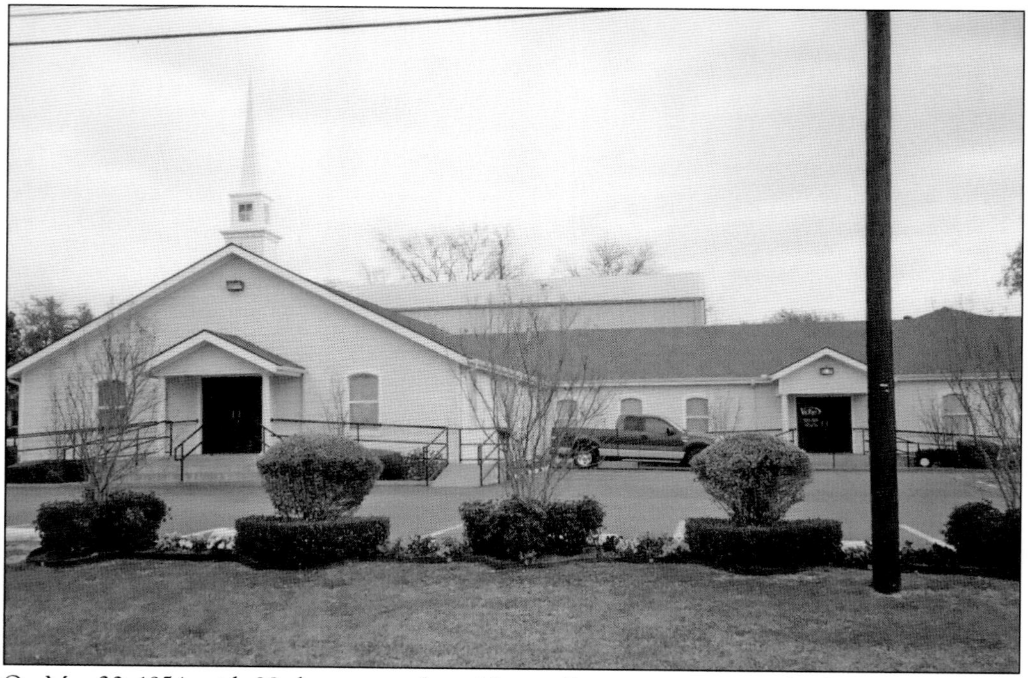

On May 30, 1954, with 28 charter members, Victory Baptist was organized. They called Brother Odie Grammar as pastor and met in a café building until erecting their church on Ferrell Drive. Grammar served as pastor for 35 years and retired in 1988 as pastor emeritus. In June 2003, the church dedicated a new educational building and named the complex the Odie Grammar Educational Building. (Courtesy of Carol Franks.)

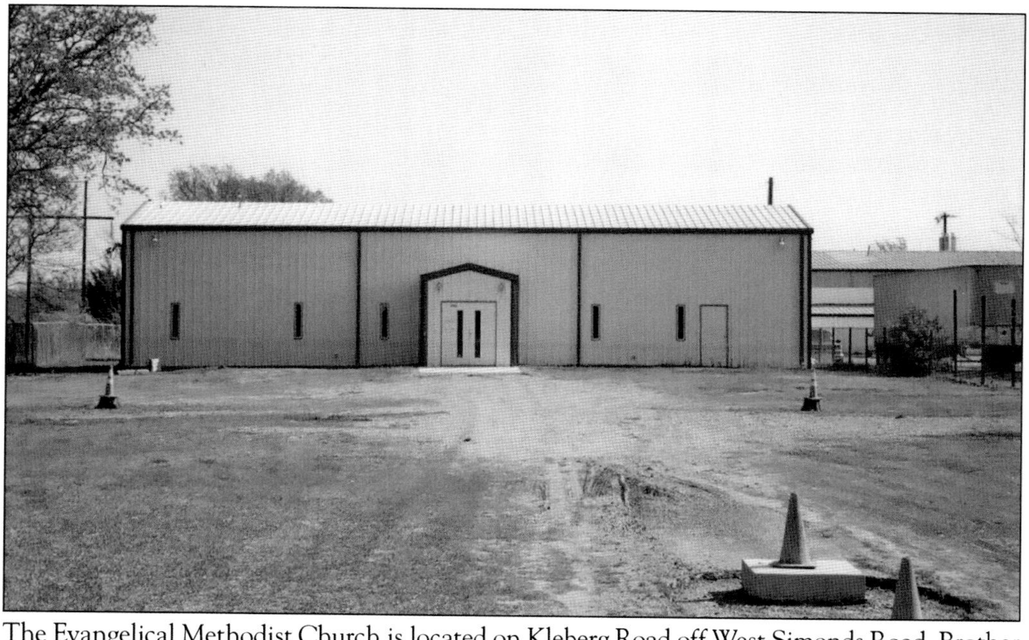

The Evangelical Methodist Church is located on Kleberg Road off West Simonds Road. Brother Louis Moran has been the pastor of the church for several years. Brother Louis and his wife, Lois Moran, have been gospel music instrumentalists and singers for over 60 years. They have won many awards for their musical abilities. (Courtesy of Carol Franks.)

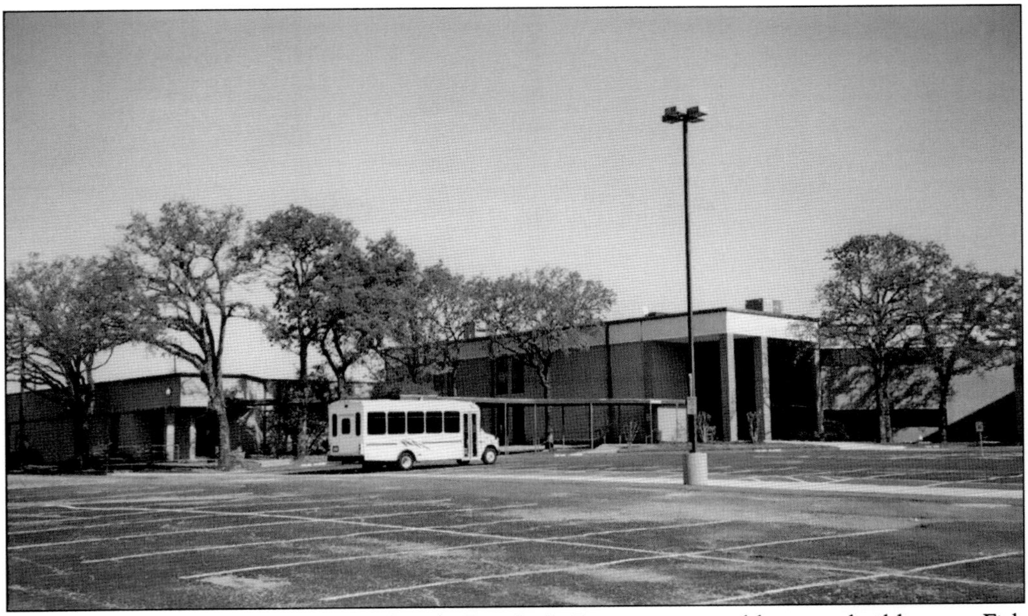

Rev. Waymon H. Evans started a church, Roadside Baptist, in an old garage building on Fisk Road and Highway 175 in June 1953. This church later became Robinwood Baptist. As the church grew, they built a sanctuary, and in 1955 more space was added. In 1964, a children's building was erected along with renovations to the old building. Additional land behind the facility was purchased for $500, and 3.5 acres beside the church was purchased for $5,000. In March 1980, a multipurpose church building was approved, and construction began in 1984 on this property. Robinwood Christian Academy was organized in 1991. A Family Life Center was erected and dedicated in May 2001. In January 2003, the center name was changed to Blessed Hope, a ministry for abused women. (Courtesy of Carol Franks.)

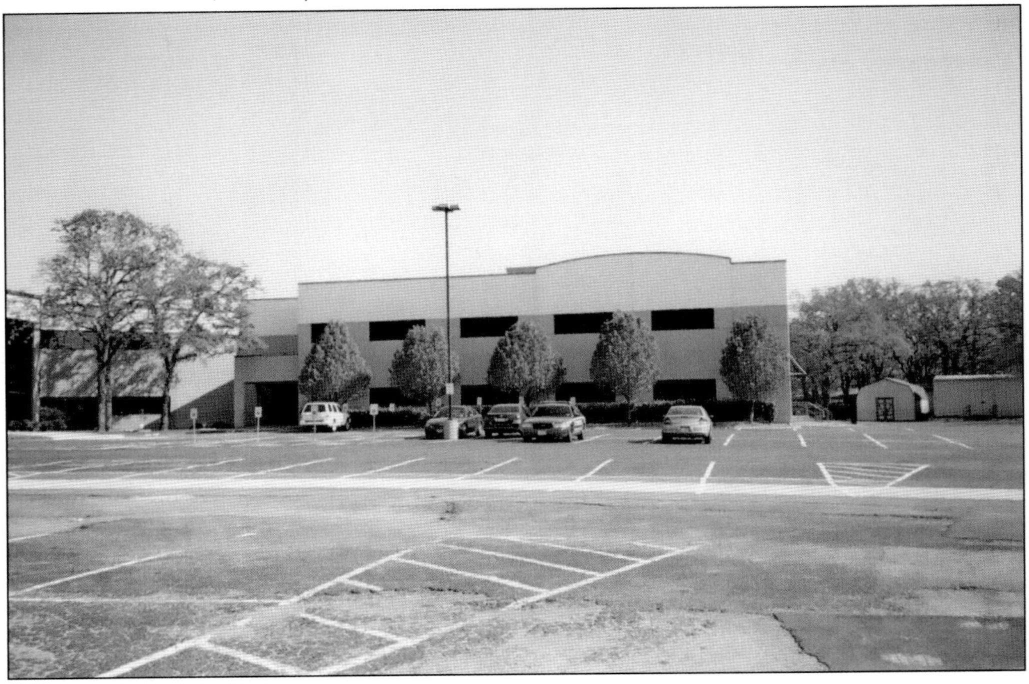

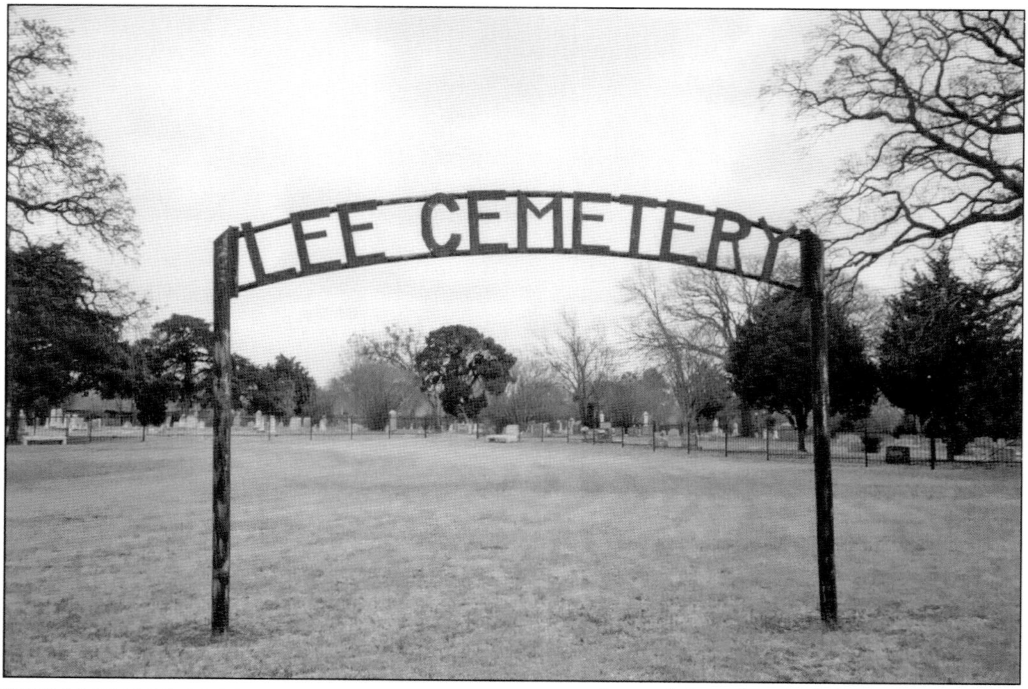

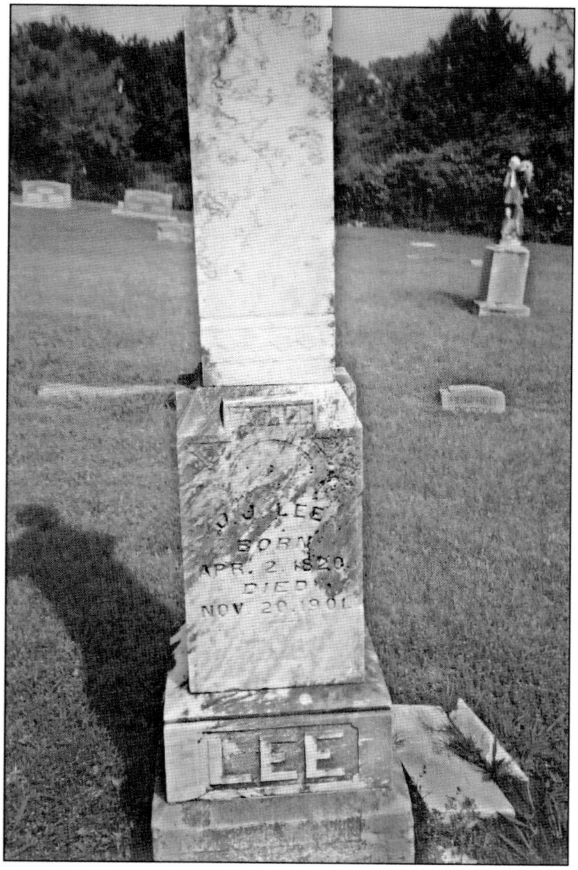

James J. Lee donated the land for the Lee Cemetery on April 29, 1870. It was the only cemetery in the southeast section of Dallas County for many years. He stipulated on the deed that no one should be charged for a burial plot. The first known burial was of Samuel T. Cravens, 12-year-old son of James and Susan Cravens. An association was formed in 1935, and the cemetery was incorporated in November 1967. It is now known as the Lee Cemetery, Inc. Ozella Sebastian, city historian, labored many hours making a list and mapping out the grave sites. (Courtesy of Carol Franks.)

In 1976, a Texas State Historical Marker was erected at the Lee Cemetery located on Highway 175 and Seagoville Road. (Courtesy of Carol Franks.)

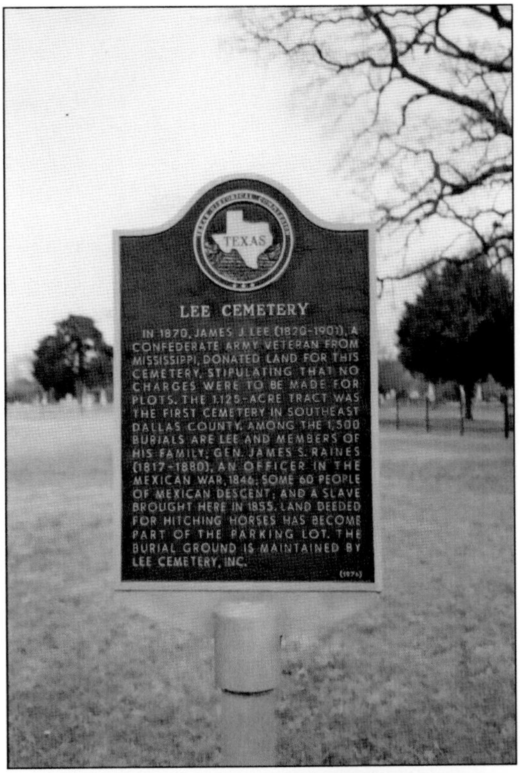

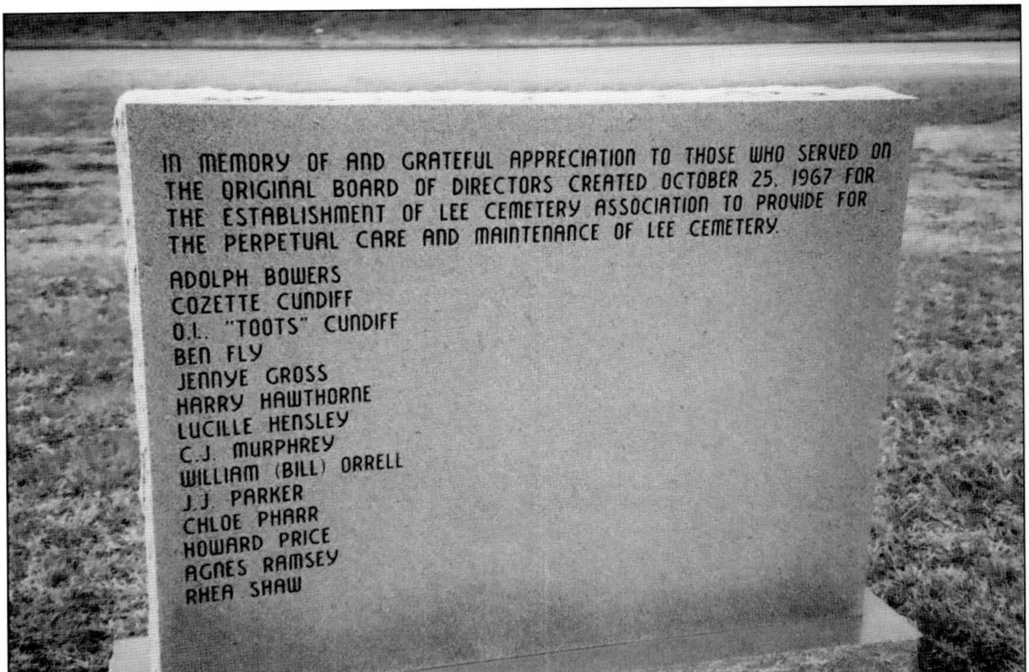

Listed on the marker are the names of the original board of directors created in October 1967 and others who worked so diligently in the establishment of the association and incorporation that oversees the perpetual care of the cemetery. (Courtesy of Carol Franks.)

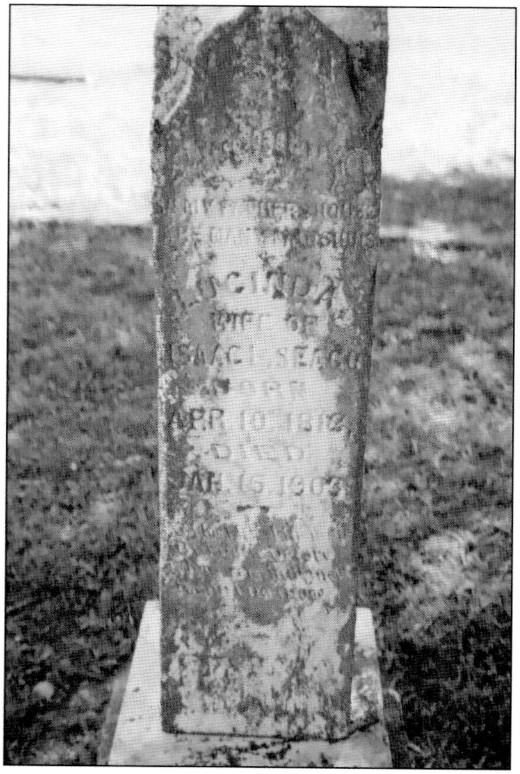

Sarah Lucinda (Garrett) Seago, mother of T. K. Seago, was born on April 10, 1813, in South Carolina. She married Isaac Seago on May 20, 1832. After his death in 1846 in the Mexican War, she moved with her seven children to Texas in 1851. She died on January 15, 1903, at the home of her daughter Cynthia (Mrs. Sam) Sullivan, in Seagoville, and is buried in Lee Cemetery. (Courtesy of Carol Franks.)

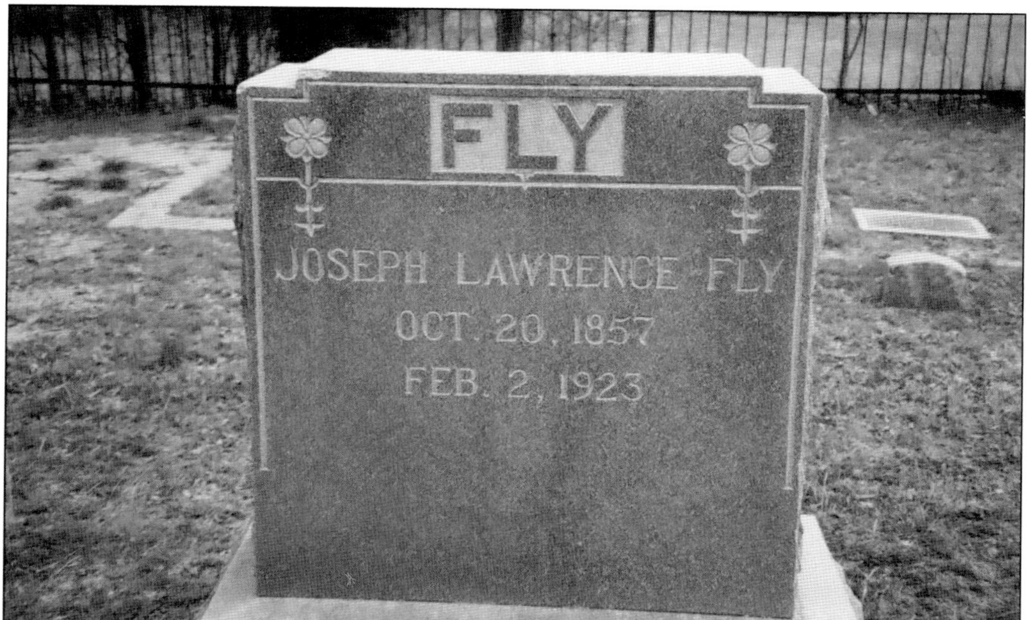

Joseph Lawrence Fly was born on October 20, 1857, and died February 2, 1923, in Seagoville. He is buried in Lee Cemetery. He became the second postmaster on July 1, 1887, and retired from this position on August 30, 1890. He also established a mercantile business and sold the first farm implements in this area and was elected justice of the peace in 1890. (Courtesy of Carol Franks.)

Six

Schools

The first known school in the Seagoville area was the old Brinegar School. It was a one-room split log building dating from the late 1860s. The curriculum consisted of the three Rs— "Reading, 'Riting, and 'Rithmetic," with a "spell down" every Friday afternoon. The second school was built about 1880 by Prof. John T. Doss and was called Woodside. It had split log seats and desks. One of the teachers earned $30 a month and paid $5 of this for room and board. The third school was a four-room frame building. About 1903, one of the rooms was destroyed by a cyclone. A total monthly budget of $195 showed the superintendent receiving $75 and the three teachers receiving $40 each. In 1909, one hundred sixty-six pupils were enrolled in the nine grades. This was also the same year that the building was destroyed by fire.

In 1927, land was purchased for a high school. Classes started in the new high school in fall 1928. The first school newspaper, the *Boll Weevil*, was published by students in January 1929. That same year, a school mascot, the Dragon, was chosen along with school colors of royal blue and white. The first football team was organized and coached by Dan Gross. In the 1940s, Brother William Greenhall wrote the school song, "Dear Old Seagoville High." This school served as both a school and a community center for years.

In the late 1940s to early 1950s, the Kleberg School became a part of the Seagoville Independent School system. In 1952, M. D. Reeves donated 22 acres for a new school. The building was constructed in 1955. In September 1958, another building was erected next to the existing structure on High School Drive. These two structures became the junior high and the high school. Central Elementary was built in the early 1960s on the site of the old burned high school. The Seagoville Independent School system became a part of the Dallas Independent School District (DISD) in August 1964.

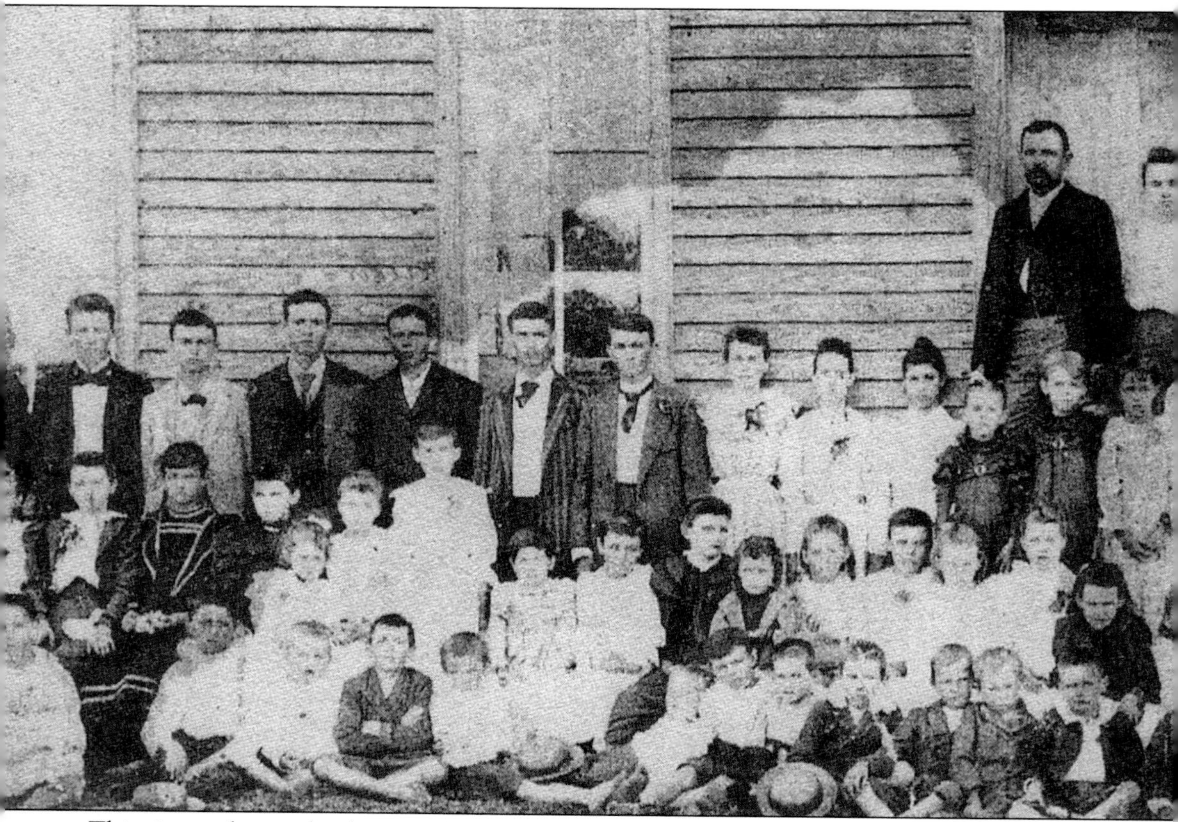

This picture shows school time in Seagoville in 1890. This is the student body of Woodside School with J. T. Doss, the principal, standing in the doorway. In the first row sitting fifth from left is his

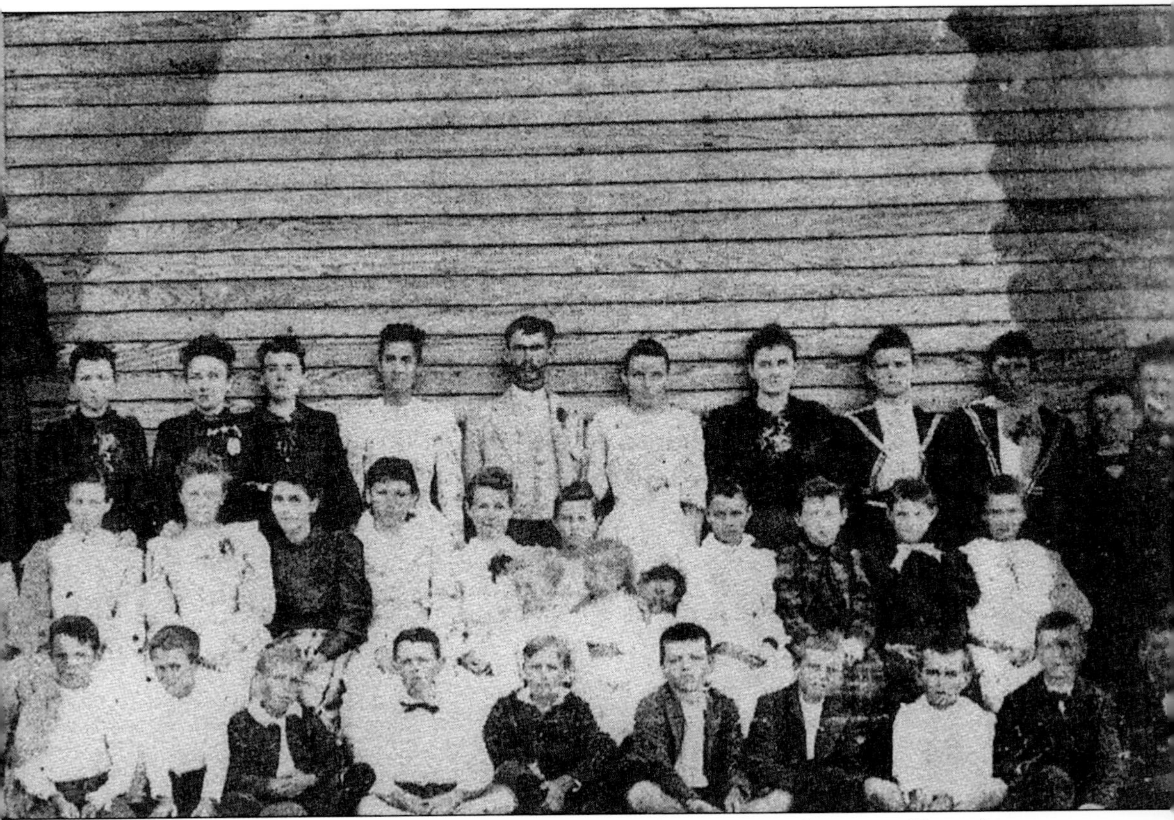

son Tom Doss, who was not old enough to go to school. Tom wanted to go and have his picture taken with the group. (Courtesy of Neal Wooley.)

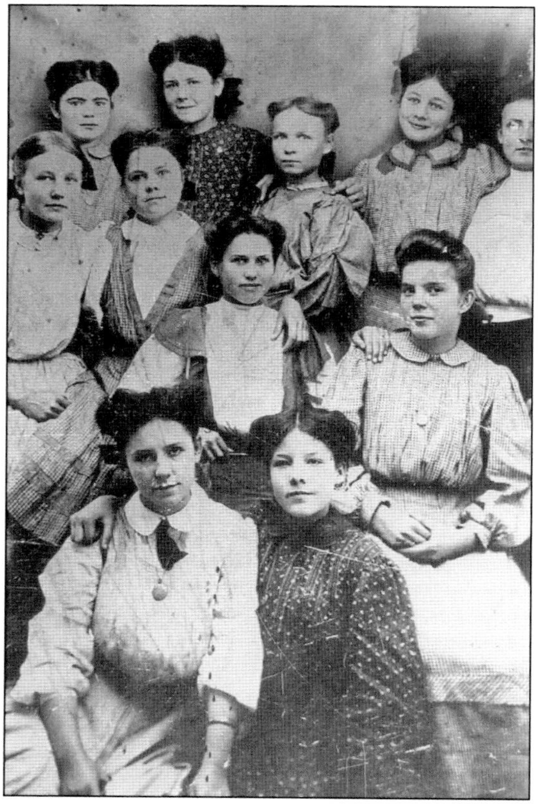

This photograph shows May 1909 Seagoville High School graduates. They are, from left to right, (first row) Ada Hurt and Callie Cardwell; (second row) Maude Wilson, Effie Thweatt, Grace Randerson, and Vera Johnson; (third row) Anabell Johnson, Annie McNutty, Ruth Fenley, Ona Wilson, and Mable Hawthorne. The group attended classes in the wooden structure located on the lower part of the 10 acres of land given by the Ben F. Fly family. (Courtesy of R. L. Glenn.)

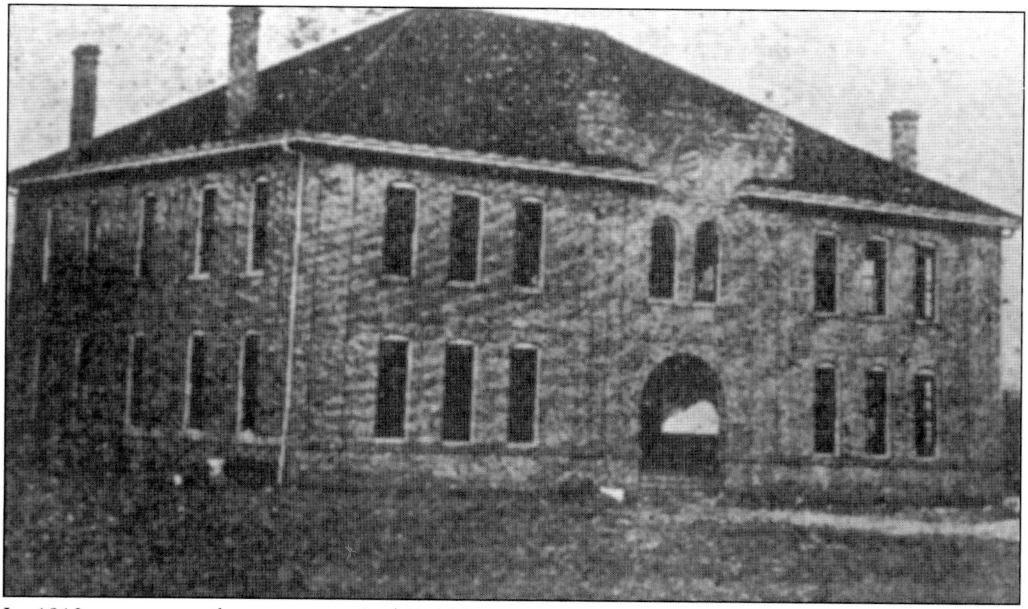

In 1910, at a cost of approximately $10,000, a new two-story brick school was built on North Kaufman Street on land donated by Ben H. Fly. The building had eight rooms with the four rooms downstairs for the lower grades and the four rooms upstairs for the higher grades. It was called the High School and later became known as the Old Red School House. (Courtesy of Neal Wooley.)

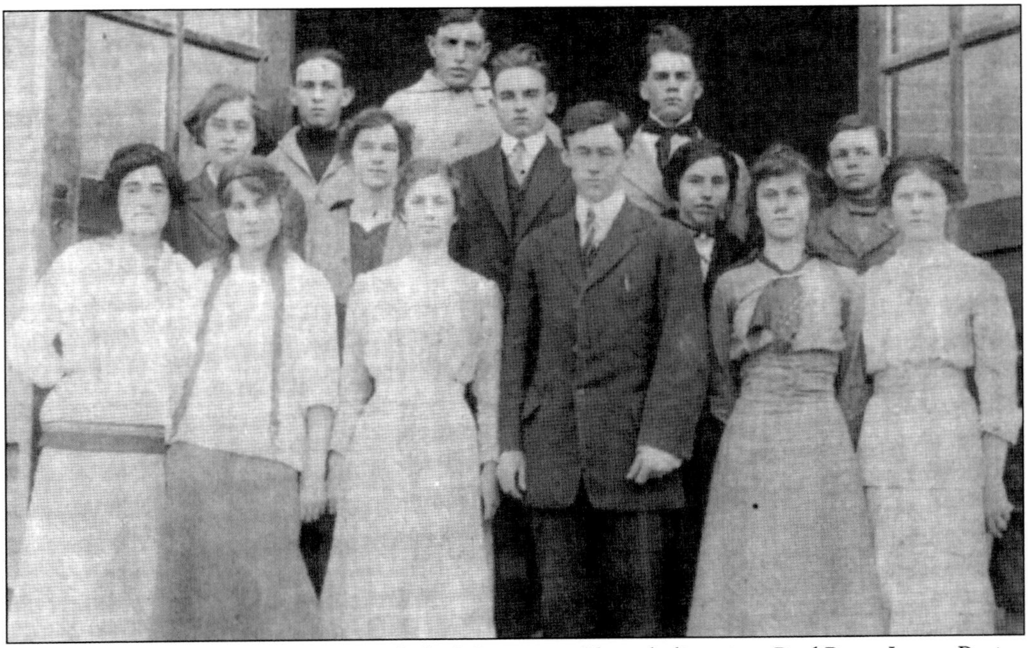

The graduating class of 1914–1915 includes J. Lawrence Fly, valedictorian; Paul Petty, Lester Pruitt, Fisher Stark, Cally Fly, Agnes Brockette, Roxie Robinson, Nora Ballard, and other unidentified members. W. L. Mitchell was superintendent, and LaVada Ratliff taught English, history, and Latin. (Courtesy of Neal Wooley.)

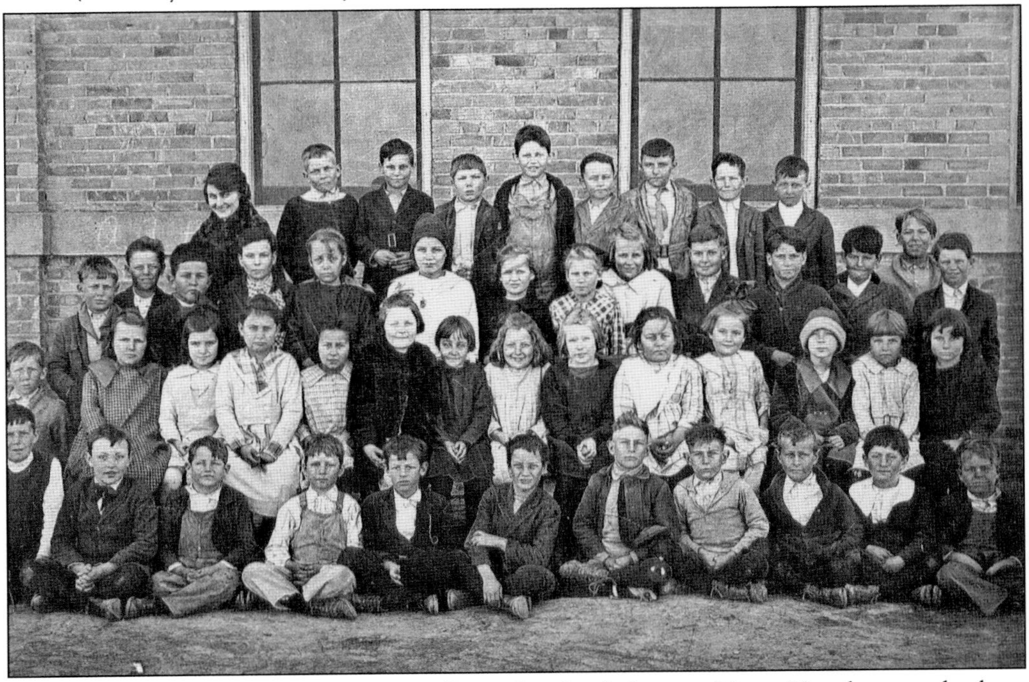

Some of the people in the 1920 Seagoville grade school class are Harry Hawthorne, who later became mayor of Seagoville for several years; Elmer Hurt, who became a pilot and built and repaired airplanes; and Edgar Robinson, who liked sports and music. Others include Kenneth Hurt, Claudine Petty, Reagan Glenn, and Thelma Crouch. (Courtesy of R. L. Glenn.)

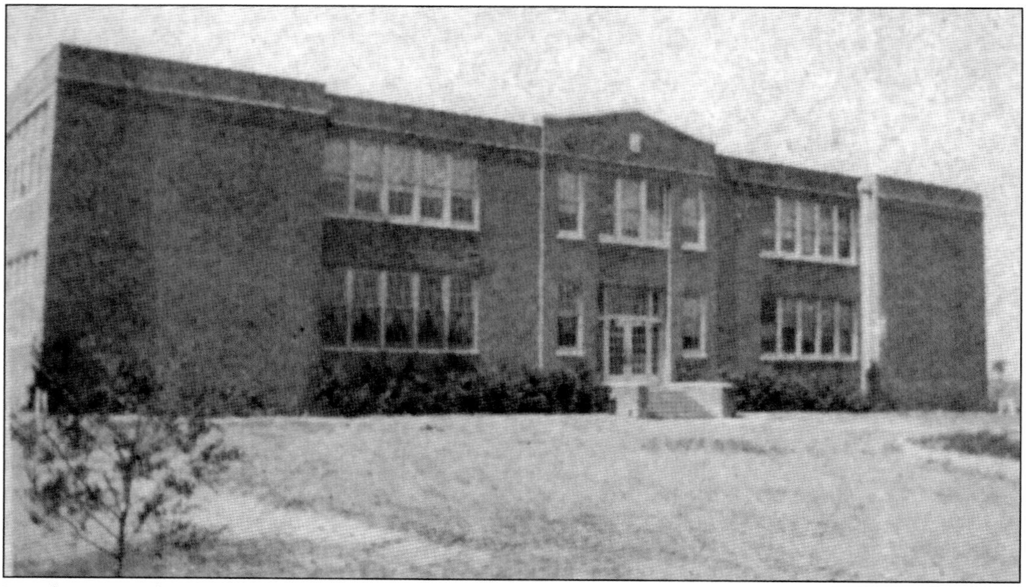

Land was purchased from Reagan Hawthorne on North Kaufman Street for a new two-story brick high school. It was built in 1928 at a cost of approximately $60,000 to $70,000. There were 12 rooms with later additions of a large gymnasium, auditorium, cafeteria, agriculture workshop, and homemaking building. The school was destroyed by fire in September 1957 after the first Friday night football game of the season. (Courtesy of Neal Wooley.)

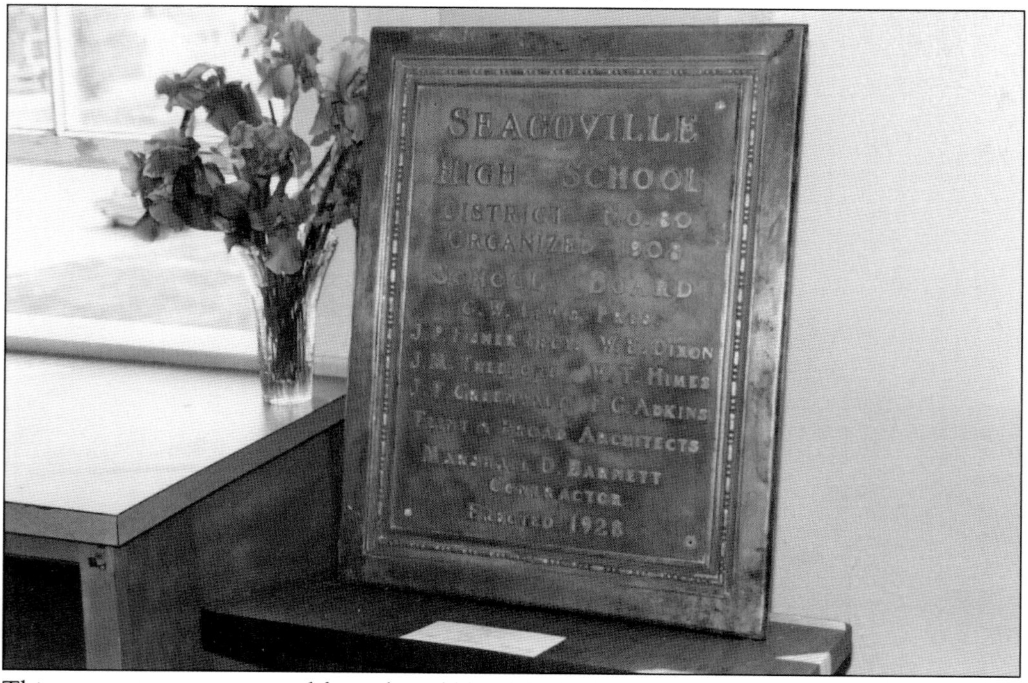

This cornerstone was rescued from the rubble of the high school fire in September 1957. It reads: Seagoville / High School / District No. 80 / Organized 1908 / School Board / G. W. Lewis Pres / J. P. Fisher Secy. W. E. Dixon / J. M. Thedford W. T. Himes / J. F. Greenawalt F. G. Adkins / Flint & Board Architects / Marshall D. Barnett / Contractor / Erected 1928. (Courtesy of Carol Franks.)

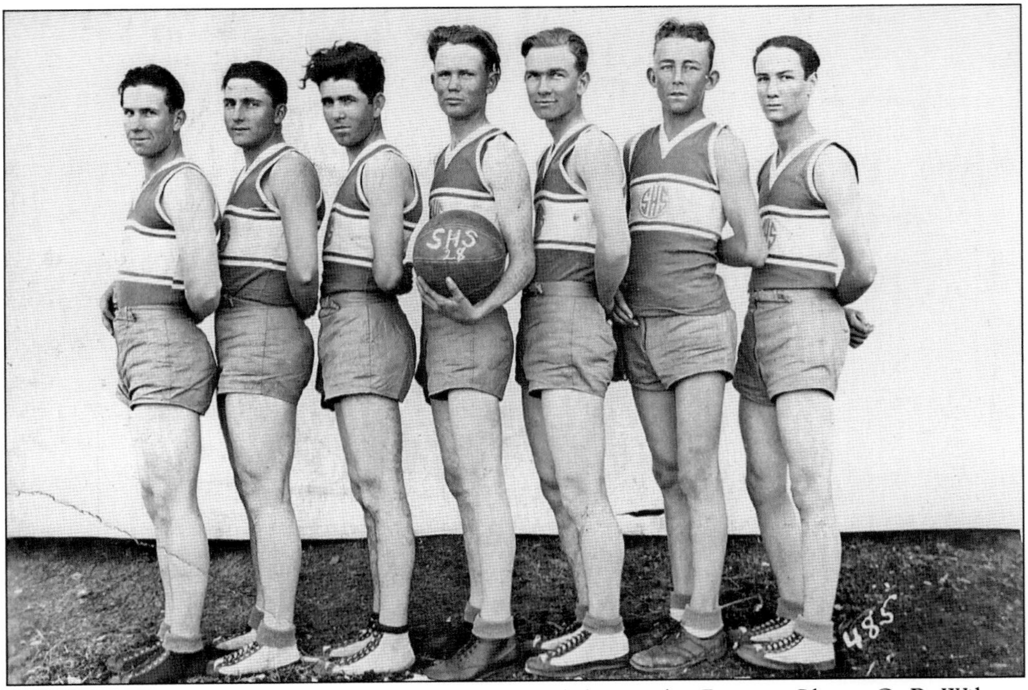

The 1928 boys' basketball team consisted of, from left to right, Reagan Glenn, O. B. Wilson, Paul Tiner, O. F. Mathis, Harry Hawthorne, I. R. Roberts, and Edgar Robinson. (Courtesy of R. L. Glenn.)

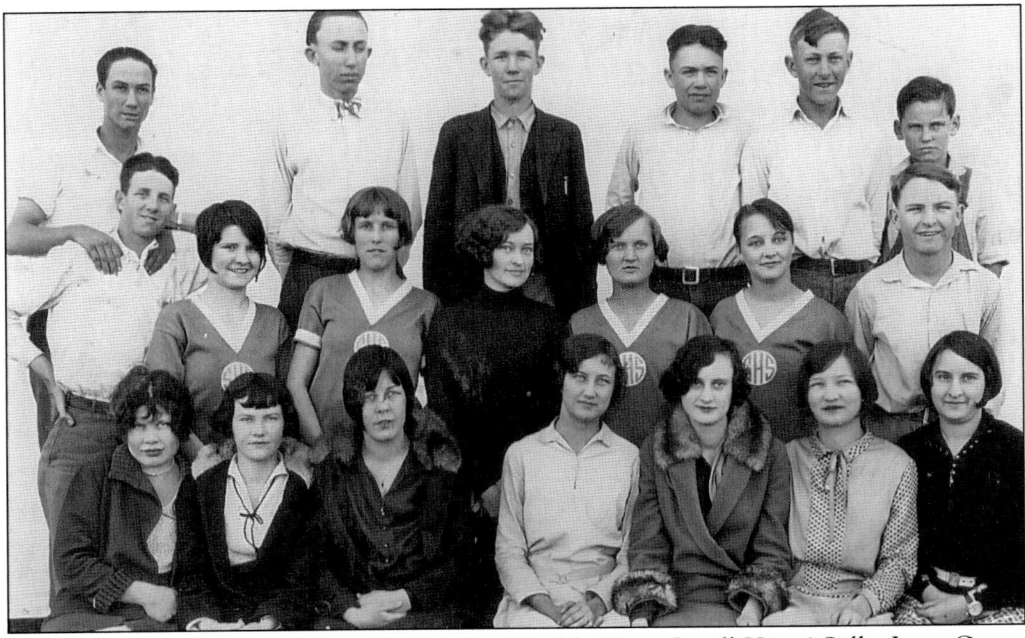

The 1928 class is, from left to right, (first row) Goldie Doss, Jewell Hitt, ? Sulla, Lena Grace, Daisy Goodman, Marie Comerine, and Mary Carder; (second row) George Hurt, Claudine Petty, Cleo Mathis, ? McTeaker, Alta Davidson, Reba Toal, and William Crawford; (third row) Edgar Robinson, Youl Riddles, unidentified, Loyd Ballard, Thomas Lee Miller, and Smell Forman. (Courtesy of R. L. Glenn.)

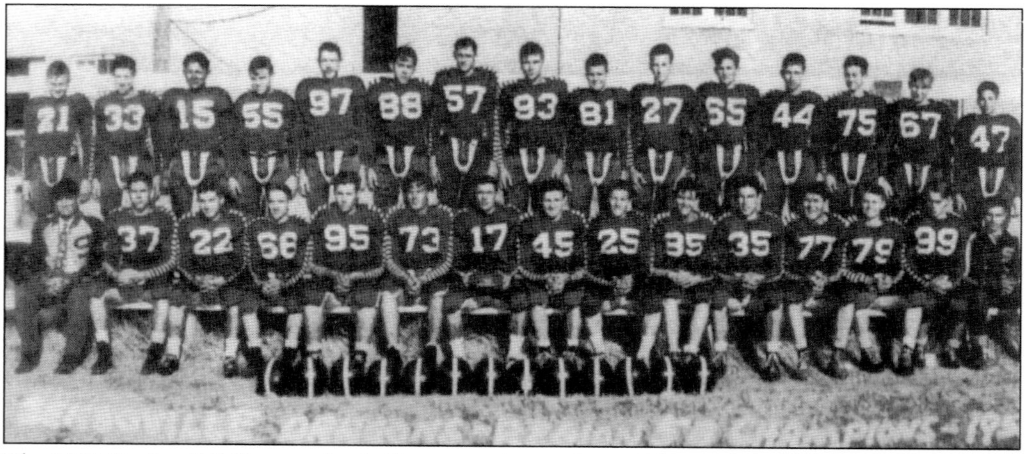

The 1950 Region 5-B Dragon football team is shown above. They went 11-1 and were selected to represent district 18-B in the state playoffs for the regional title. Regional was the highest honor for a class B team to win. Their coach was I. D. Thompson, who was also selected the greater Dallas area's coach of the year in this classification. (Courtesy of Neal Wooley.)

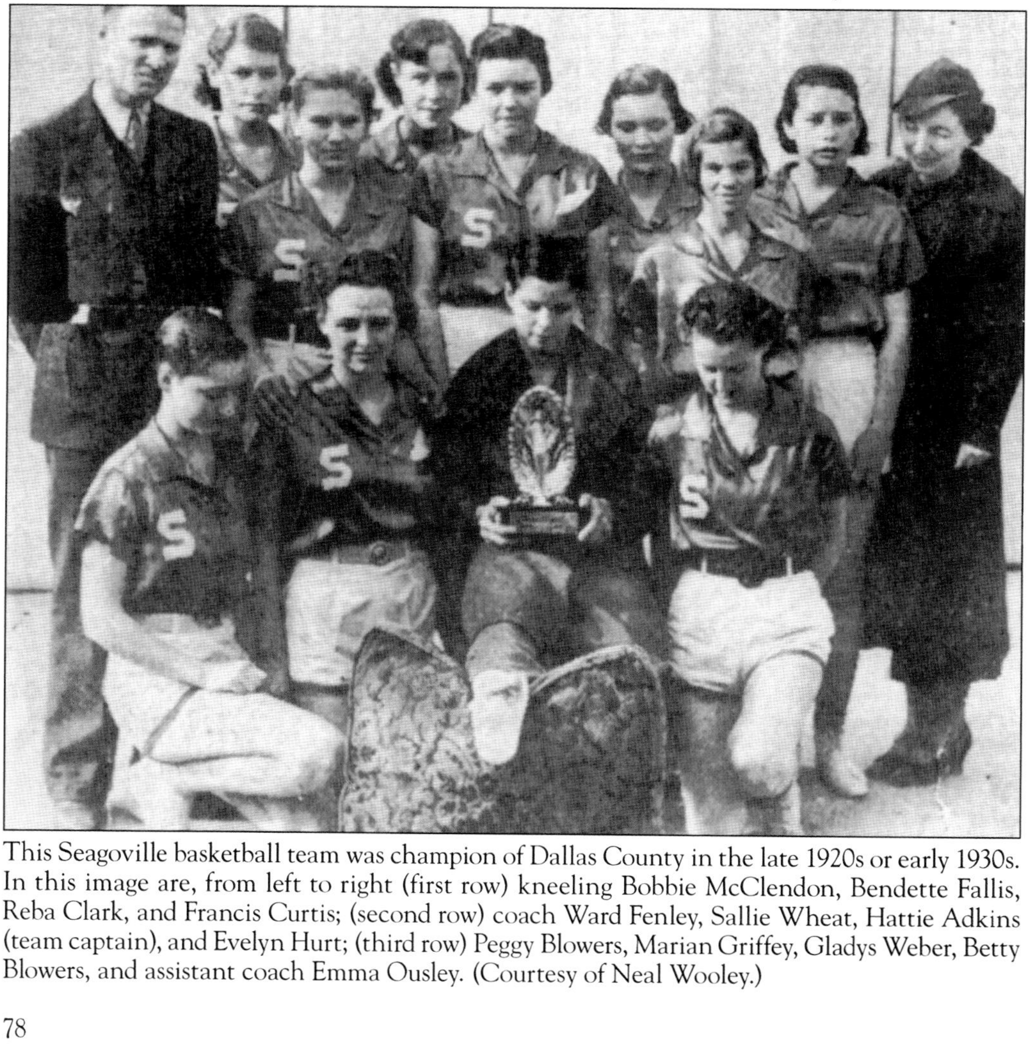

This Seagoville basketball team was champion of Dallas County in the late 1920s or early 1930s. In this image are, from left to right (first row) kneeling Bobbie McClendon, Bendette Fallis, Reba Clark, and Francis Curtis; (second row) coach Ward Fenley, Sallie Wheat, Hattie Adkins (team captain), and Evelyn Hurt; (third row) Peggy Blowers, Marian Griffey, Gladys Weber, Betty Blowers, and assistant coach Emma Ousley. (Courtesy of Neal Wooley.)

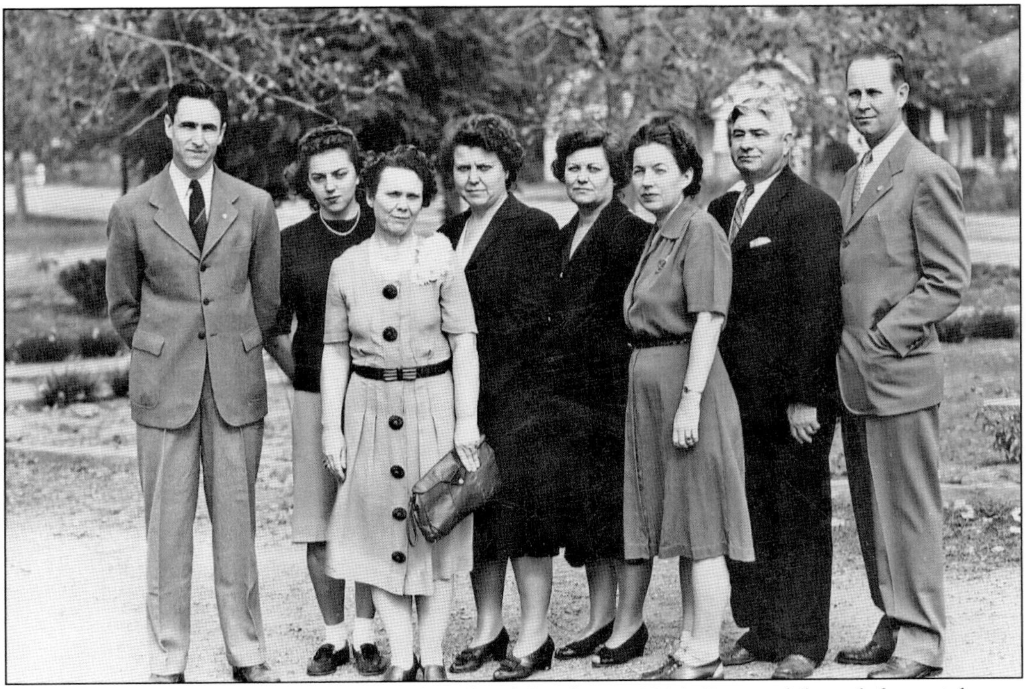

This is a picture of the Seagoville High School faculty in 1946. Pictured from left to right are James R. (Jimmy) Phillips, LaJuana Hampton, Anita Hunt, Ruby Price Taylor, Lourae Price Smith, Emma Ousley, Jack Derden, and Charles Tergerson (superintendent). Jimmy Phillips led the girls' basketball team to three state championships. When a game was played, the town closed up and only the night watchman was left. (Courtesy of Barbara Taylor Shepherd.)

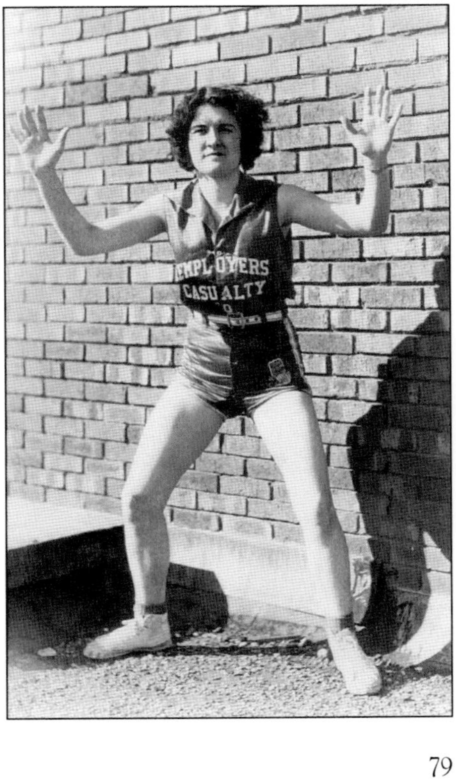

Claudine Petty (Glenn) was born and raised in Seagoville and played basketball for Moody Insurance based in Galveston. She began working for Moody's when she graduated from high school. Claudine was an outstanding basketball player. One of her teammates was Babe Didrikson Zaharias. The team won a national championship in 1931. (Courtesy of R. L. Glenn.)

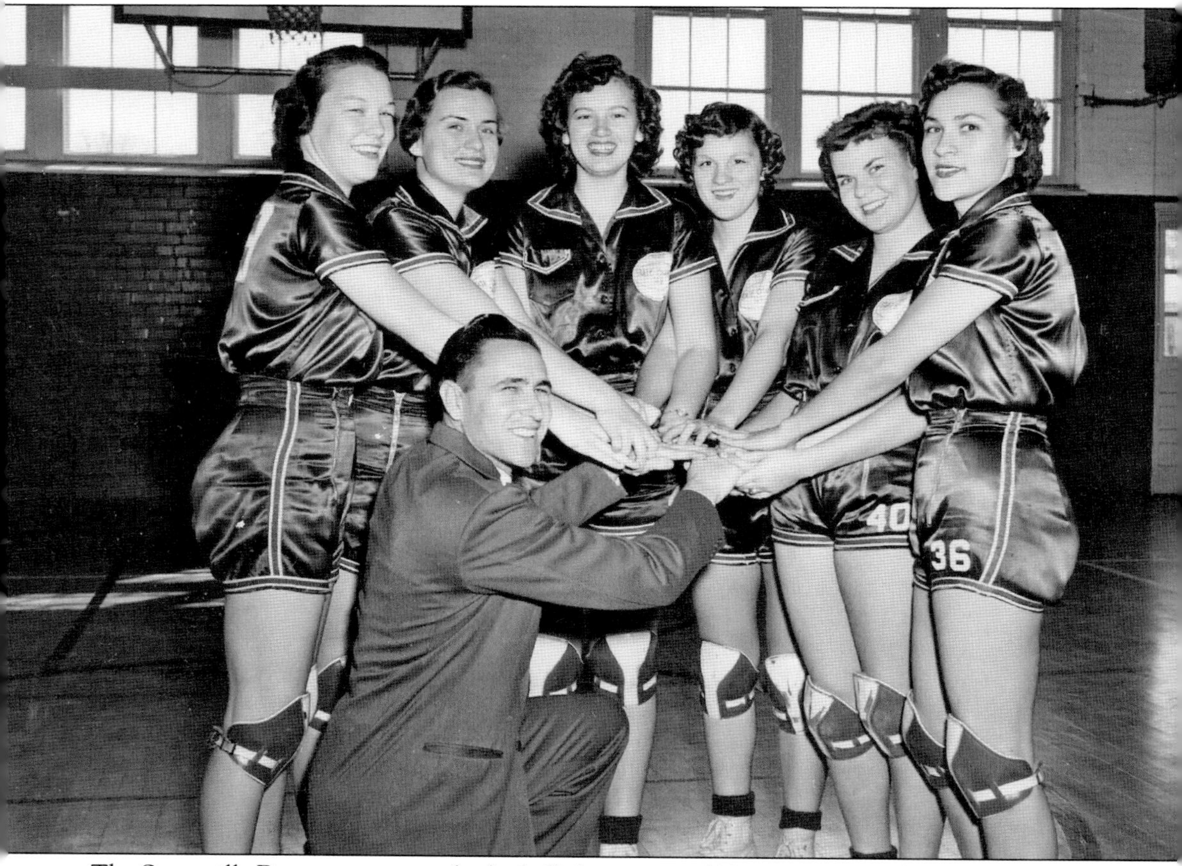
The Seagoville Dragonettes, state basketball champions of 1949, were greeted by Iowa fans along with Seagoville supporters. They were then transported by bus to their accommodations until game time. Of the two games played, the Dragonettes won the first contest and Wellsburg, Iowa, won the second game. The Dragonettes continued to be successful at Texas state meets as they won second place in 1950 and third place in 1951. (Courtesy of the Phillips family.)

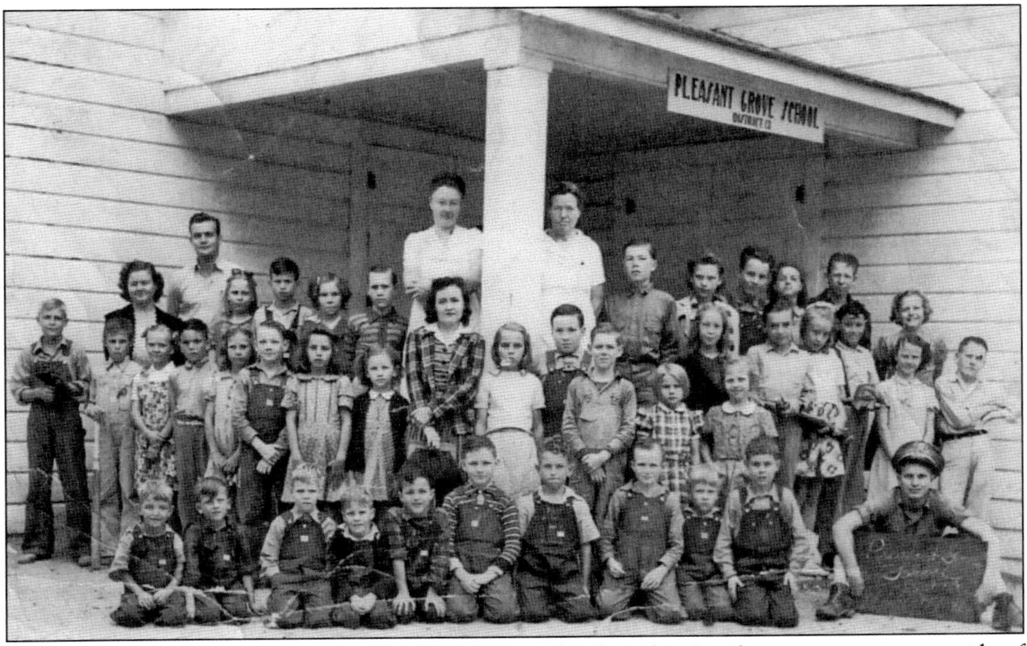

This is a group of students at the Pleasant Grove School in the Combine community outside of Seagoville in 1941 or 1942. Students from this school later fed into the Seagoville Elementary School. After being annexed into the Seagoville school system, the Pleasant Grove building was moved onto the grounds of Seagoville High School on North Kaufman Street. This building served as classrooms for the seventh and eighth grades in the 1950s. (Courtesy of Floy Ballantine.)

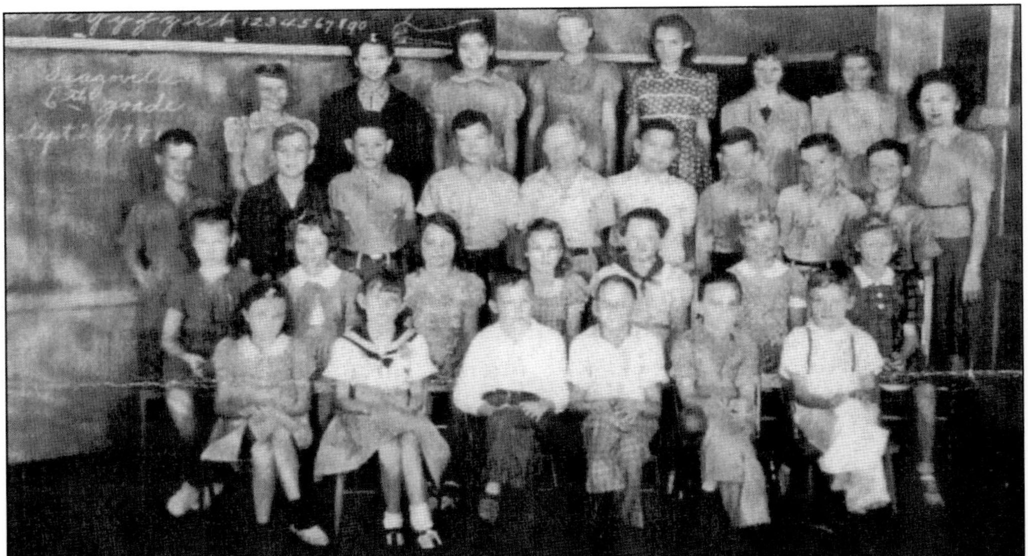

Pictured is the Seagoville sixth-grade class with Reba Phillips as the teacher. This was originally the fifth grade but became the sixth grade because it was the year the school district added a 12th grade. It was also the last year Reba Phillips taught at Seagoville. She left in February 1942 after World War II broke out. (Courtesy of the Phillips family.)

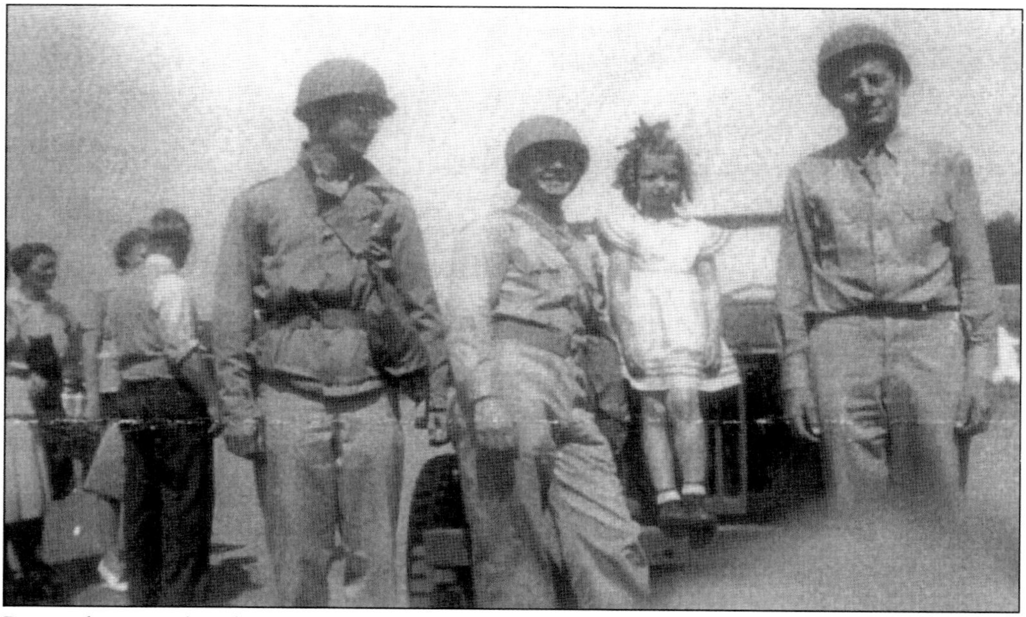

Pictured is a war bond party held at the Seagoville Grammar School in the fall of 1938. Martha Raye Glenn Richardson was the lucky little girl pictured with the soldiers. A person could buy a $25 war bond and ride in the jeep. Delia Glenn, Martha Raye's grandmother, bought several bonds. The jeep was the first in Seagoville, as they were developed for use in World War II. (Courtesy of the Seagoville Historical Commission.)

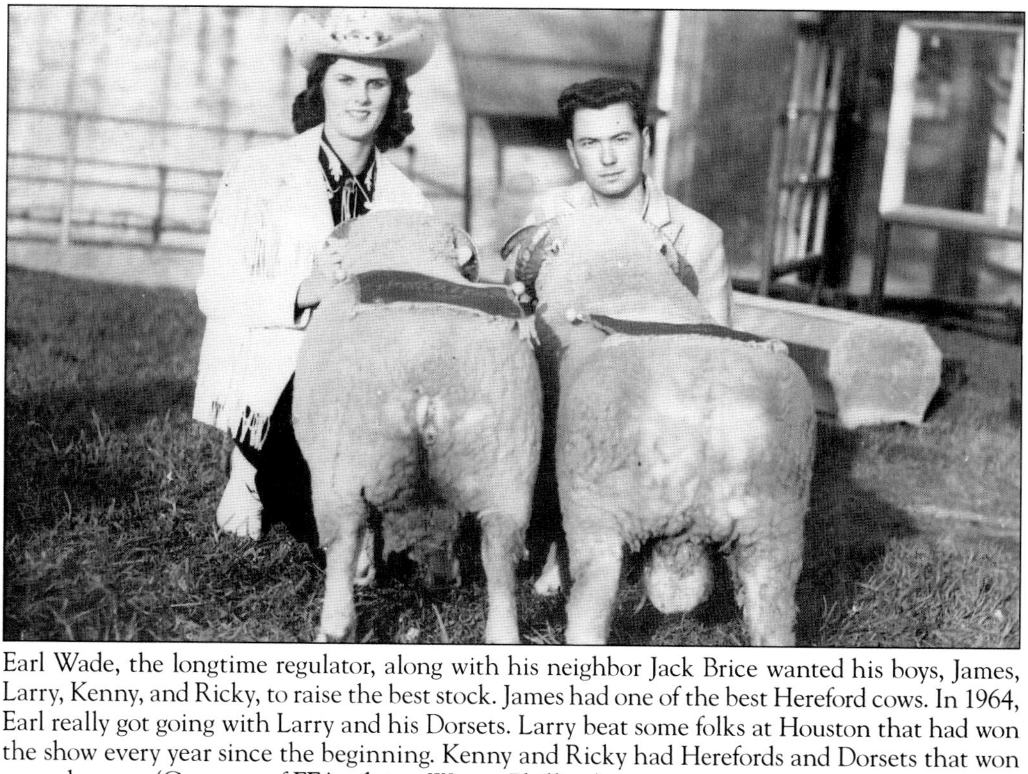

Earl Wade, the longtime regulator, along with his neighbor Jack Brice wanted his boys, James, Larry, Kenny, and Ricky, to raise the best stock. James had one of the best Hereford cows. In 1964, Earl really got going with Larry and his Dorsets. Larry beat some folks at Houston that had won the show every year since the beginning. Kenny and Ricky had Herefords and Dorsets that won many honors. (Courtesy of FFA adviser Wayne Phillips.)

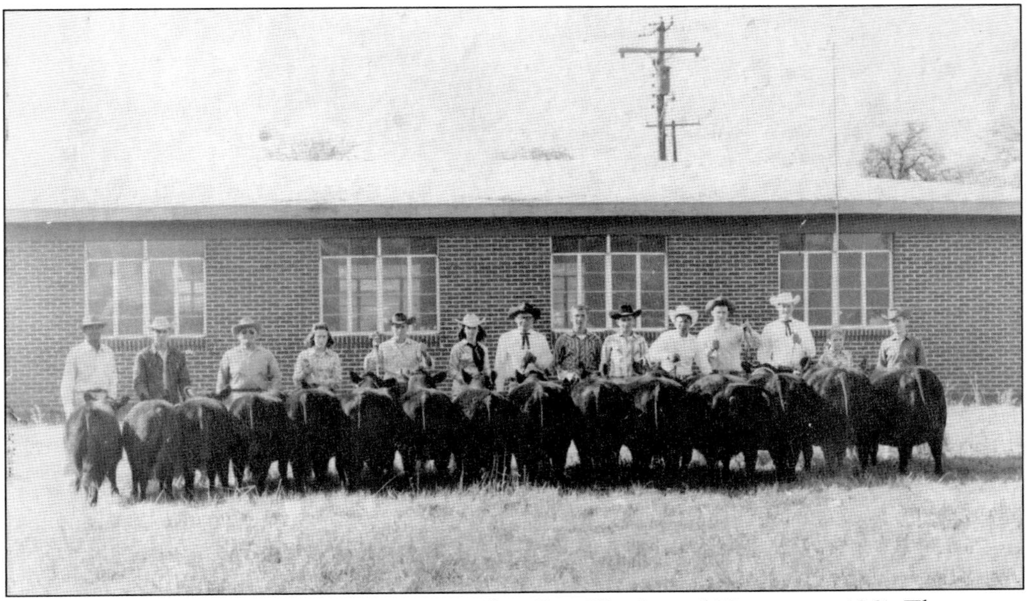

This is a group of Angus heifers shown in Dallas, Fort Worth, and Houston in 1961. There were many winners, including a reserve champion at Dallas and several class winners. In this photograph are, from left to right, an unidentified employee of Nelson farm, Bobby Thomason, Nile Hoffman, Pat Hoffman, Doug Thomason, Barbara Ogletree Yarbrough (FFA Sweetheart), Ronald Hoffman, Leroy Dixon, Baleriano Rodriguez, Danny Nix, Johnny McDonell, Denny Nelson, Prissy Price, and Teddy Price. (Courtesy of FFA adviser Wayne Phillips.)

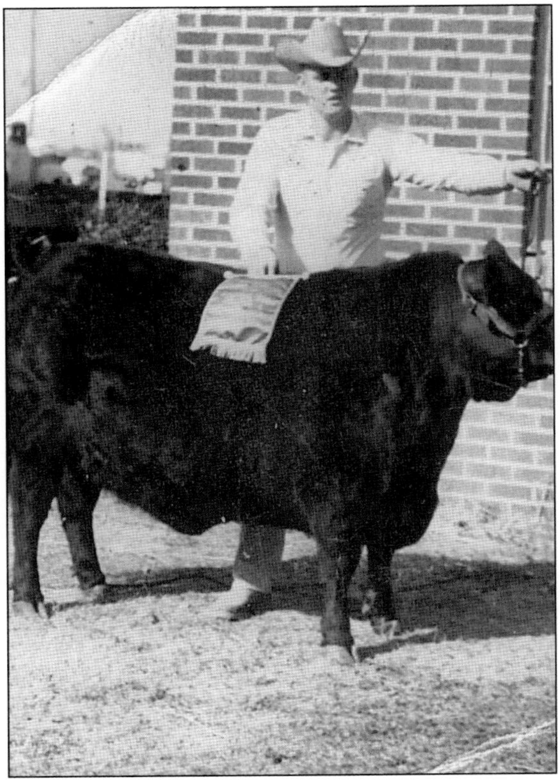

In 1962, at the local project shows, Johnny McDonell won or placed in every division. Angus cattle were his first love. He was very helpful to other exhibitors and was instrumental in helping the chapter in winning several good-housekeeping awards. After graduating, McDonell went on the road as herdsman for several Hereford and Angus herds and worked on one of the largest Southdown flocks in the country. (Courtesy of FFA adviser Wayne Phillips.)

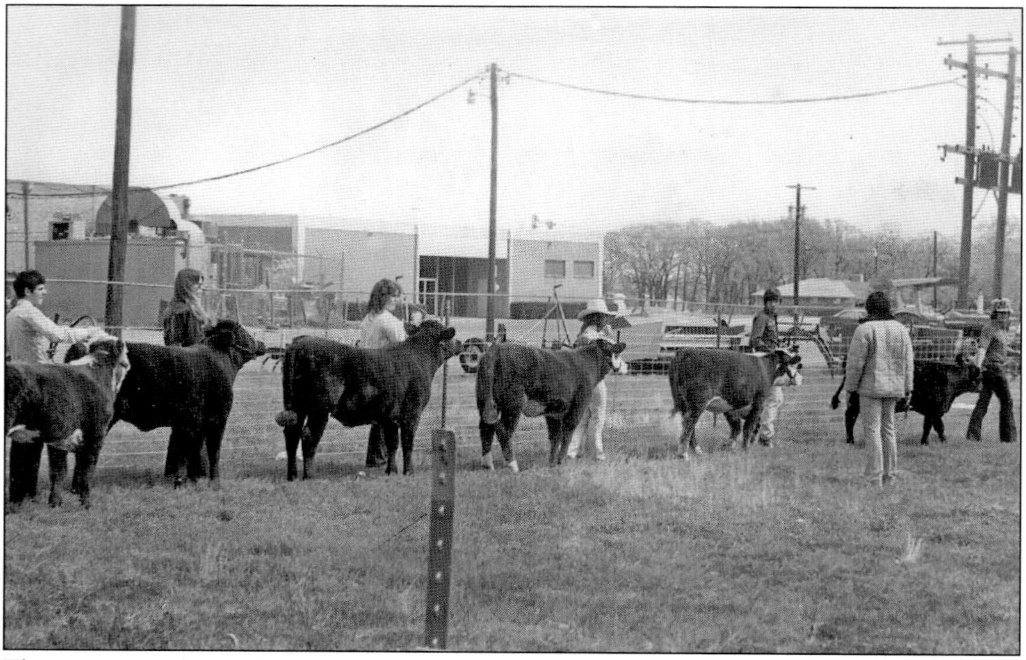

This is a group of young heifers being shown in the area behind the Town and Country shopping center in 1982. From left to right are Mike Rucks, Becky Buster, Laurie Smith with her Shorthorn, Tracy Battson with her Polled Hereford, Randy Hinton (?) with his Hereford, and Terri Sims with an Angus. (Courtesy of FFA adviser Wayne Phillips.)

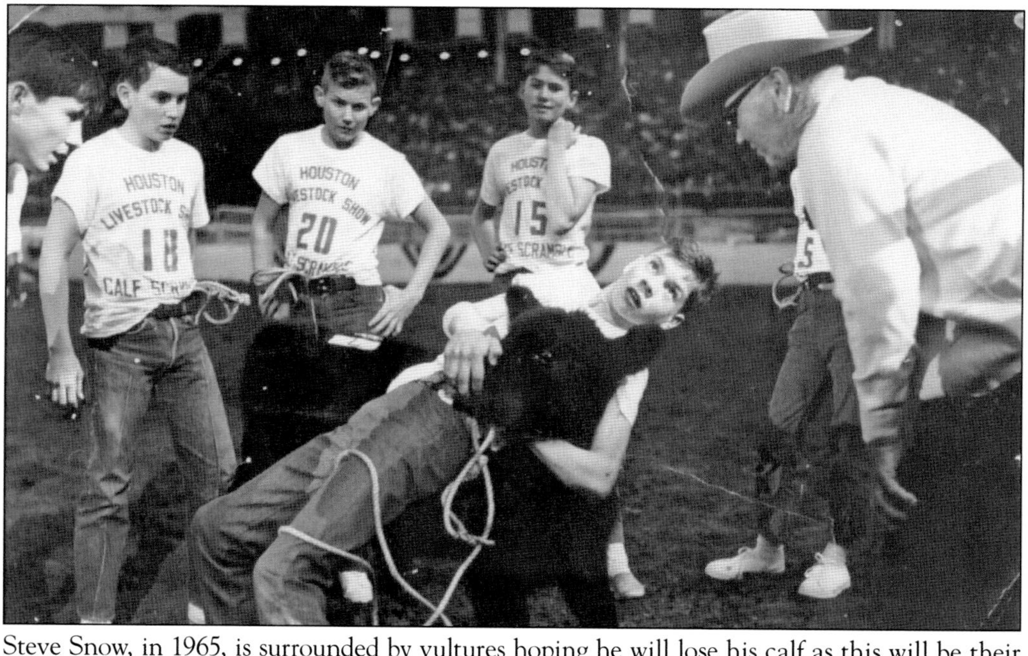

Steve Snow, in 1965, is surrounded by vultures hoping he will lose his calf as this will be their only chance. Steve endured and selected a Santa Gertrudis heifer for the next year. Some of the other Houston show winners include Doyle Loveless, Charles Hillin, Dick McGaughy, Bill Ridgell, Jimmy Stark, Mike Thomas, Wendel Schoenberger, and Terry Tunnell. Denny Nelson won a certificate by winning in the judging contest. (Courtesy of FFA adviser Wayne Phillips.)

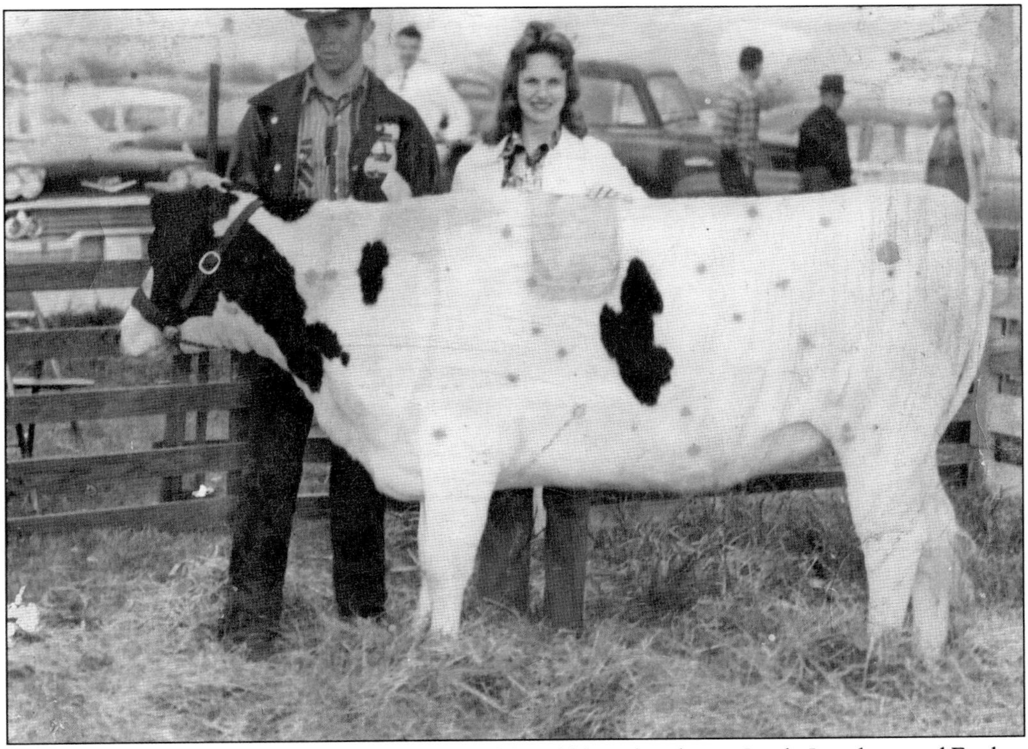

Jimmy Stark is descended from at least three of the old-line families—Stark, Landess, and Fenley. Jimmy was a top scholar, FFA chapter president, and calf scramble winner. He married an FFA chapter sweetheart. Stark raised beef cattle, but his Holstein heifer project holds the all-time record for net profit. Annette Smith is the FFA Sweetheart who won the queen's contest at the North East Texas livestock show. (Courtesy of FFA adviser Wayne Phillips.)

Dick McGaughy says he rode in the back of a pickup truck to enter the calf scramble at Houston in 1960. He was accompanied by Charles Hillin and a boar hog. They were both successful. Dick had many projects—pigs, sheep, and cattle. He is shown with Annette Smith, the FFA Sweetheart who became queen of the North East Texas show. Dick is a grandson of a pioneer area doctor, Dr. Ridgell. (Courtesy of FFA adviser Wayne Phillips.)

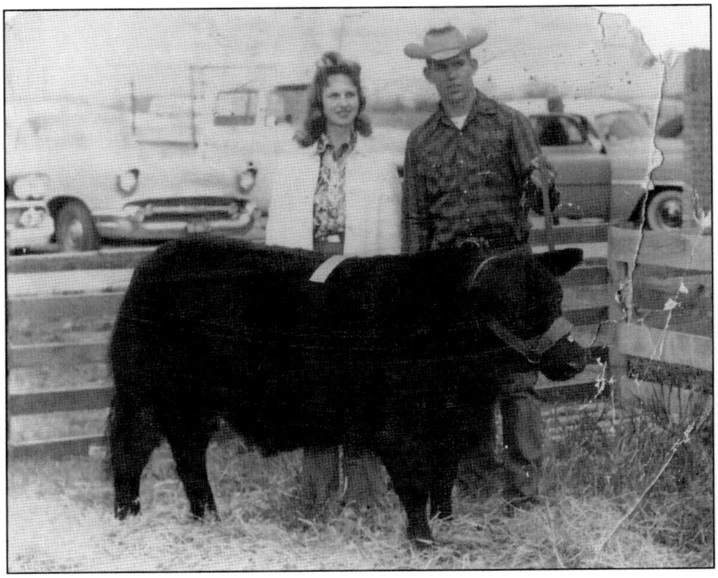

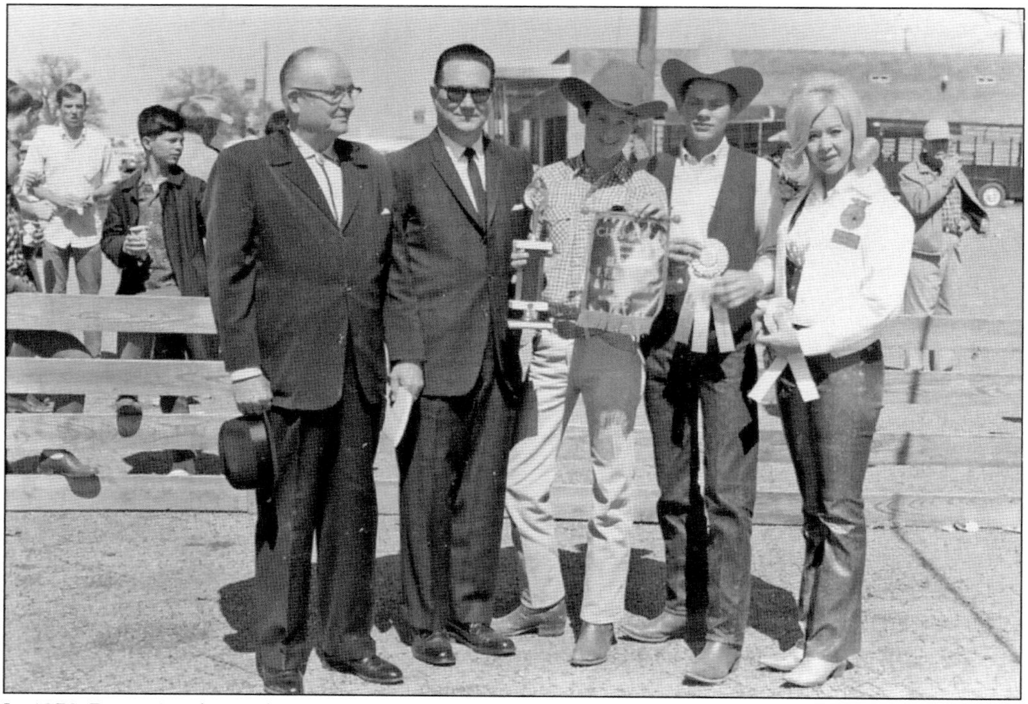

In 1970, Bragg Stockton, director of occupational education (DISD), and Weldon Griffith, facilitator, presented a trophy for champion showman Larry Morris and a rosette for reserve champion Jim Ballentine. Also pictured is Charlotte Glenn, FFA Sweetheart. This was an award coveted by FFA members. Morris and Ballantine were frequent winners. Other notable showman winners were Lee Paul Smith in the Shorthorn show at Houston and Wendel Schoenberger showing Denny Nelson's first-place Shropshire wether lamb at Dallas, while Denny was showing his Angus heifer to reserve championship. (Courtesy of FFA adviser Wayne Phillips.)

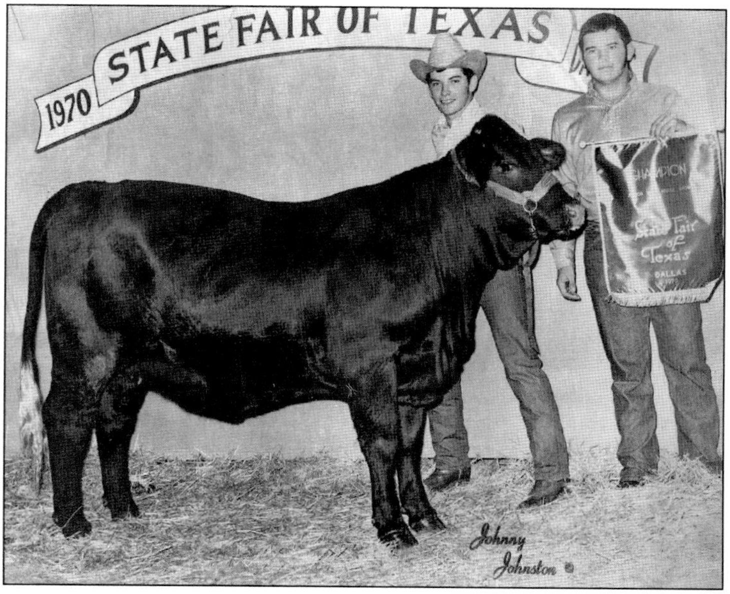

Joe Scott is smiling because he beat his brother Terrell for the state fair championship in 1970. The tide was turned at Fort Worth, where Terrell won. Other good Santa Gertrudis were owned by Joel Davis, Reagan L. Glenn, Donald Kindser, Steve Snow, and Jim Ballantine. The Scotts also raised some Brahmas as did Stepper Sebastian, Joe Hale, Joe Scott, and Sammy Scott. (Courtesy of FFA adviser Wayne Phillips.)

In 1959, Jackie Ballard had an outstanding flock of Shropshires. However, likely his greatest feat was with a Southdown ram lamb he bought from his neighbor, Billy Davis. He fitted him, took him to the Oklahoma state fair, and beat one of the biggest breeders that had not been defeated in the ram lamb class in three years. Jackie farmed for a time and was president of the area five FFA association. (Courtesy of FFA adviser Wayne Phillips.)

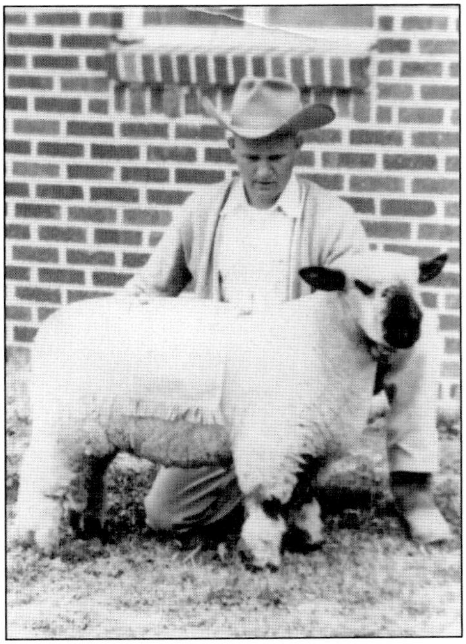

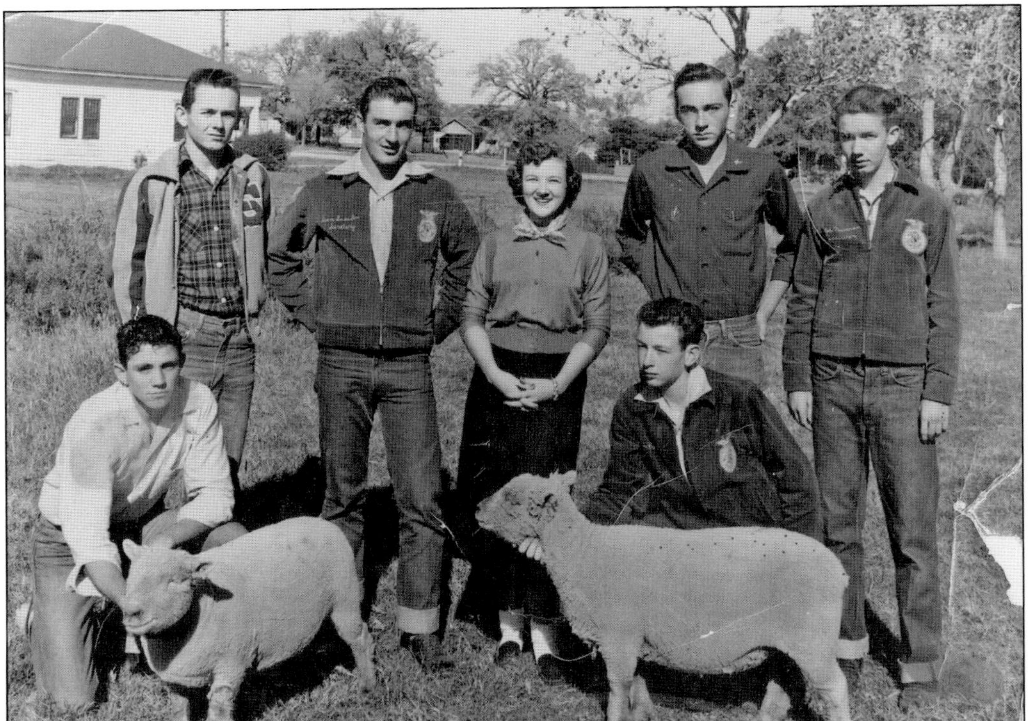

In this 1954 photograph are, from left to right, (kneeling) Paul Davis and Dan Prescott; (standing) Raymond Gregg, football quarterback; Dean Snowden, who became a successful builder and businessman in Arlington; FFA Sweetheart Charlotte Allen Blessing; Doyle Loveless; and Ralph Newman. Paul Davis won the Ben Griffin tractor-driving contest, and Doyle Loveless was the first Houston calf scramble winner. Loveless got sick and could not show, so Dean Snowden showed for him. (Courtesy of FFA adviser Wayne Phillips.)

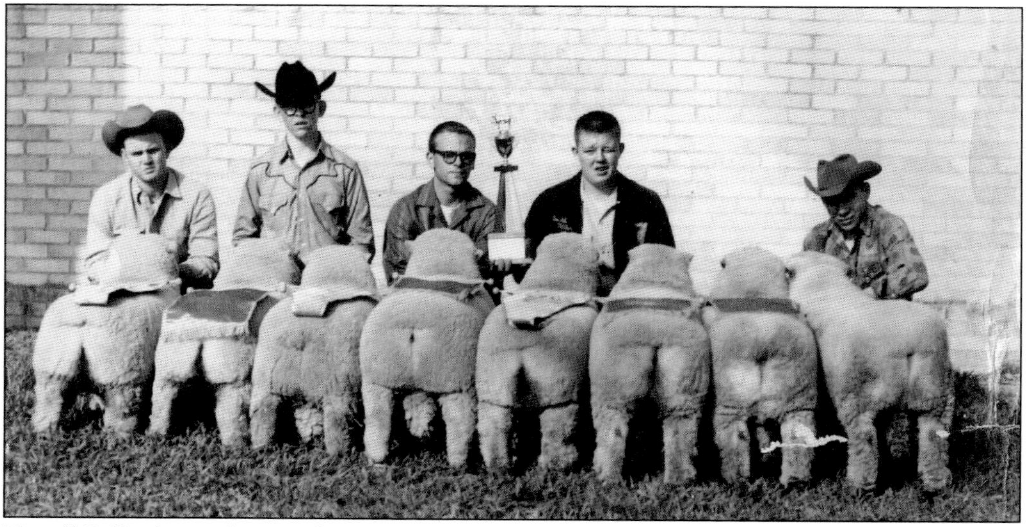

Newell Ballard won the very first premier exhibition award offered by the show in 1962. He won all that was to be won in the Southdown and Shropshire breeds. The holders are, from left to right, Johnny McDonell, Joel Hitt, Newell Ballard, David Miller, and Grady Doss. Doss won many awards with his Shropshire ram, the pinnacle of which was the championship of the open show at Fort Worth. (Courtesy of FFA adviser Wayne Phillips.)

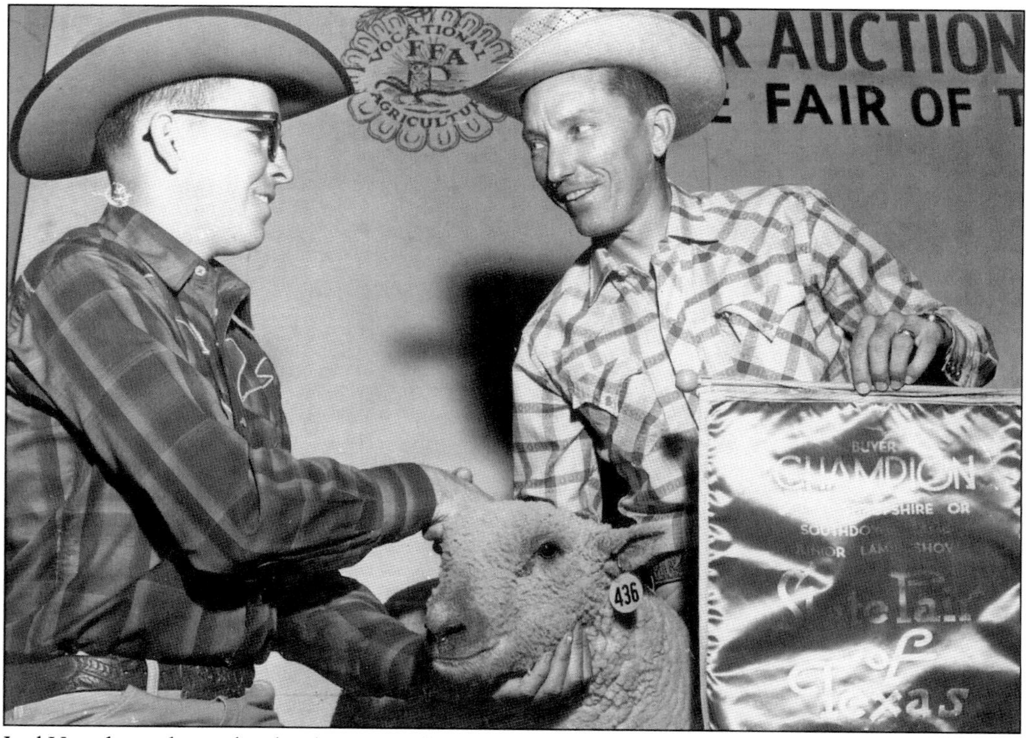

Joel Hitt showed a wether lamb in 1963 that won the Ellis County fair. This lamb, costing $25, was born and raised in Seagoville. It also won grand champion at the Texas State Fair. Joel and Mike Thomas followed Newell Ballard with some top Southdowns. Others having good Southdowns were Sidney and Mark Goodson, Elvin Chapman, Gene Altom, Lavoy Dixon, Dan Watkins, Tim Ramsey, and Larry Harris. (Courtesy of FFA adviser Wayne Phillips.)

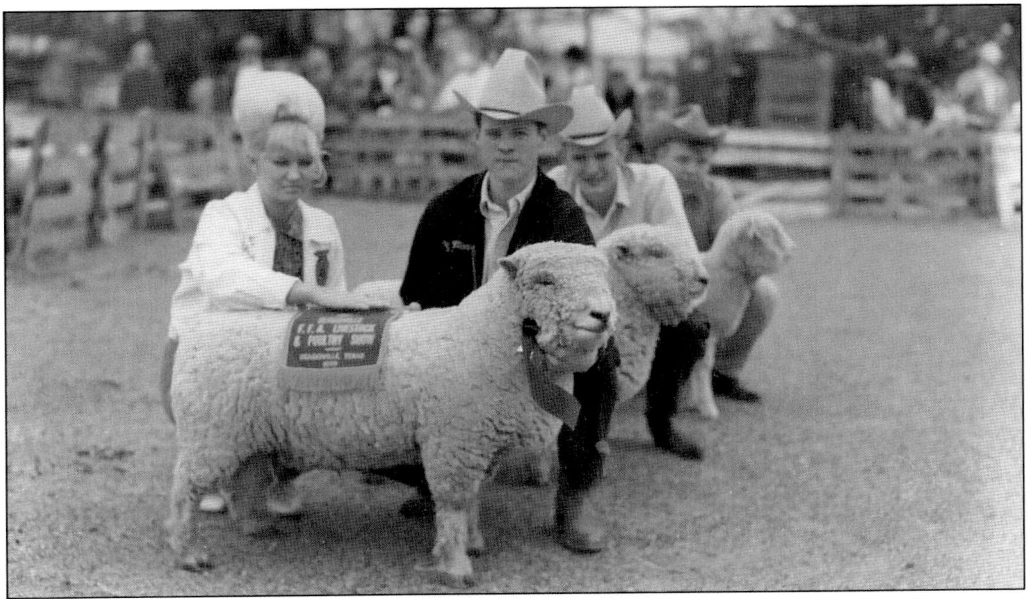

In 1969, James and Larry Morris kept the Southdown sheep banners coming after the success of Newell Ballard, Joel Hitt, Mike Thomas, Larry Dixon, the Cades, Larry Harris, and Dan Watkins. An excellent flock won them many honors at North East Texas, Fort Worth, Houston, and Seagoville. Pictured from front to back are Charlotte Glenn, FFA chapter sweetheart; Larry Morris; James Morris; and Stanley Coker. The Coker boys—Ronald, Stanley, and Larry—had some good Dorsets. (Courtesy of FFA adviser Wayne Phillips.)

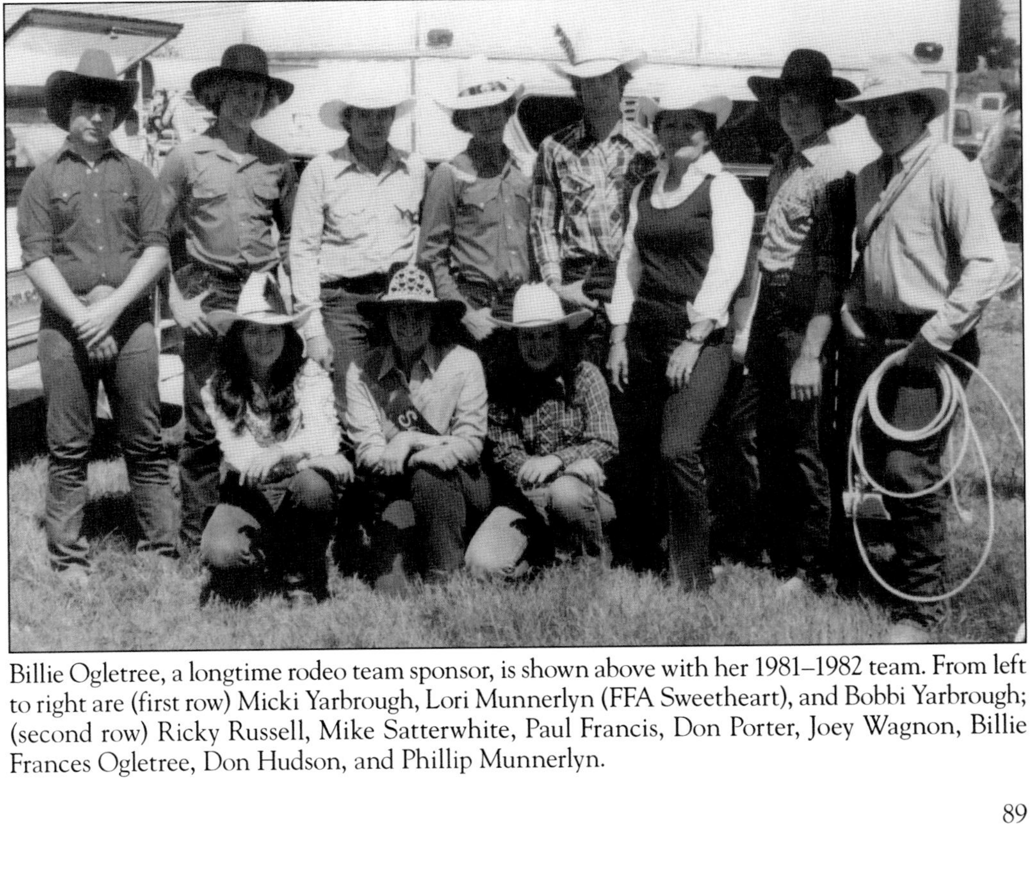

Billie Ogletree, a longtime rodeo team sponsor, is shown above with her 1981–1982 team. From left to right are (first row) Micki Yarbrough, Lori Munnerlyn (FFA Sweetheart), and Bobbi Yarbrough; (second row) Ricky Russell, Mike Satterwhite, Paul Francis, Don Porter, Joey Wagnon, Billie Frances Ogletree, Don Hudson, and Phillip Munnerlyn.

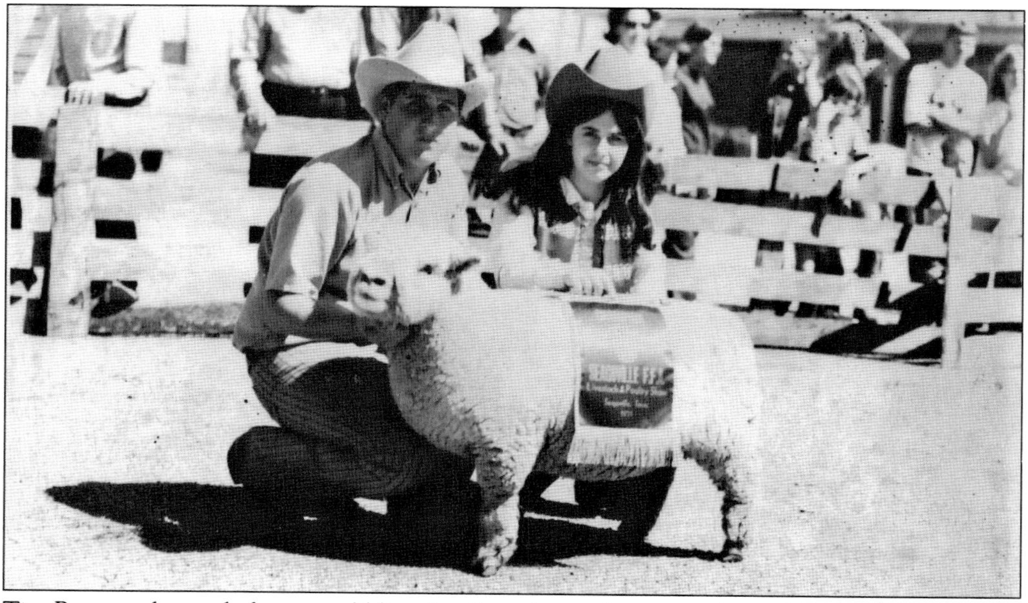

Tim Ramsey descends from an old-line family and raised some good Southdown sheep. He also helped with the family cattle and farming operations. Ramsey is presently a fireman and local businessman. He poses here with Lynn Thomas, FFA Sweetheart in 1973. (Courtesy of FFA adviser Wayne Phillips.)

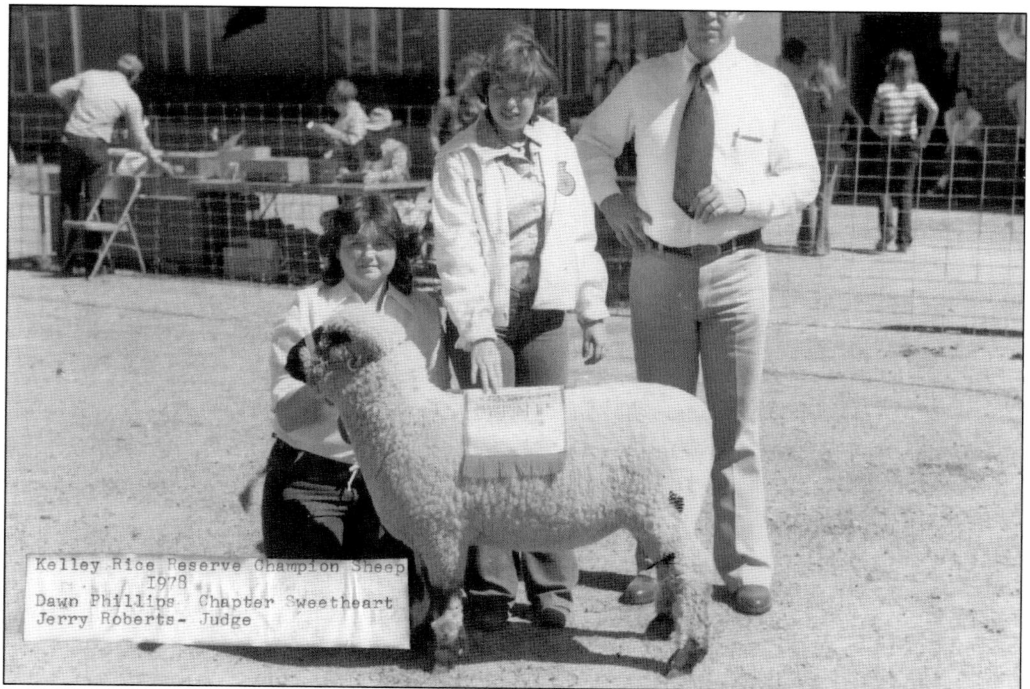

Kelly Rice spent much time with her grandmother Hattie Mae Harrell, and she raised this good Hampshire ewe. Jerry Perkins, her uncle, also raised good Hampshires. Jackie, Jimmy, and Donna Childers, another Seagoville family, also raised good sheep. In 1978, Kelly is shown with Dawn Phillips, FFA chapter sweetheart, and judge Jerry Roberts. (Courtesy of FFA adviser Wayne Phillips.)

Seven

HOMES

Homes in the Seagoville community in the beginning were often constructed of logs similar to the one occupied by the Leamon Cox family. In the early 1900s, more modern houses began to evolve, like the Cobb and Fenley homes. Many of the present-day residences were built in the prosperous times preceding and shortly after World War I.

As the Depression began to ease, more homes were built. E. A. Robinson and Ode Simmons built many houses in and around Seagoville in the 1920s, 1930s, and early 1940s. In the later 1940s and early 1950s, housing developments began to spring up. C. M. Duncan and M. D. (Pappy) Reeves were some of the early builders. Steve Philpot was another developer.

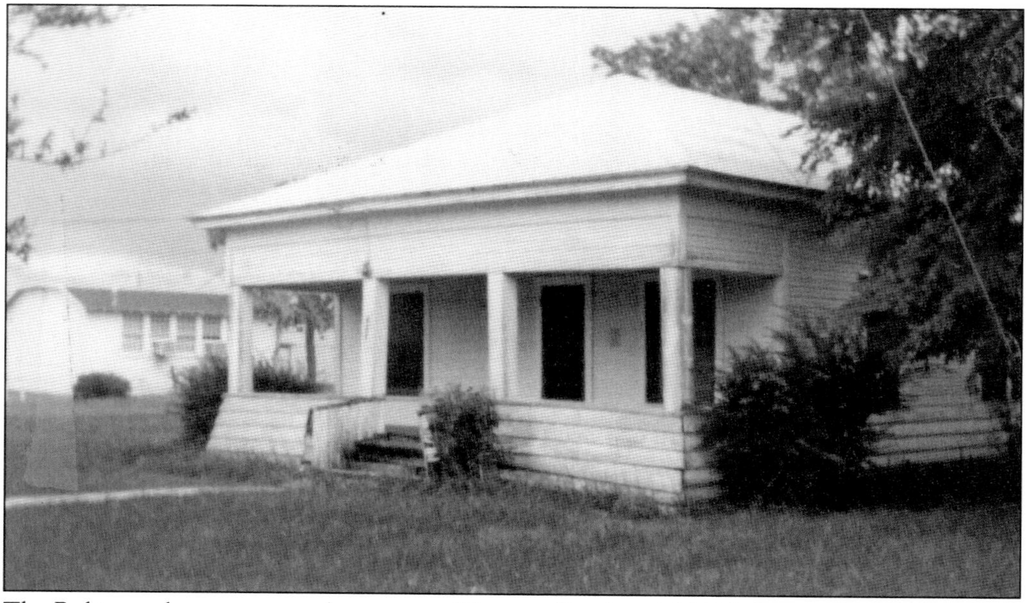

The Robinson house was on the corner of Farmers Road and Old Highway 175, now known as North Kaufman Street. It was built in 1906 by Edgar Alfonzo Robinson and Ode Simmons. There was a smokehouse, a chicken house, outdoor toilet, and a double garage coming off Farmers Road. The well was dug in 1906 at a location that was found by Ode Simmons, who used a water witch cut from a tree on Ward Fenley's property at the corner of Farmers Road and Watson Street. It took two weeks to hit water, which was very cold but had a strong metallic taste. The well still stands on property at Old Highway 175 and Farmers Road. (Courtesy of Gwen Robinson Gaida.)

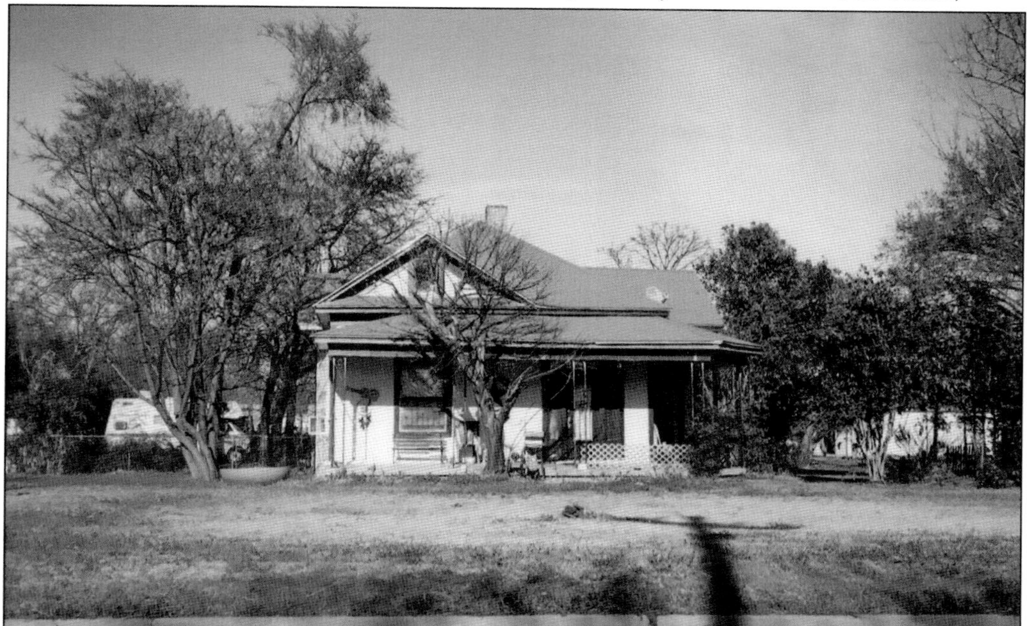

This one-story house with the wraparound porch is a Texas classic. It was known as the Hunsaker home and was built in the early 1920s. Several families have lived on this property and always kept it neat. (Courtesy of Kathryn Ballard.)

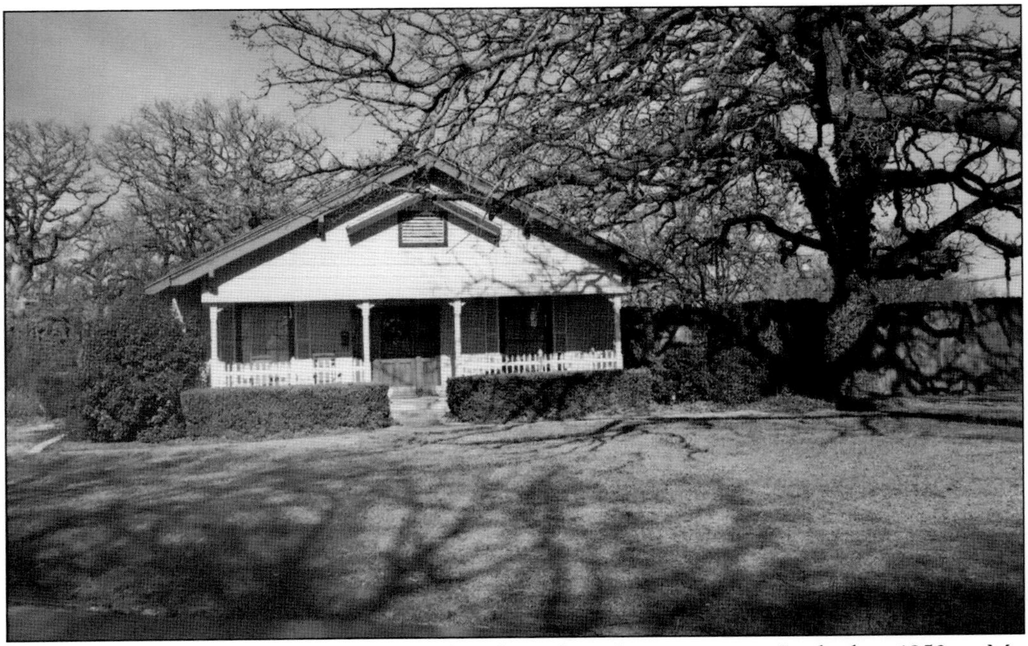

Maggie Williams's house was surrounded by a large farm for many years. In the late 1950s, a Mr. Duncan and a Mr. Reeves bought the land and divided it up into lots. Thus, many homes made use of the land known as Duncan-Reeves addition. A road from Highway 175 now known as Hall Street was created as a direct route. (Courtesy of Kathryn Ballard.)

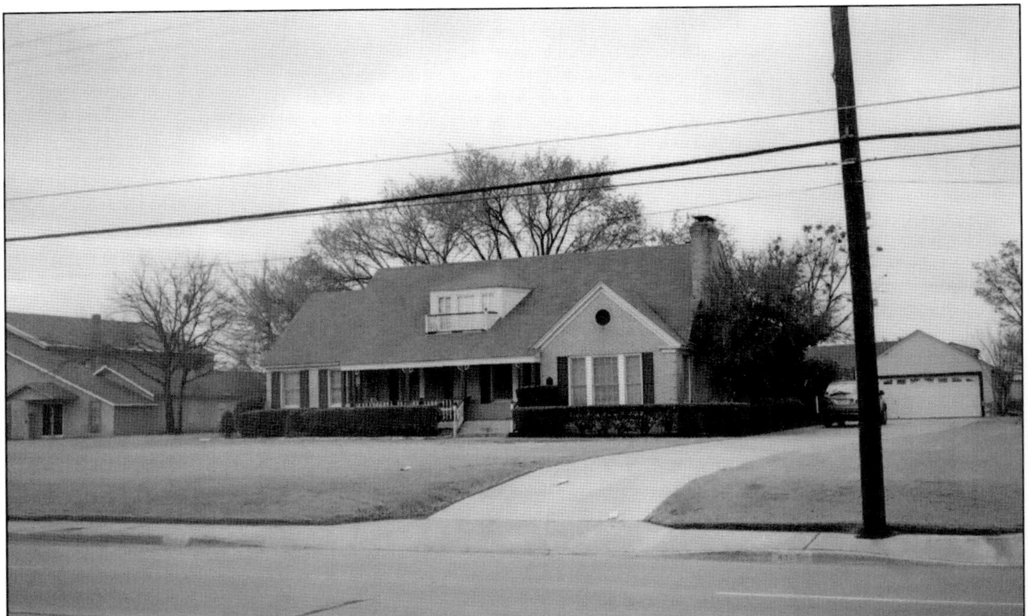

Bette Jo and Robert L. Carter are the present owners of this home. It has one story and a half-brick veneer, two baths, one kitchen, three bedrooms, and one fireplace. Reagan and Kathleen Hawthorne built this home in the late 1930s and lived there for many years. They had one daughter, Topsy. (Courtesy of Kathryn Ballard.)

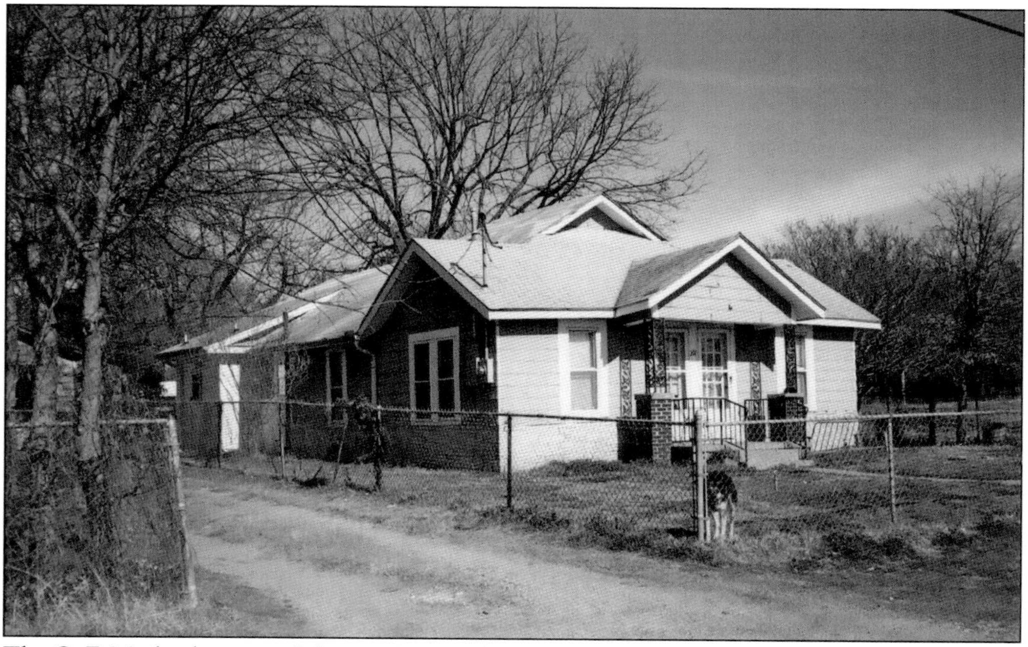

The O. F. Mathis house on Johnson Street is known as the Crouch house and was built in 1928. Here the Crouches raised three daughters—Ruth, Thelma, and Bertha. Ruth married Ben Nash and moved directly behind the Crouch home. Thelma married Ross Durham and moved around the corner on Cypress Street. Bertha married O. F. Mathis and lived in the duplex. All three couples lived in these homes the rest of their lives. (Courtesy of Kathryn Ballard.)

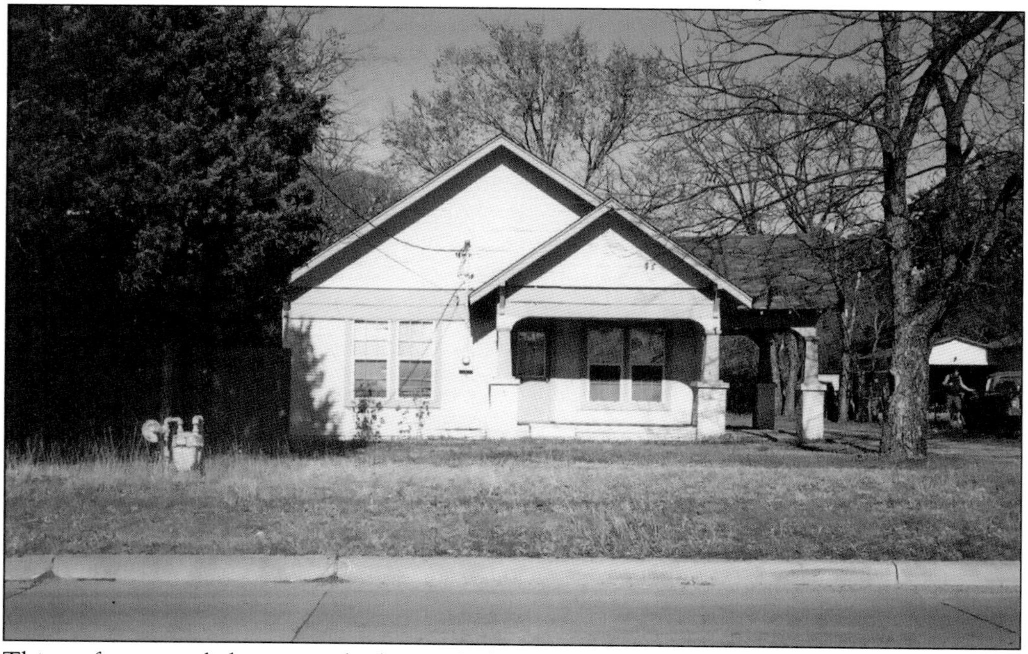

This craftsman-style house was built in 1934 by Jake Ryherd and J. V. Adkins. The material for the house came from the second floor of Ada Andrews's house next door. This house, located at 620 North Kaufman Street, was the home of Frank and Molly Hurt, who are the parents of Billie Frank Hurt Phillips. (Courtesy of Billie F. Hurt Phillips.)

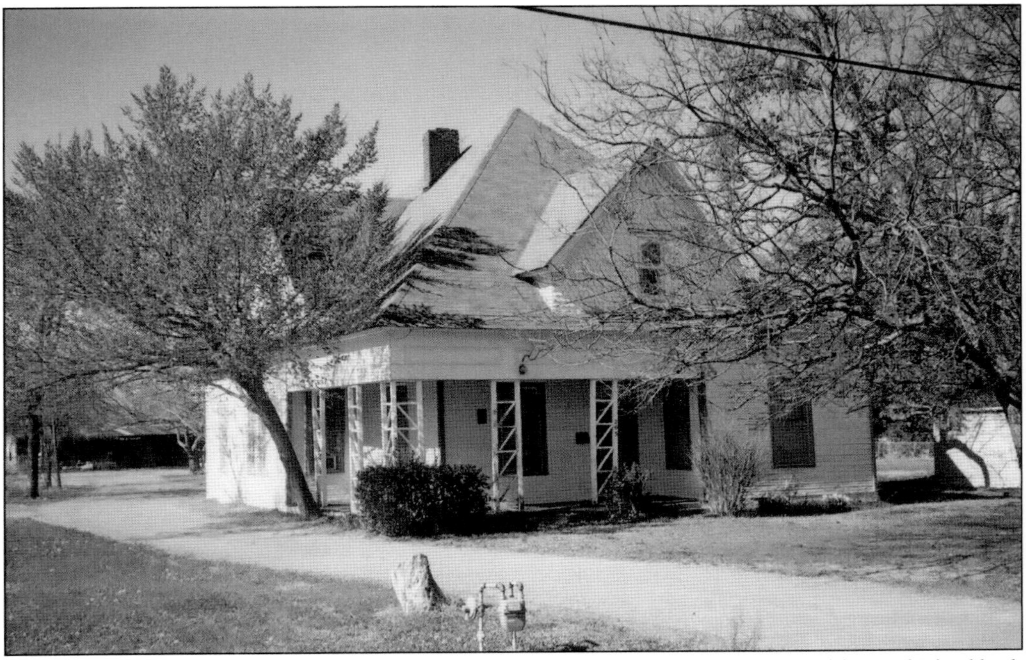

The Munroe Thedford house was built around 1910. Callie and Mun, the children of Thedford, were raised here at 103 Water Street. It served as the headquarters of the Thedford dairy, which encompassed more than 50 acres and required many helping hands. Mun Thedford was the dairyman at the Thedford dairy for many years. (Courtesy of Kathryn Ballard.)

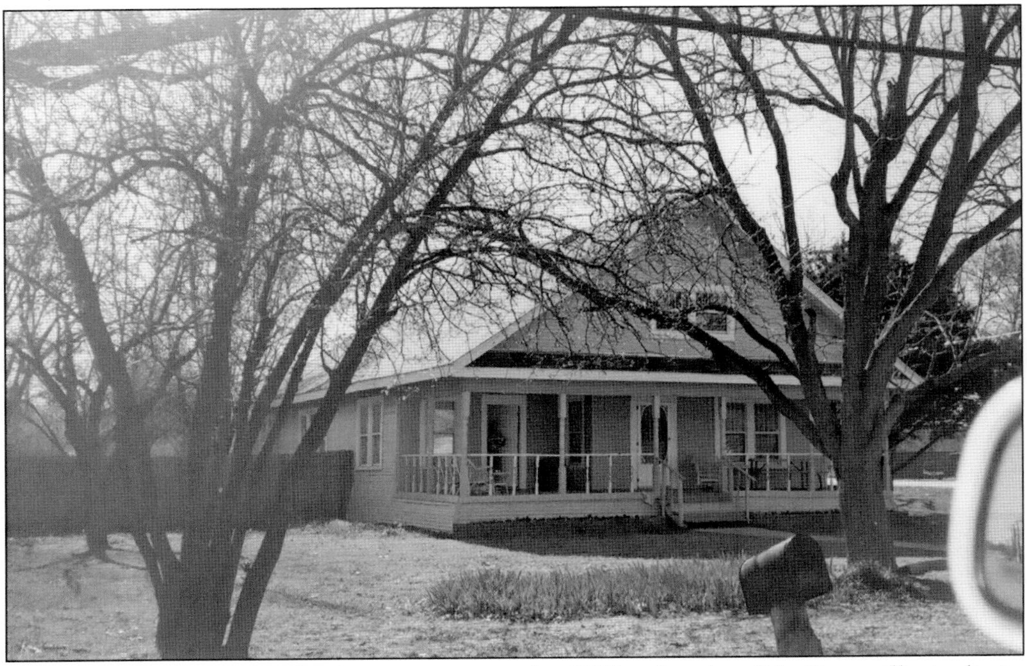

This was known as the Reading house, constructed in 1920 at the edge of the Seagoville city limits and Dallas County on Highway 175, now known as South Kaufman Street. R. R. Reading and his wife, Gladys, raised two sons, R. L. and Glen, and one daughter, Gladys, there. The parents lived there for the rest of their lives. (Courtesy of Kathryn Ballard.)

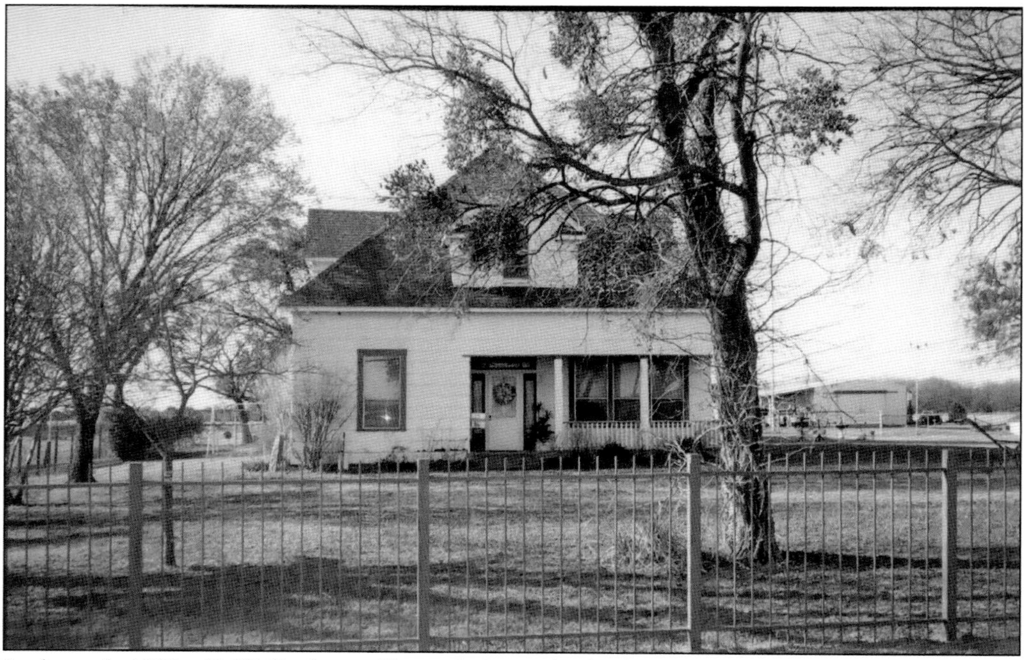

In the early 1900s, G. W. Fenley and his wife, Lizzie, built a home for their family, which included Ruth Landess, Chloe Pharr, and George Ward. The farm was large and required several hands, who were fed by Lizzie in the spacious kitchen. The Fenley's granddaughter, Peggy, now lives in the house. (Courtesy of Kathryn Ballard and Billie Frank Phillips.)

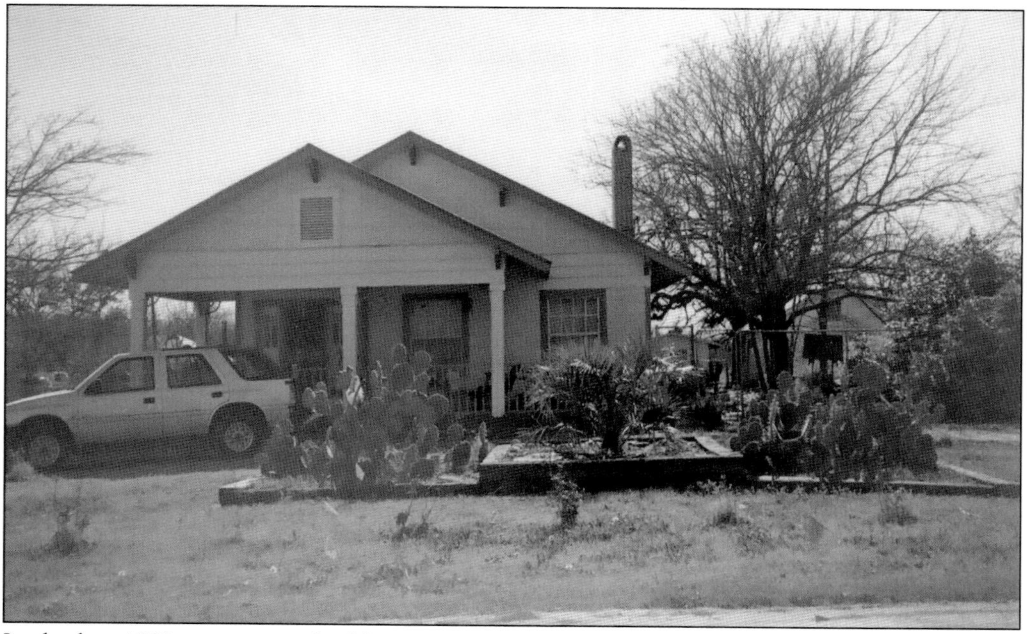

In the late 1920s, two sisters had homes next to each other, and they were constructed exactly alike. Maggie (Mrs. R. F.) McClung and Beulah (Mrs. W. T.) Dixon lived all their lives in these two houses. W. F. McClung owned the hardware store, and the McClungs had one daughter, Grace, an accomplished pianist. Beulah Dixon had three daughters—Earline Wright, Virginia Dixon Middlebrook, and Addie Lee Lewis. (Courtesy of Kathryn Ballard.)

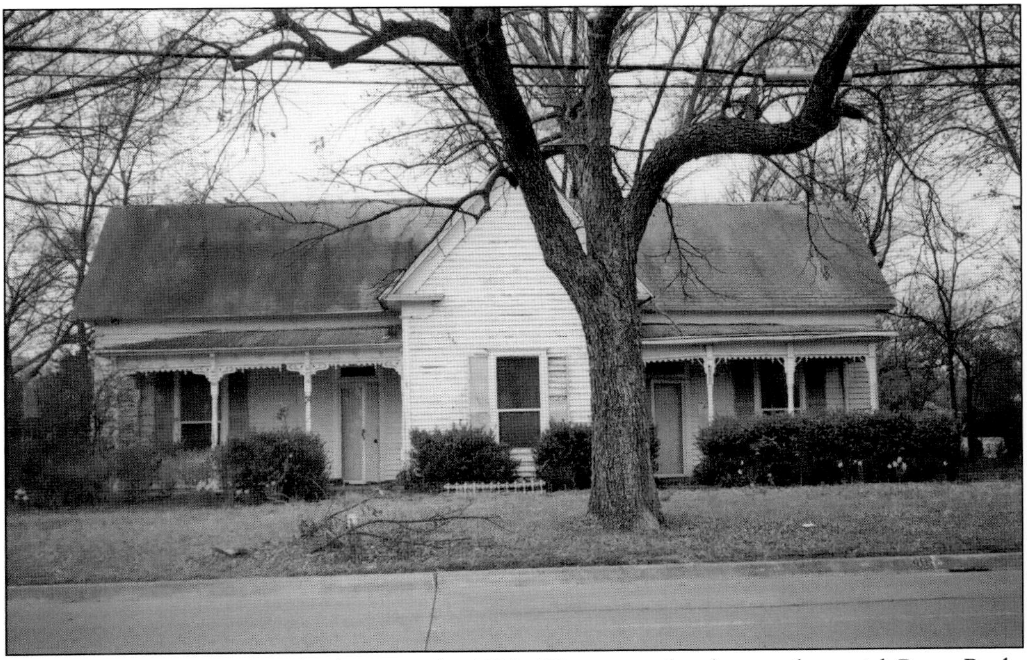

The Russell family lived in this house in the 1930s. There were four boys and one girl, Peggy Ruth. Later the Swaim family resided here with their children. In the 1950s, Mildred Cruthirds moved in with two daughters, Carolyn and Ruth, and one son, Tom. Each family maintained the house and kept it in good condition. The gingerbread trim is still intact. (Courtesy of Kathryn Ballard.)

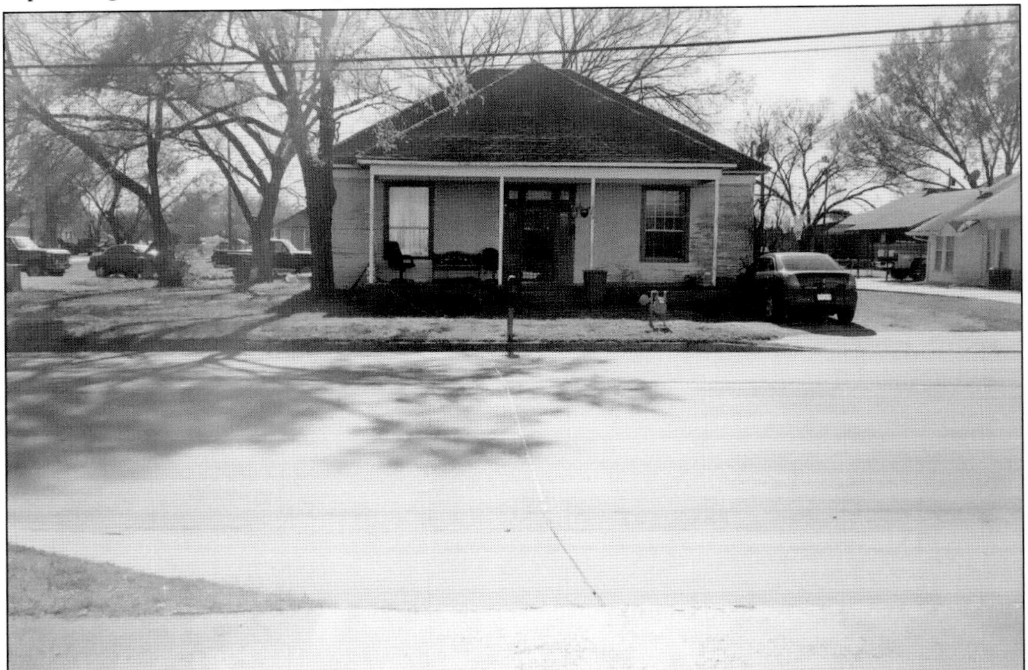

The W. T. Himes house, located on North Kaufman Street, is a 1921 Texas classic. It consisted of one bath, one kitchen, and four bedrooms. The Himes resided here for 30 years. They had one son, W. T. Himes Jr. (Courtesy of Kathryn Ballard.)

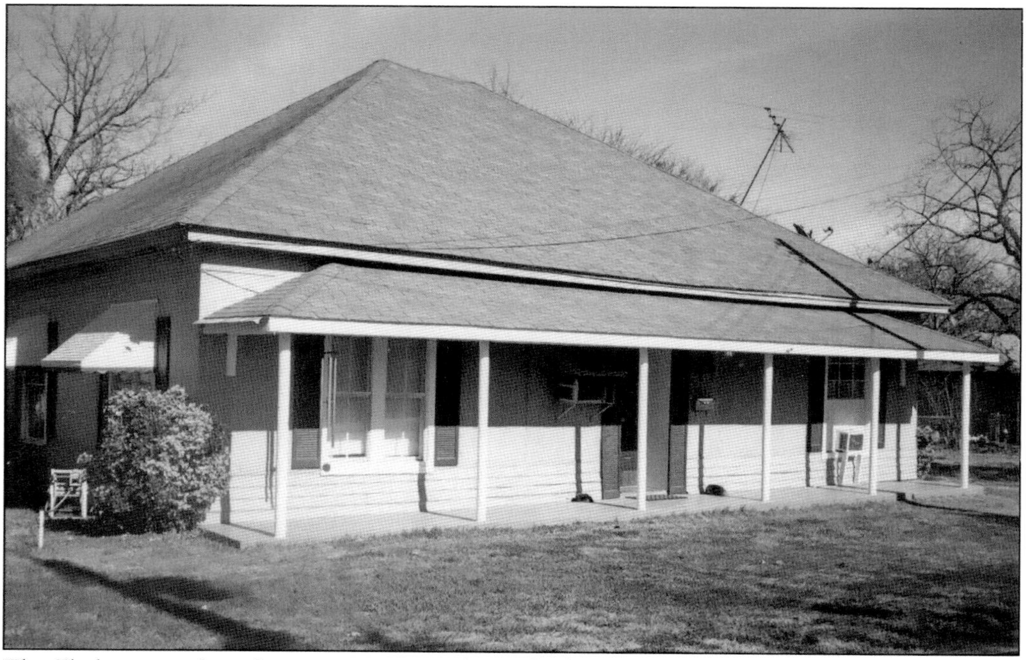

The Fly house with its long sweeping porch was built in the 1920s. The Fly family lived there for 20 years with their boys—Ben, J. Lawrence, and Walter, who made names for themselves from Dallas to Washington, D.C. The residence passed from family to family. (Courtesy of Kathryn Ballard.)

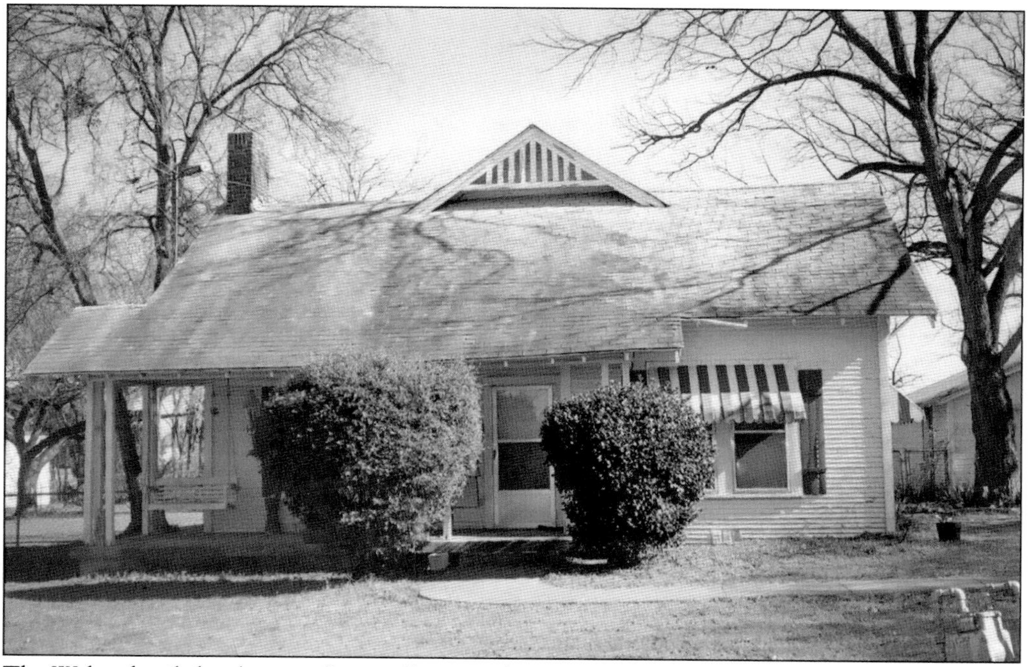

The Weber family has been in Seagoville since the 1800s. Hubert Weber and Mary Ida decided on Farmers Road in Seagoville for their craftsman residence, built in 1935. They had one daughter, Linda. Mary Ida told Mollie Hurt she was going to find a place and build so Mollie could see her house every day. (Courtesy of Kathryn Ballard.)

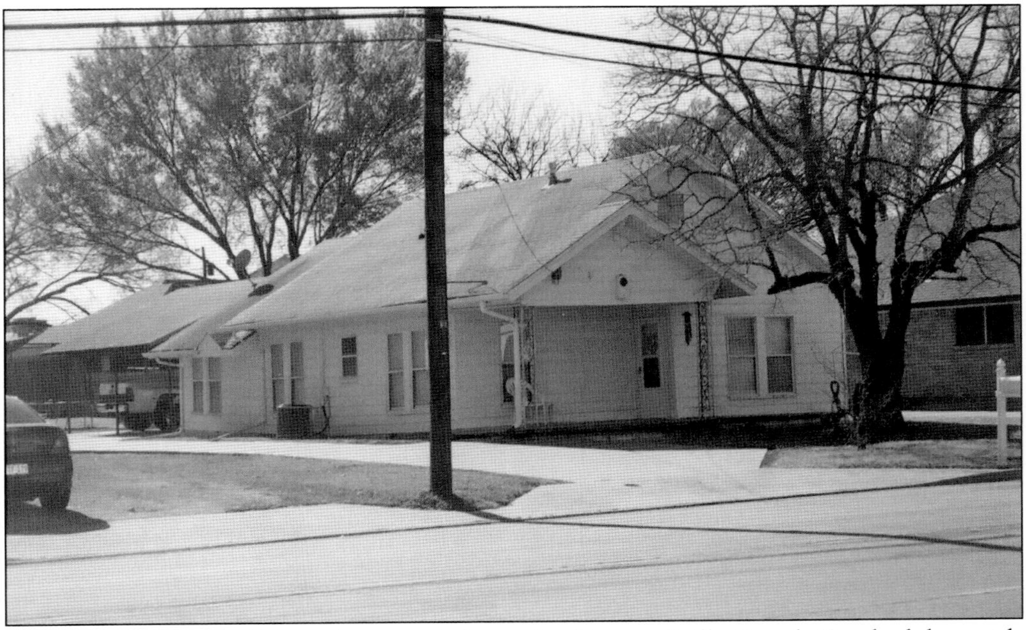

Pictured is the Hurt's 1920s craftsman-style home. Jim Hurt and Lilly Crouch Hurt had three girls and two boys. Jim owned a hamburger stand that was known for its delicious burgers. Many people patronized his establishment. Lilly was a dressmaker who made dresses for ladies in Seagoville as well as Nancy Cobb and her family in Dallas. (Courtesy of Kathryn Ballard and Billie Frank Phillips.)

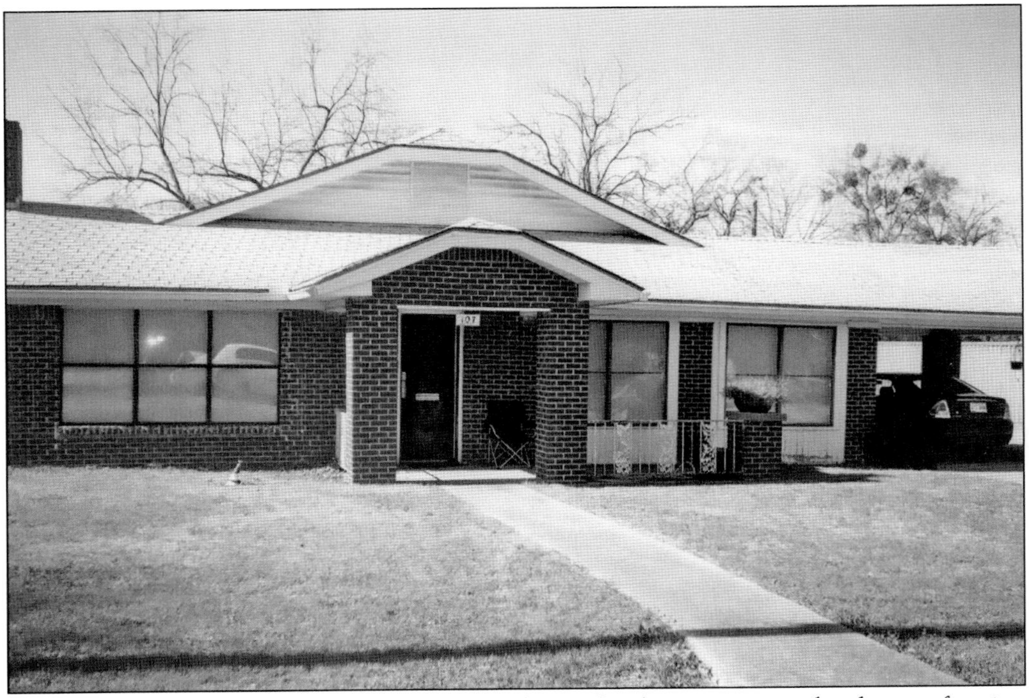

John Curtis and Pauline Curtis resided in this house for the many years that he was farming close to Malloy Bridge Road. They had one daughter, Frances Ballard. Frances was postmistress of Seagoville for 30 years, from 1940 to 1970. (Courtesy of Kathryn Ballard.)

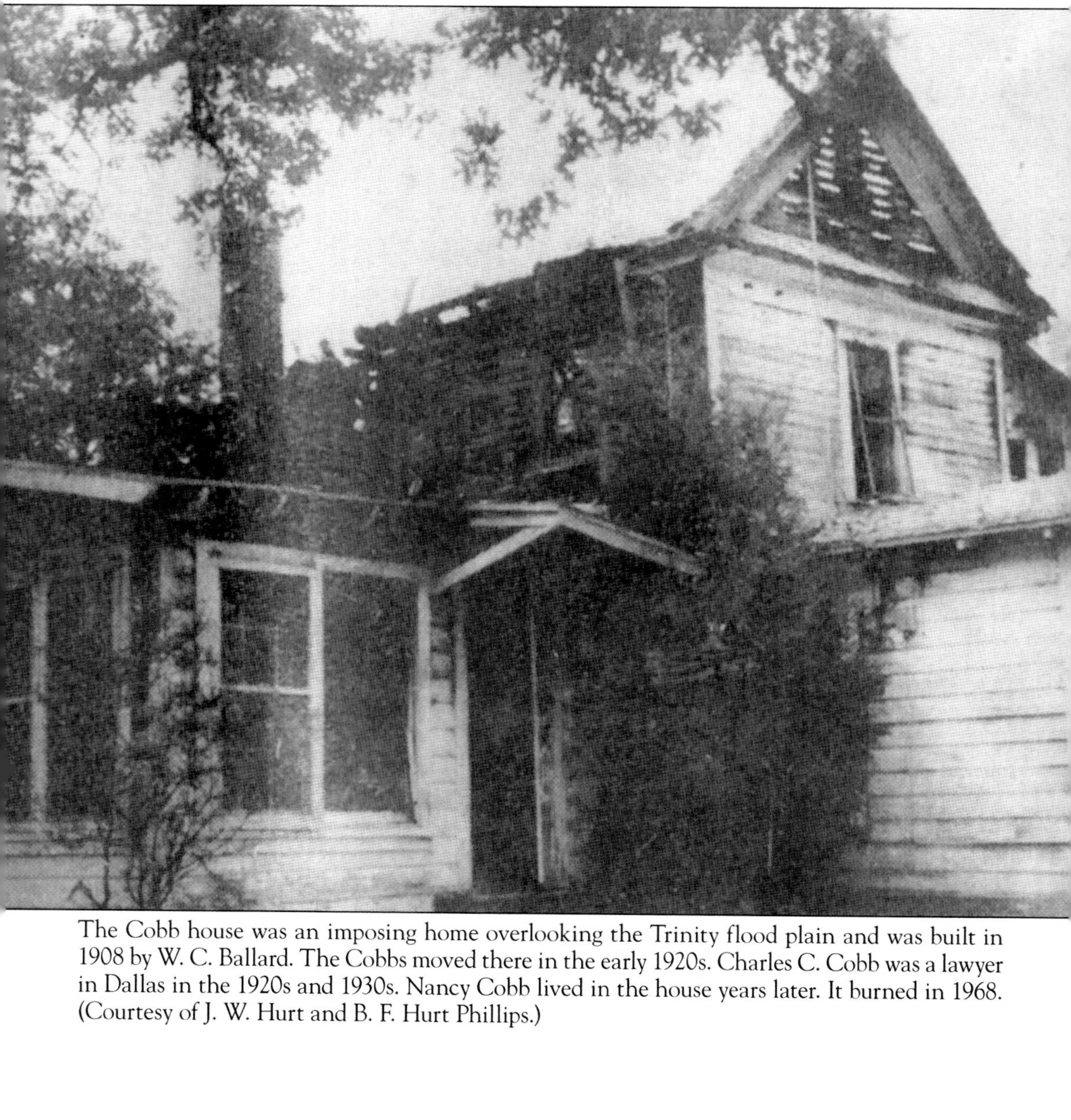

The Cobb house was an imposing home overlooking the Trinity flood plain and was built in 1908 by W. C. Ballard. The Cobbs moved there in the early 1920s. Charles C. Cobb was a lawyer in Dallas in the 1920s and 1930s. Nancy Cobb lived in the house years later. It burned in 1968. (Courtesy of J. W. Hurt and B. F. Hurt Phillips.)

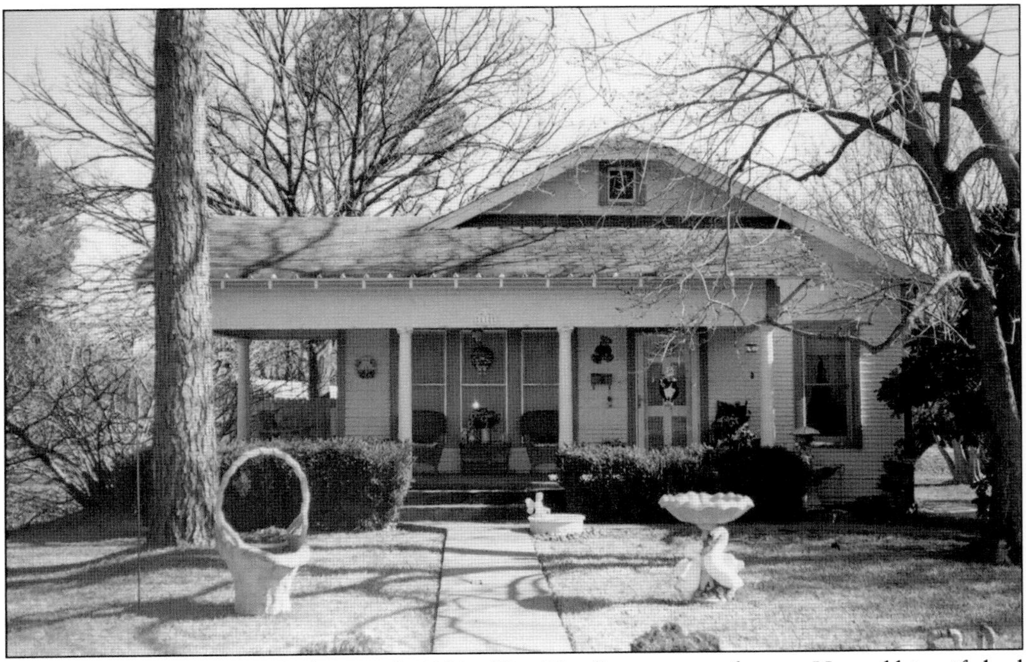

The Ledbetter house was built in early 1920s. "Bun" Ledbetter was a farmer. He and his wife had one daughter, Lorena. Lorena and her husband, Raymond Hawthorne, lived three doors down the street. The present owners have renovated the house to its present condition. (Courtesy of Kathryn Ballard.)

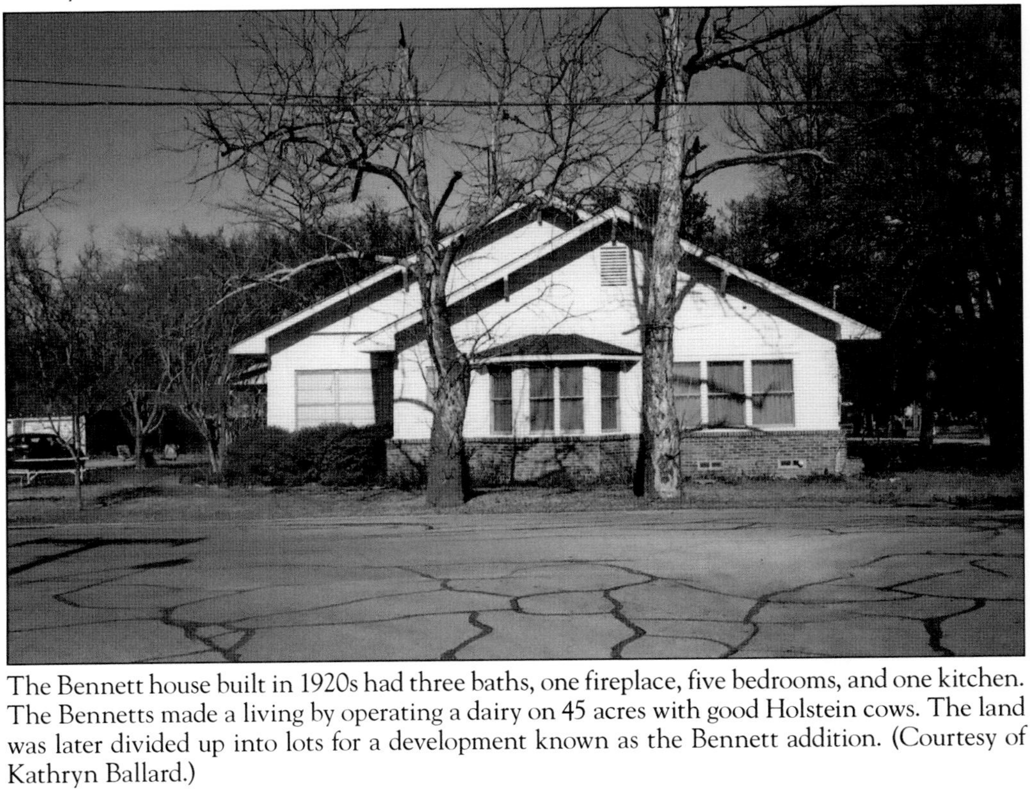

The Bennett house built in 1920s had three baths, one fireplace, five bedrooms, and one kitchen. The Bennetts made a living by operating a dairy on 45 acres with good Holstein cows. The land was later divided up into lots for a development known as the Bennett addition. (Courtesy of Kathryn Ballard.)

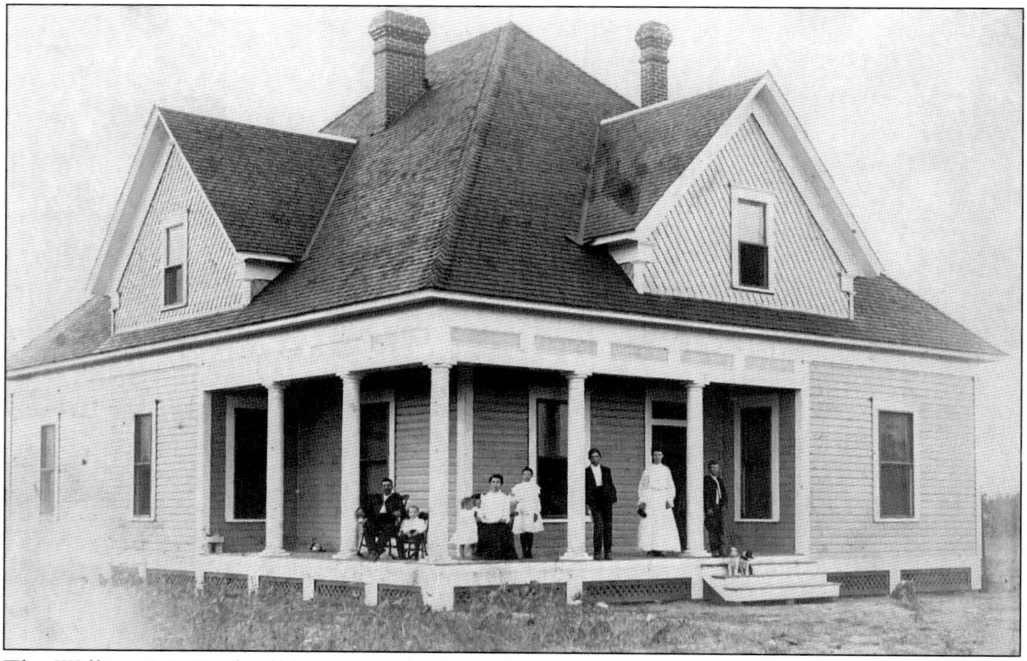

The William M. Cardwell home was built in 1904 at 209 Water Street, Seagoville, Texas. The family on the porch includes, from left to right, William M. Cardwell, Asa Cardwell, Charles W. Cardwell, Sarah Jane McIntyre Cardwell, Callie Cardwell, Lee O. Cardwell, Delia Cardwell, William O. Cardwell, and two pet pups. This house burned in 1938. (Courtesy of R. L. Glenn.)

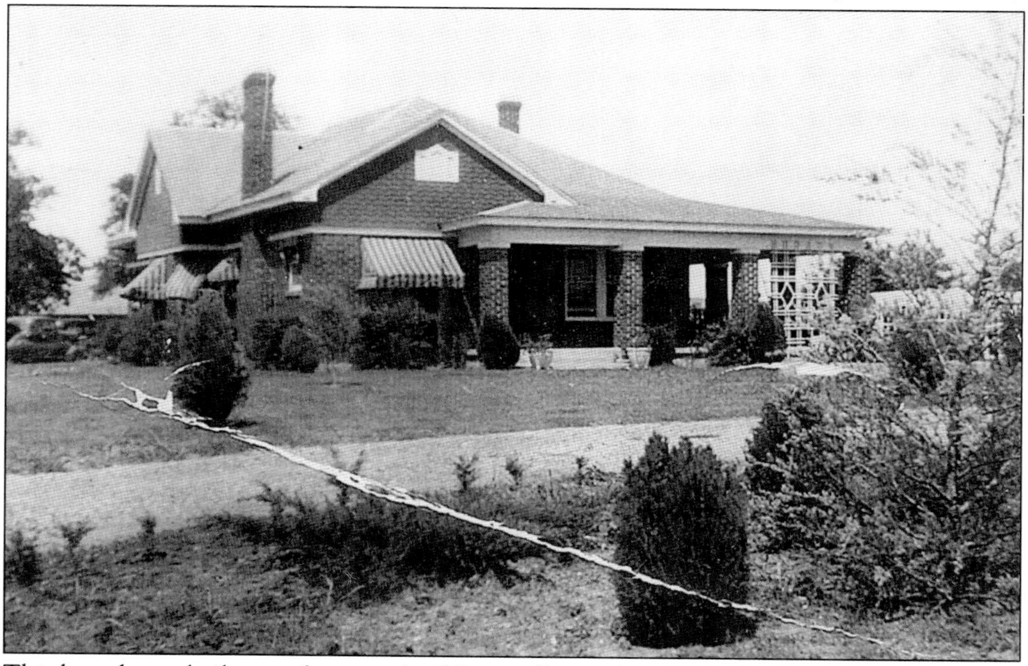

This large home built on a farm north of Seagoville was known as the Price place. L. A. Price owned the Price Construction Company. Price built the first levees along the Trinity River in Dallas County. This stopped the major flooding in the fertile river bottomland. (Courtesy of Kathryn Ballard.)

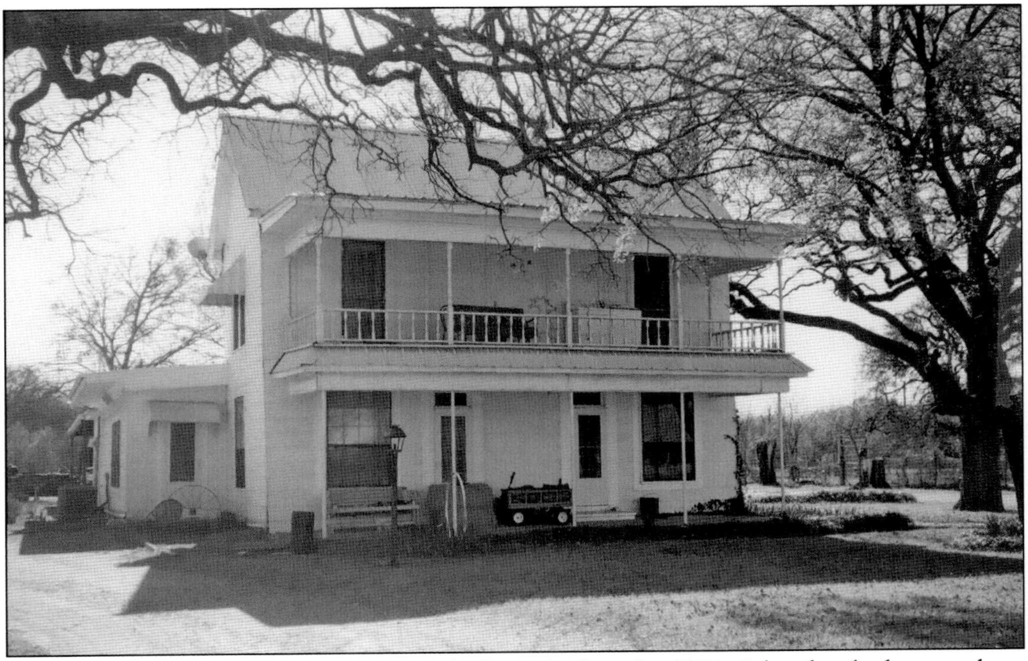

Timothy Leon Ramsey owns this house, which was built in the 1930s. It has four bedrooms, three baths, a living room, and a den. George Ward and Vina Fenley raised their children, George and Jane, in this Texas plains house. The Fenleys moved to Albuquerque, New Mexico, in the early 1940s. (Courtesy of Kathryn Ballard.)

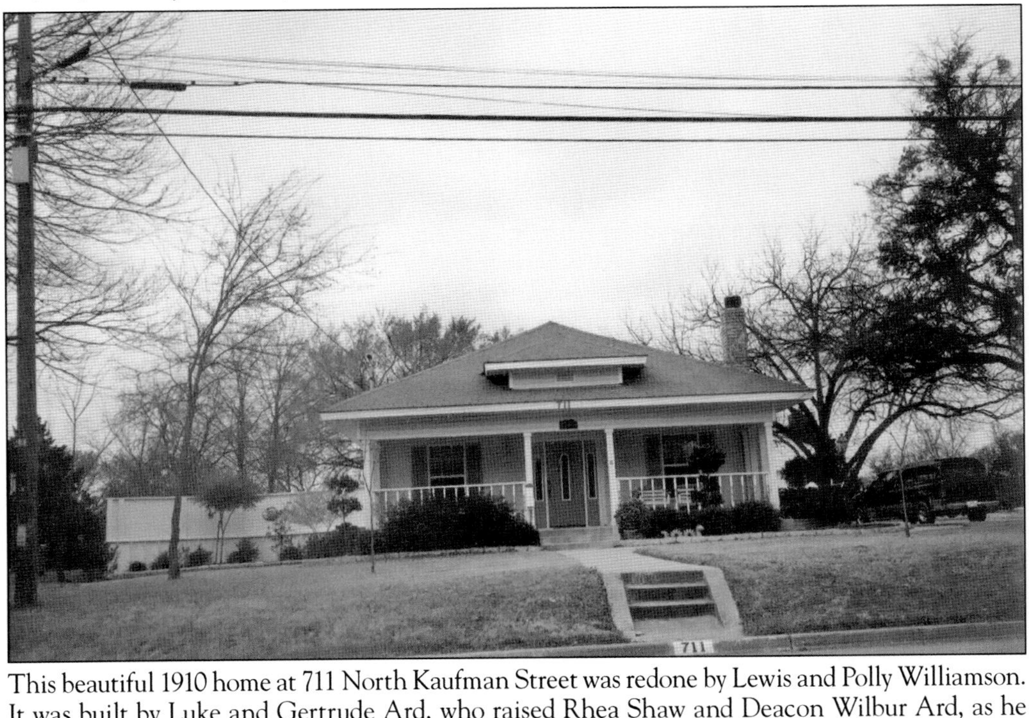

This beautiful 1910 home at 711 North Kaufman Street was redone by Lewis and Polly Williamson. It was built by Luke and Gertrude Ard, who raised Rhea Shaw and Deacon Wilbur Ard, as he was called on the *Early Bird* radio program. Wilbur was another outstanding son of Seagoville. (Courtesy of Kathryn Ballard.)

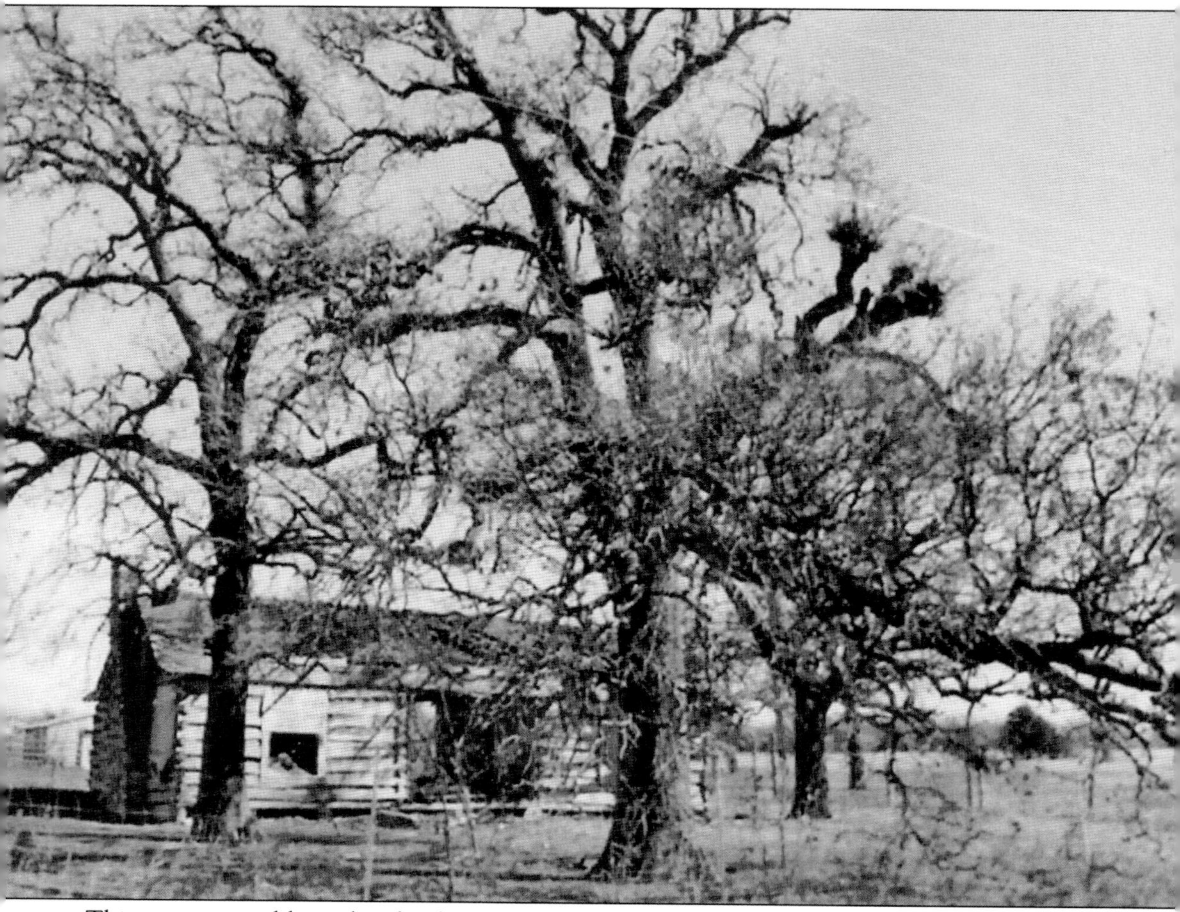

This was a typical log cabin for this area. The rooms were usually 16 feet by 16 feet, as this was about as large as the available trees would provide. There was an opening in the middle of the cabin called a dogtrot, and often such cabins had a fireplace on either end. Leamon Cox and his family lived here from the early 1930s to the late 1940s. This old log house had acres of fruit trees, peaches, plums, a big blackberry patch, and vegetables of all kinds. The family also raised hogs and pigs. There was a smokehouse used to smoke hams and bacon, and the pork meat was salted so it would cure. Leamon Cox also had cows that produced all the milk and butter the family could use. They even had enough to give away to people in the community. (Courtesy of Floy Ballantine.)

Eight

Around Town

Seagoville has always been blessed with fine people, from the first settlers to the present. Its citizens pay tribute to veterans with the monument dedicated to those who served in World War I and II. Seagoville sent 268 men and women of a population of 720 to World War II.

Residents have provided strong leadership in city government, schools, and churches. Local farmers and stockmen have been some of the best.

The city strives to provide many services such as water, sewage, fire protection, and police protection to its citizens at affordable rates. Seagoville also provides playing fields for both adult and youth recreation activities.

The schools have very satisfactory facilities, with one school featuring an award-winning design. Teachers are attracted to Seagoville because of the small community atmosphere.

Religious freedom is in evidence by the number of churches and faiths in the town.

It has been said Seagoville is the best kept secret in Dallas County. This could well be true, but Seagoville is also the best kept secret in the country.

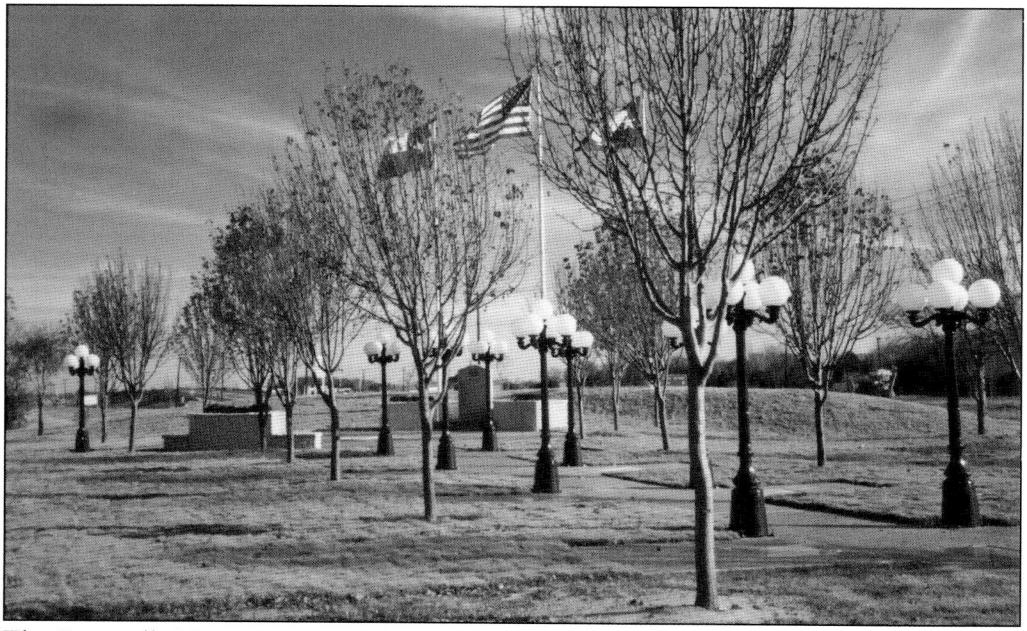

The Seagoville Veterans Memorial Plaza Park was dedicated on December 5, 1999. The city donated the land for the park with the projected cost estimated at $50,000. Funding came from the Lions Club selling 4-inch-by-8-inch granite bricks for $100 each and from a grant of $25,000 from the Seagoville Economic Development Corporation. Many people also donated free labor and materials at cost or at discount for this project. (Courtesy of Carol Franks.)

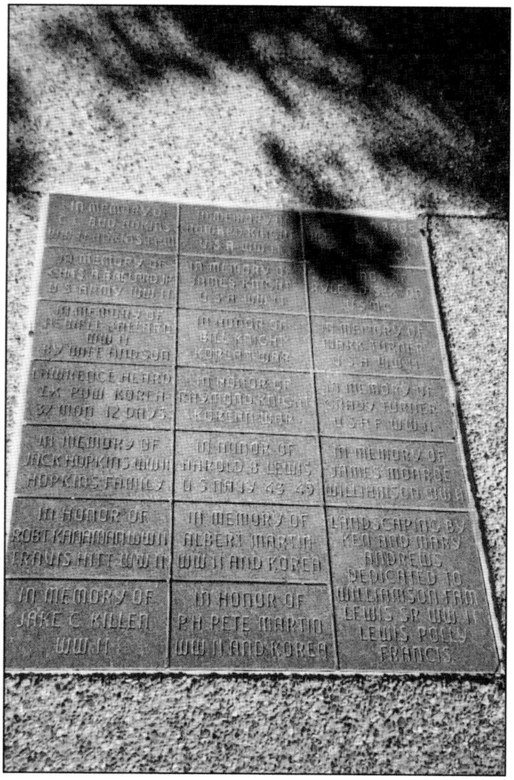

The granite bricks were inscribed with the names of veterans being honored or memorialized from World Wars I and II, the Korean Conflict, and the Vietnam War. One of the bricks included is Bryan Kirby's, who was awarded three Purple Heart medals during World War II. Also, many citizens supported the project by having individual family names inscribed on some of the bricks, which were placed in the concrete sidewalks over the park area. (Courtesy of Carol Franks.)

Fulps Monument Company prepared the marble monument on which the names of veterans killed in action or who died in service are inscribed. Below the names listed on the monument is the inscription, "Dedicated to the men and women who have served our country and especially to those listed above who gave their lives, may we never forget their sacrifice. Seagoville Lions Club 1999." (Courtesy of Carol Franks.)

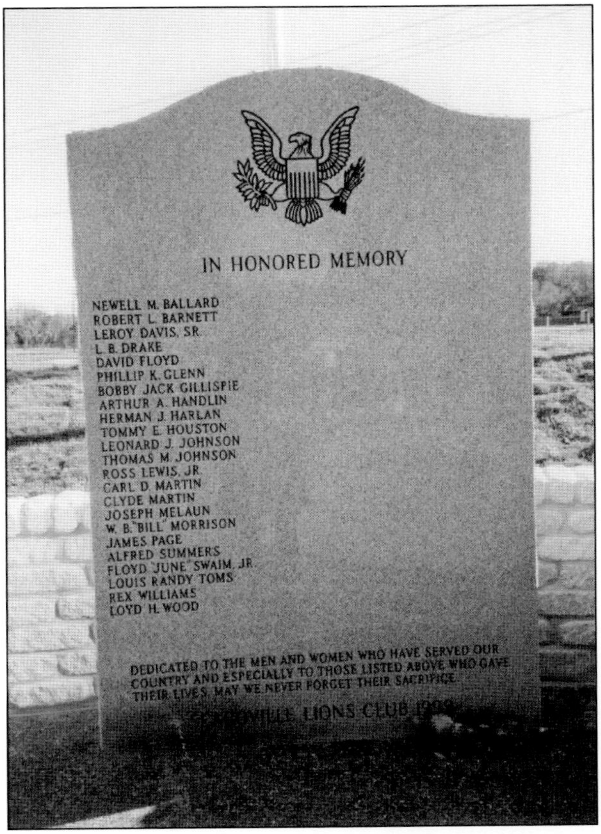

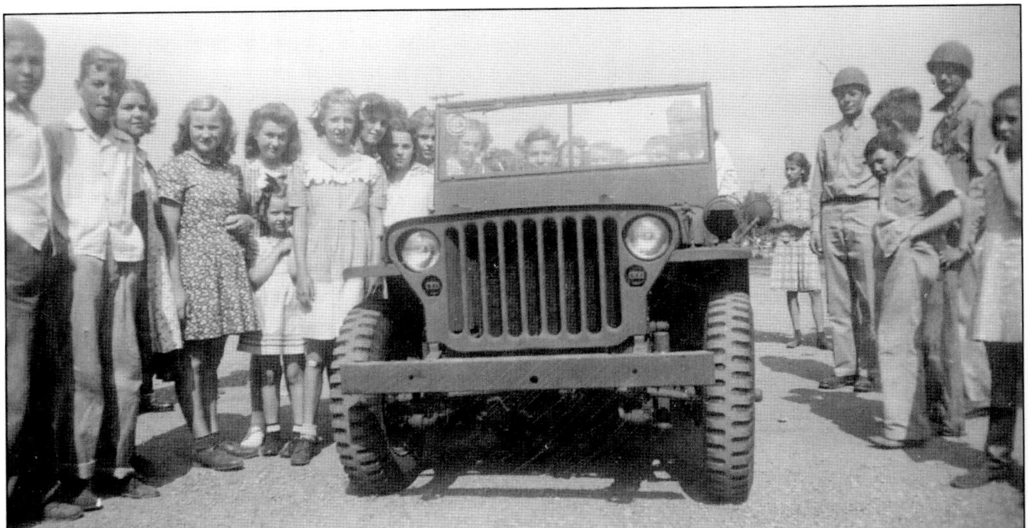

There was much change in 1942. Teachers and others were going to war. Financing for the war was important, and the sale of war bonds was promoted by soldiers coming to communities such as Seagoville and giving rides in the then unheard of army jeep for those buying a $25 bond. In this group of students are Martha Raye Glenn Richardson, Billie Frank Hurt Phillips, and Mary Ann Pollan Wilkirson. (Courtesy of the Phillips family.)

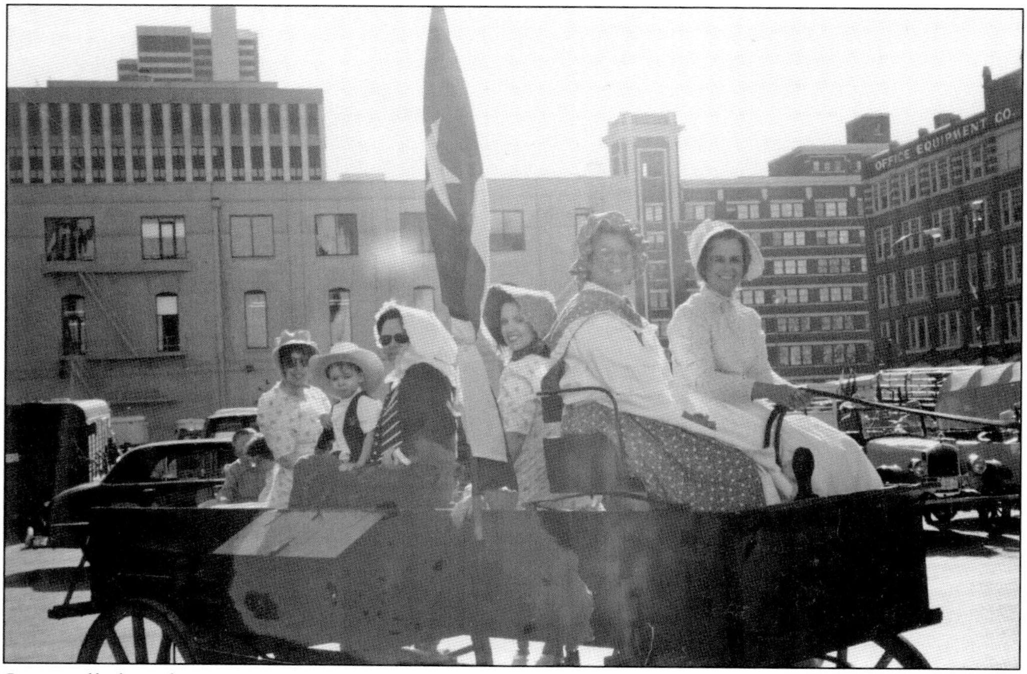

Seagoville has the most authentic participants in the sesquicentennial celebration for Dallas. Joe Priest led the horsemen, and O. F. Mathis led the teamsters. The driver of this wagon that made the trip around Texas is Barbara Ogletree Yarbrough. Others on board are, from left to right, Dawn Holston, David Bingham, Gay Leigh Bingham, Kathleen Phillips, and Melba Mathis. (Courtesy of the Phillips family.)

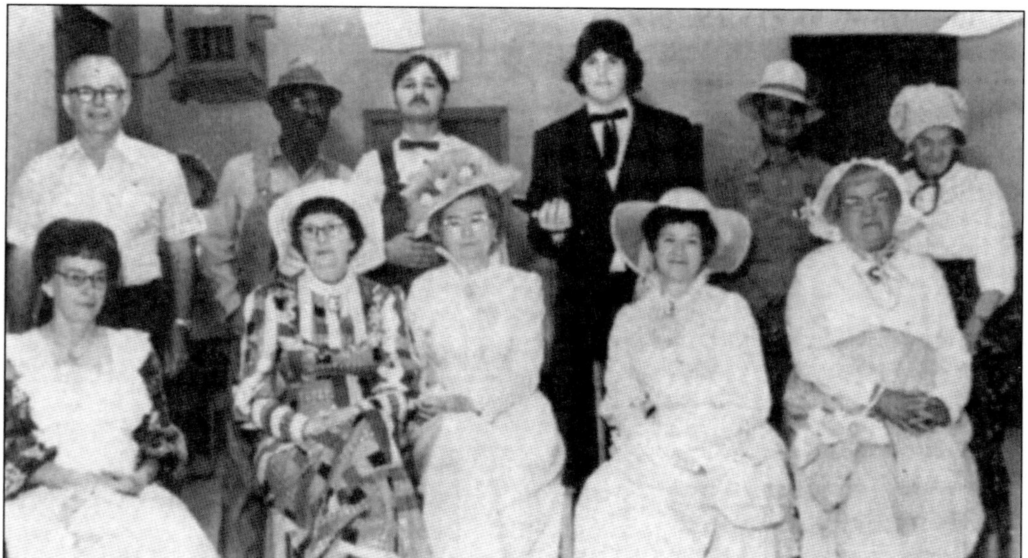

Seagoville celebrated its centennial in May 1979. The Centennial Week was May 6 to 12 and was sponsored by the chamber of commerce. Some of the royal court are, from left to right, (first row) Wilma Johnson, Virgie Hammers, Gladys Garrett, Willie Adams (queen), and Margie Spurgeon; (second row) Lamar Johnson, Willie Helms, Stepper Sebastian (king), David Mayne, Grady Franks, and Jewell Ballard.(Courtesy of Neal Wooley.)

O. F. Mathis was a man seen around town more than anyone else. He was the only person who had a team Sowell trained enough that they could walk among the flowers and vegetables without stepping on them. He is attired in the standard clothes from the 19th century—bib overalls and a straw hat—and is catching up to the wagon to throw his bundle of oats on it. (Courtesy of Delta Mathis.)

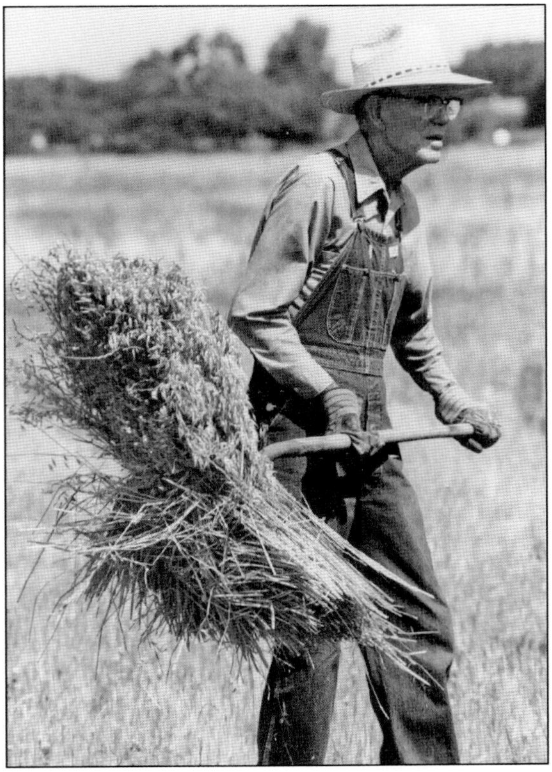

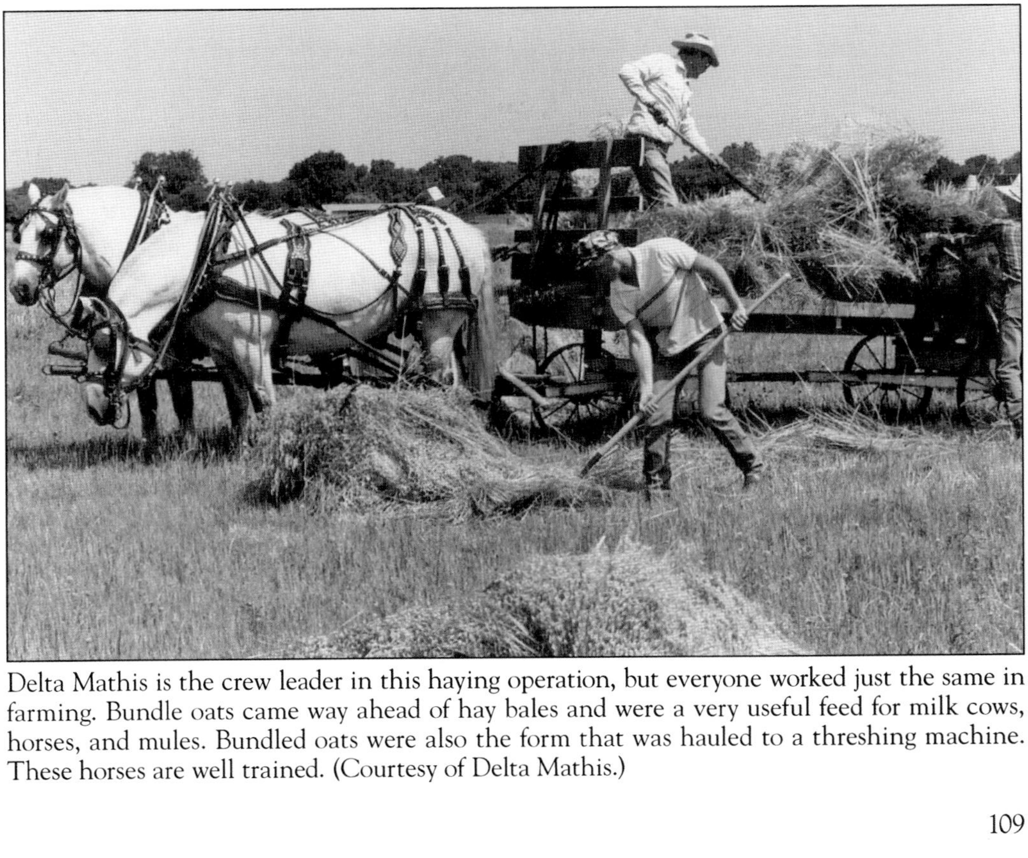

Delta Mathis is the crew leader in this haying operation, but everyone worked just the same in farming. Bundle oats came way ahead of hay bales and were a very useful feed for milk cows, horses, and mules. Bundled oats were also the form that was hauled to a threshing machine. These horses are well trained. (Courtesy of Delta Mathis.)

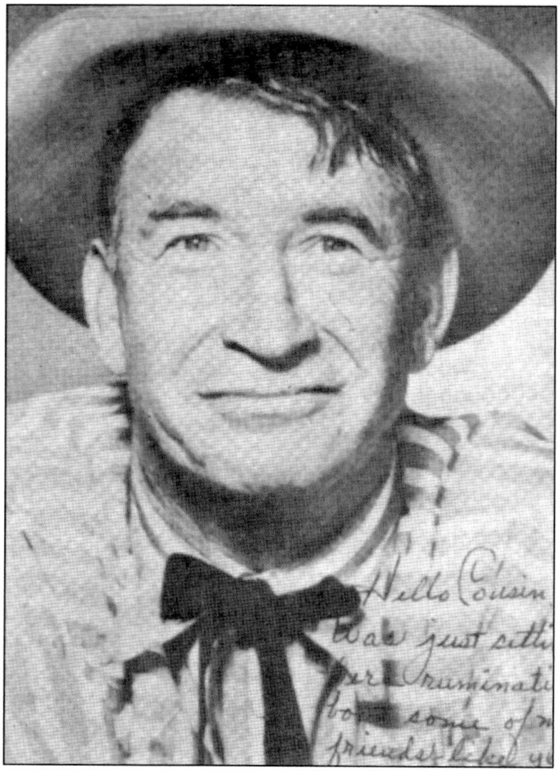

Chill Wills, son of Bob Wills, was born on Johnson Street. Dr. Childers asked his mother why they picked the name Chill. She replied that he was born on a hot July day, and Chill was the coolest thing she could think of at the time. In interviews, Chill always acknowledged Seagoville as his birthplace. He starred with John Wayne and Spencer Tracy in movies and was the voice of Francis the Talking Mule. (Courtesy of Neal Wooley.)

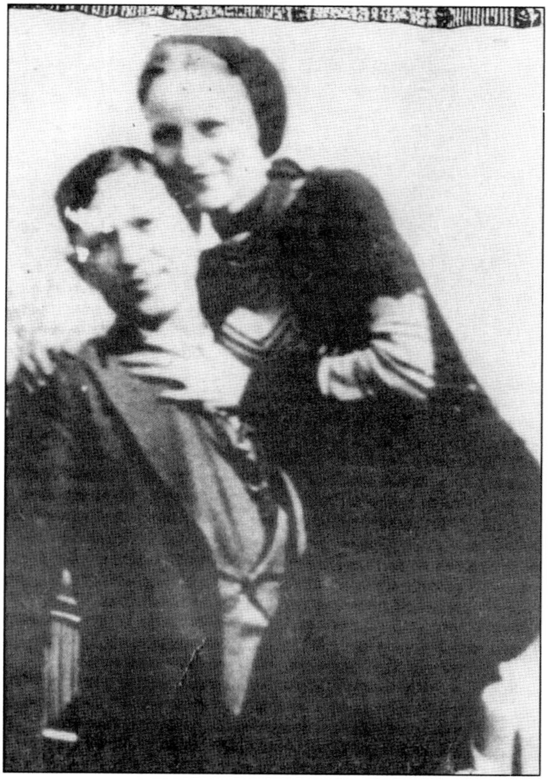

Seagoville is truly Bonnie and Clyde country. They had relatives in the area who gave them ammunition they practiced with. They would drive behind Jim Hurt's hamburger stand to be served. When Warner Brothers made the movie *Bonnie and Clyde*, the studio used many local roads, a cornfield, and a sand pile owned by Otis Ramsey. A house on Johnson Street was duplicated in a studio in Dallas for the movie. (Courtesy of Neal Wooley.)

Seagoville Central Park was dedicated on March 25, 1979, and renamed C. O. Bruce Central Park, in honor of a longtime resident of Seagoville. The park started with tennis courts and ball fields. Later a walking trail around the lake was added, and in 2008 a new accessible playground was installed. The playground was funded by a grant from the Seagoville Economic Development Corporation. (Courtesy of Carol Franks.)

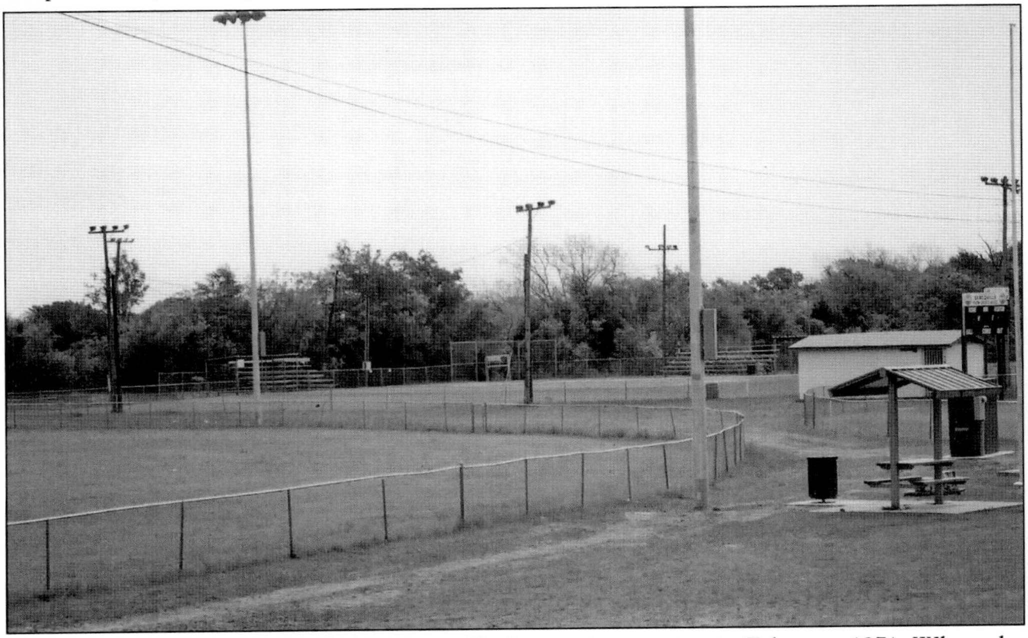

J. W. "Toady" Bearden started the Seagoville Sports Association in February 1971. When the baseball park was built, it was named the Bearden Park in honor of his many hours spent with the association and in coaching the teams. He was a member of the U.S. Marine Corps Reserve, a local fireman, and a longtime resident of Seagoville. Many citizens of Seagoville have supported this park with their time and donations. (Courtesy of Carol Franks.)

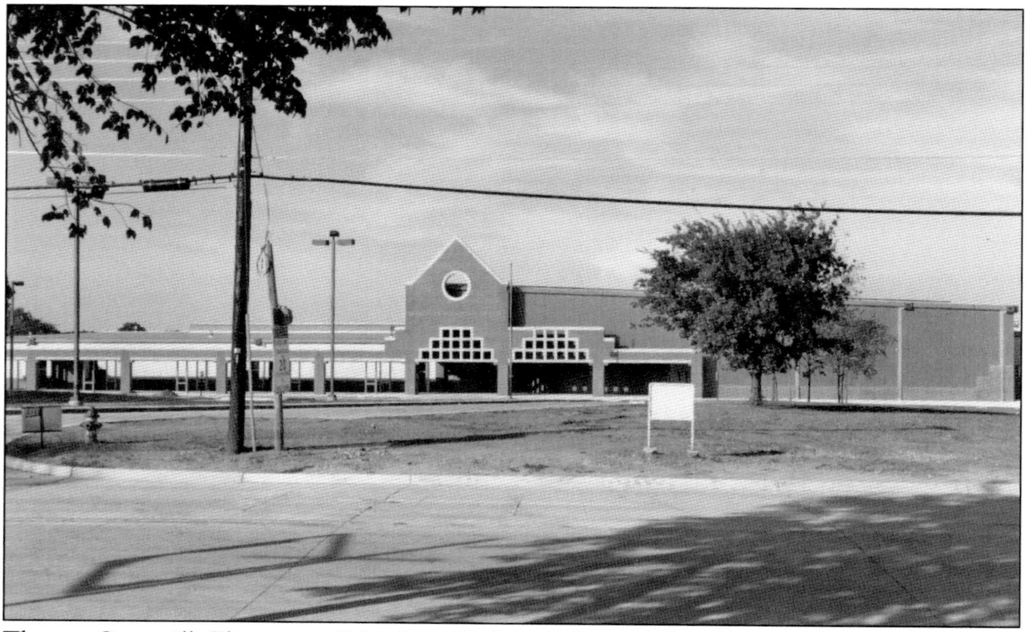

The new Seagoville Elementary School was built on 11.5 acres behind the old two-story elementary school on North Kaufman Street in 1986. The cost was approximately $4 million, and the school started with grades kindergarten through fourth. It now houses pre-kindergarten through second grades. (Courtesy of Carol Franks.)

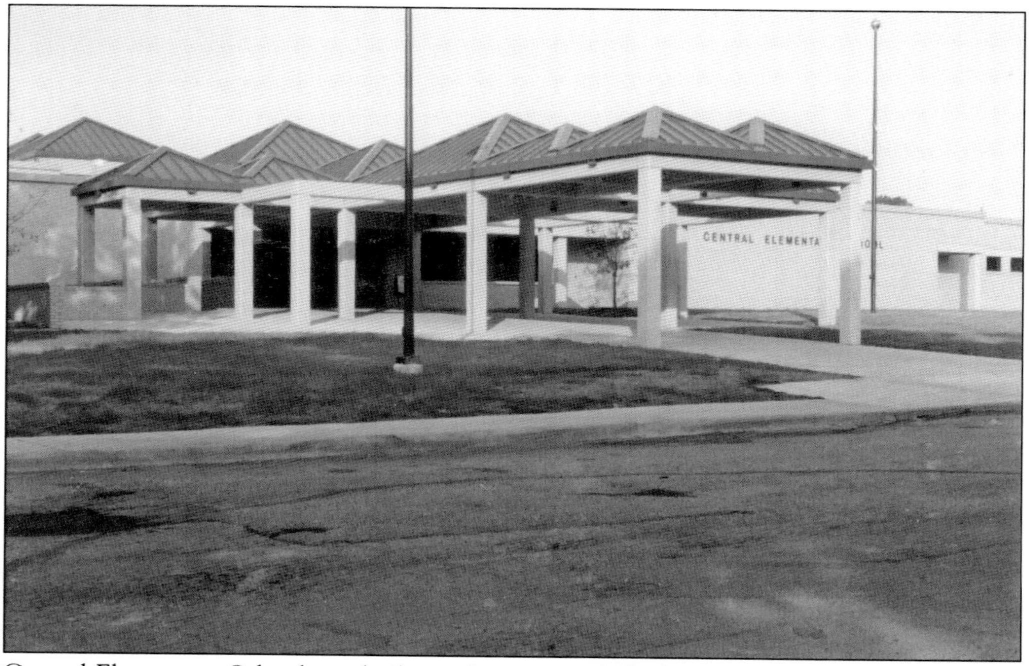

Central Elementary School was built on the corner of Shady Lane and Jack Street at a cost of $2.6 million, and classes began in fall 1987. It started with grades five through six and now houses third through fifth grades. The old central site on North Kaufman Street later became the Seagoville Alternative School until 2008, when it consolidated with another alternative center. (Courtesy of Carol Franks.)

Herb and Belva Gibson were quite a pair. And to think they picked Seagoville for their corporate offices! It has been said they could go into one of their many discount centers and in a little while they could tell how the center was doing. Words cannot explain H. R. Gibson—entrepreneur, salesman, genius. It may be best explained by an instance in Abilene, Texas, where he was opening a discount center in July. He ordered a boxcar load of antifreeze from DuPont. "It won't work," said DuPont representatives. Herb did not like to be told he could not do something, so he requested three more boxcars. When told he could not sell antifreeze in July, he asked for two more boxcars, adding "I do not want to run out." Gibson had the television and radio stations telling about the 10 inches of snow and expected freeze every 15 minutes on opening day. The joke was that he sold six boxcar loads of antifreeze the first day. Herb opened the Seagoville center around 1938. The warehouse included rubbing alcohol, hair oil, and other personal care products. (Courtesy of Herb Gibson Jr.)

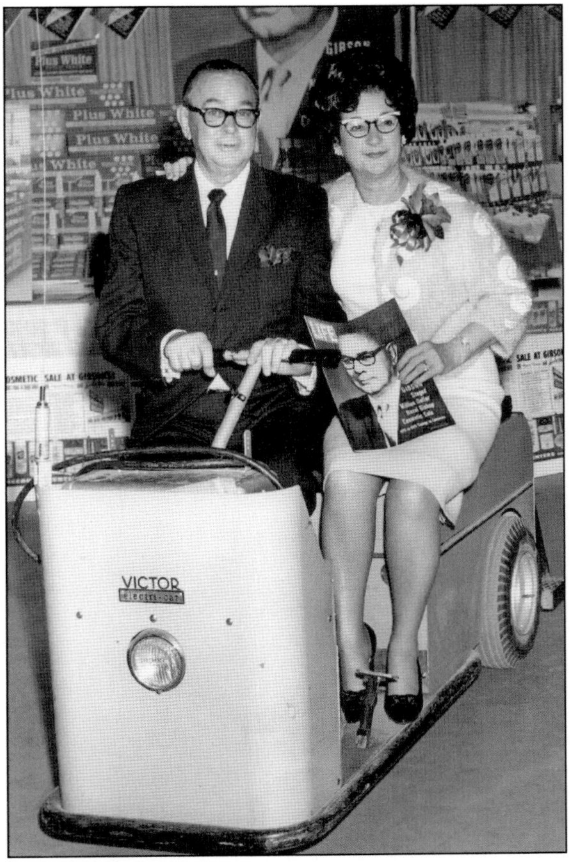

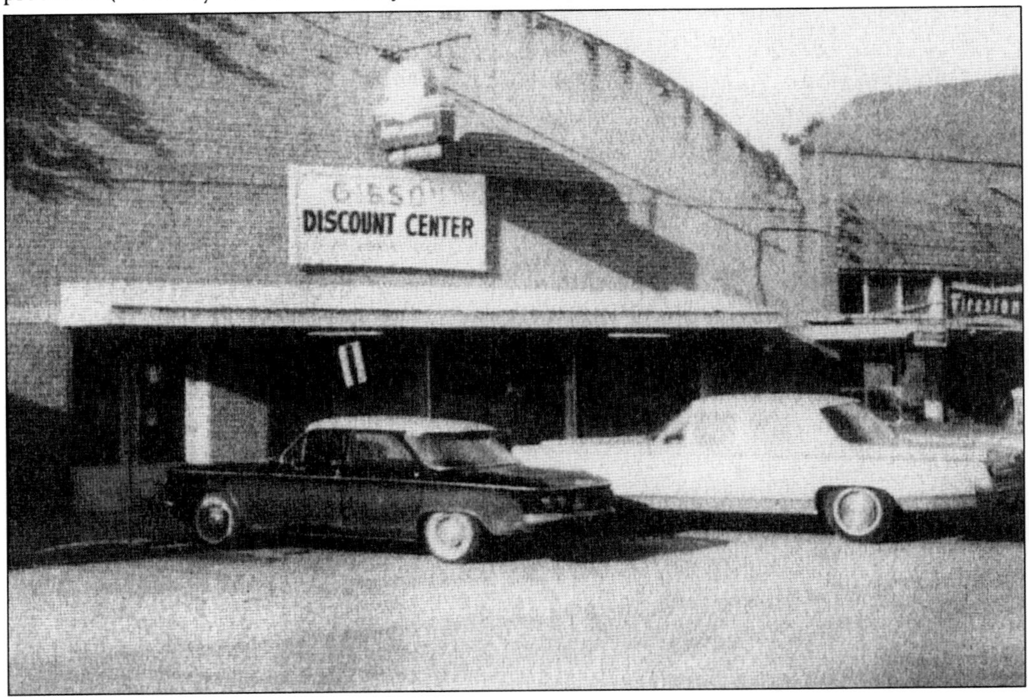

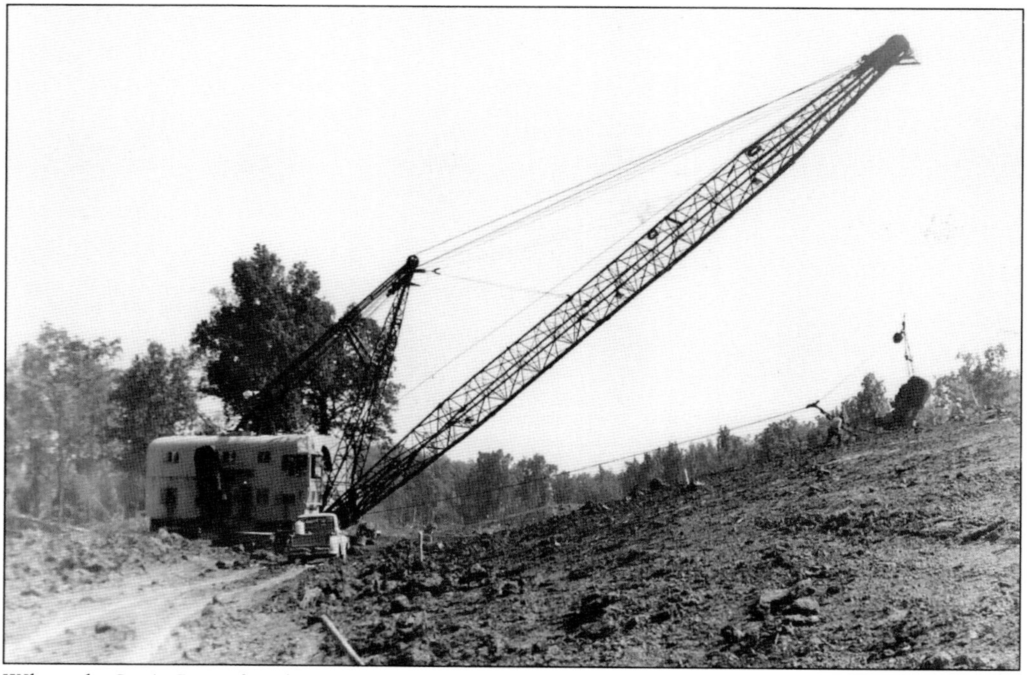

When the L. A. Price family came to Seagoville in the 1920s, they brought many things that still exist to this day. They brought draglines and other equipment plus their knowledge of operation. The draglines were used to move dirt for the levee on the Trinity River. The original operators were very helpful in training future operators. (Courtesy of Barbara Shepherd.)

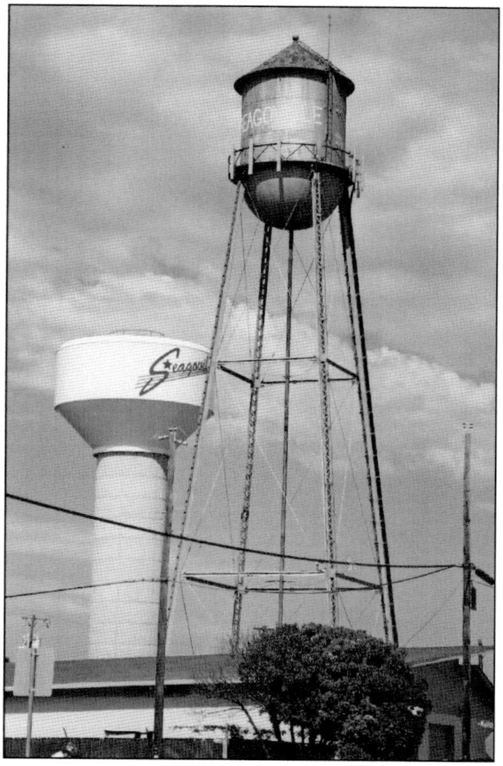

Seagoville was fortunate to have a water tower in the heart of town. It has stood as a beacon of welcome for many years. It was erected in 1929 and was in use until 1954. Artesian water flowed from deep in the earth and served the people well. (Courtesy of Carol Franks.)

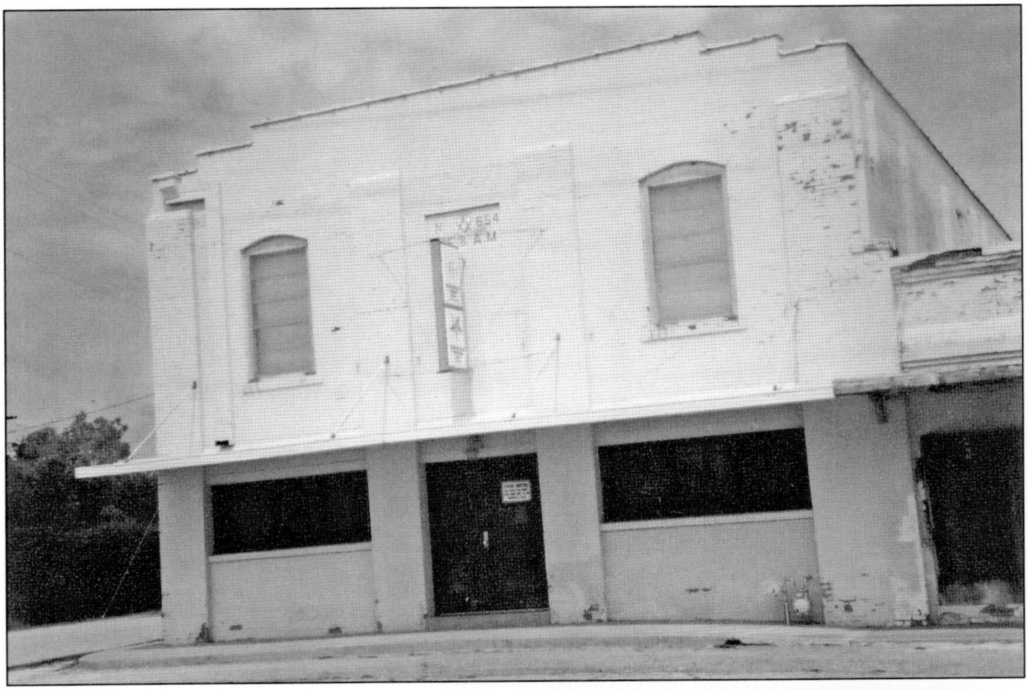

In the early 1900s, the Palace Drug store occupied the bottom floor of a two-story frame building. The Woodman of the World and Independent Order of Odd Fellows lodges were on the top floor. Much later, a brick building was erected with the Masonic Lodge, Eastern Star, and Rainbow girls on the top floor and a meat locker plant on the bottom. Now the Masonic Lodge occupies the entire building. (Courtesy of Carol Franks.)

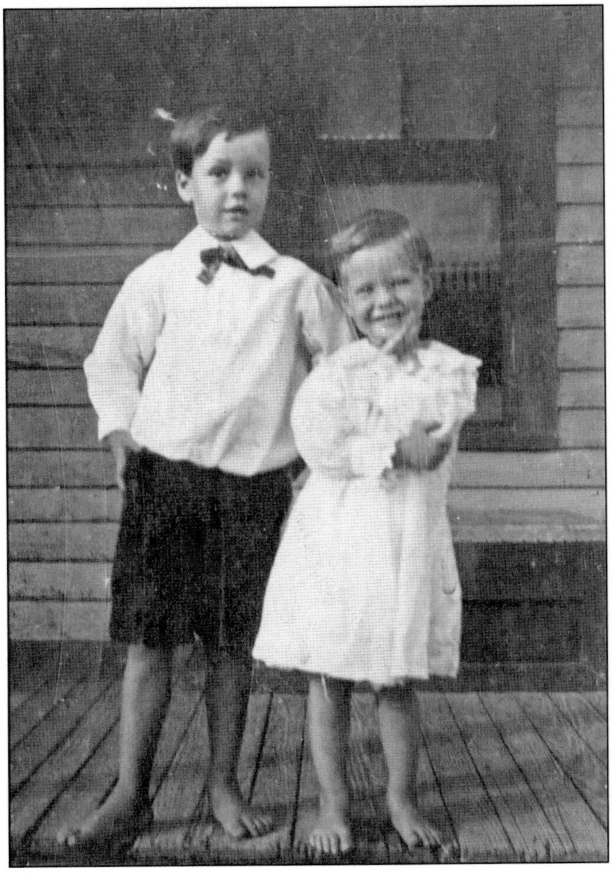

Pictured are the children of Edgar Alfonzo Robinson and his wife, Bertie Carmen—Guy Lincoln (left), age five, and Wilford Leonard, age four. They are standing on the front porch of the original Ramsey house where four of the five children—Guy, Leonard, Roy, and Lara—were born. A fifth child, Edgar, was born in a new house that was built on the corner of Kaufman Street and Farmers Road. (Courtesy of Gwen Robinson Gaida.)

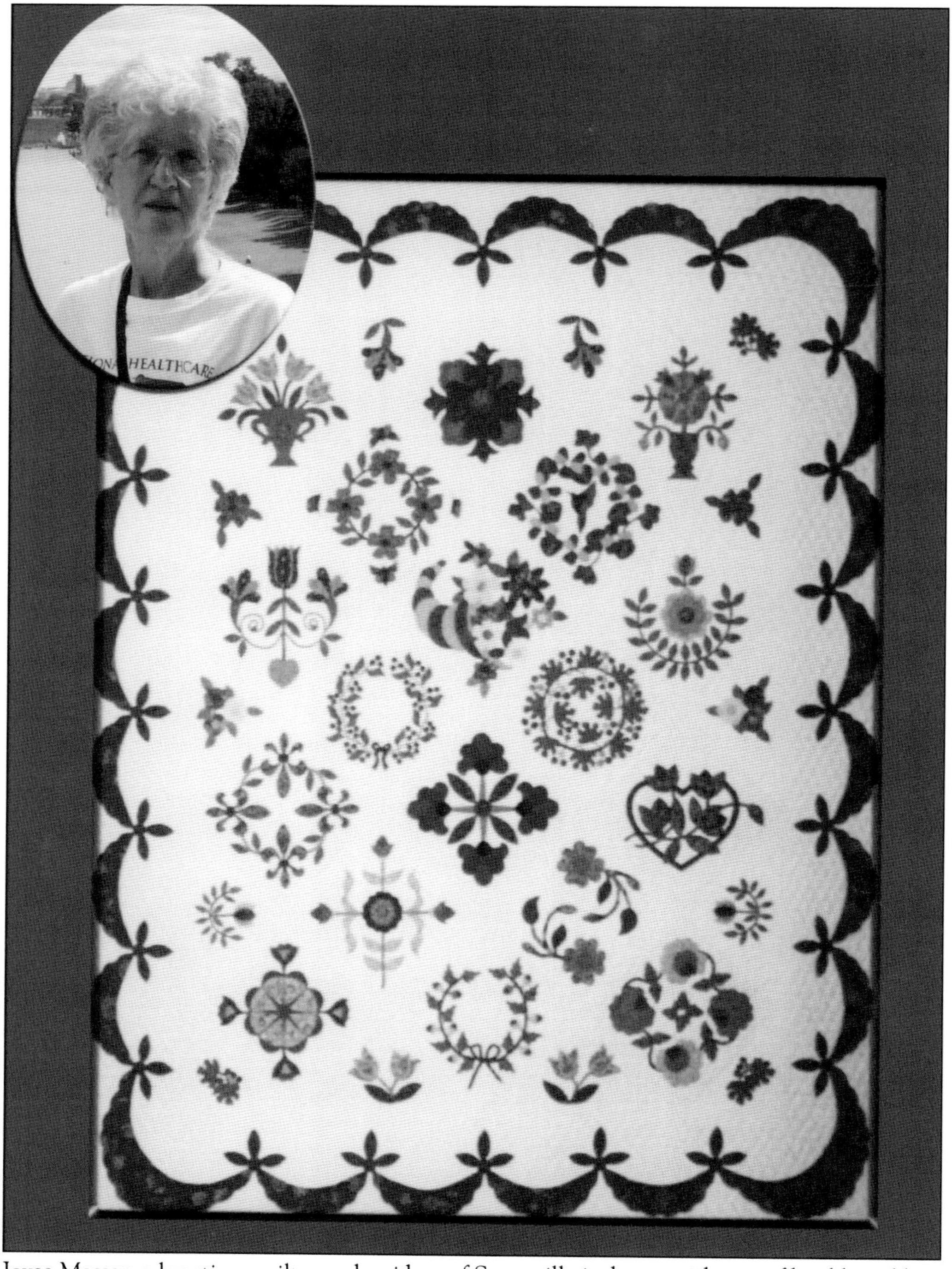

Joyce Massey, a longtime quilter and resident of Seagoville is shown with one of her blue ribbon quilts. She has entered quilts in local shows and the State Fair of Texas. She won Best of Show in the Quilters' Guild of Dallas annual show in 1990 with her Baltimore Album quilt. That quilt also won Best of Show at the 1991 State Fair of Texas. She took Best of Show with quilts in 1992, 1995, 1996, and 2000 as well.

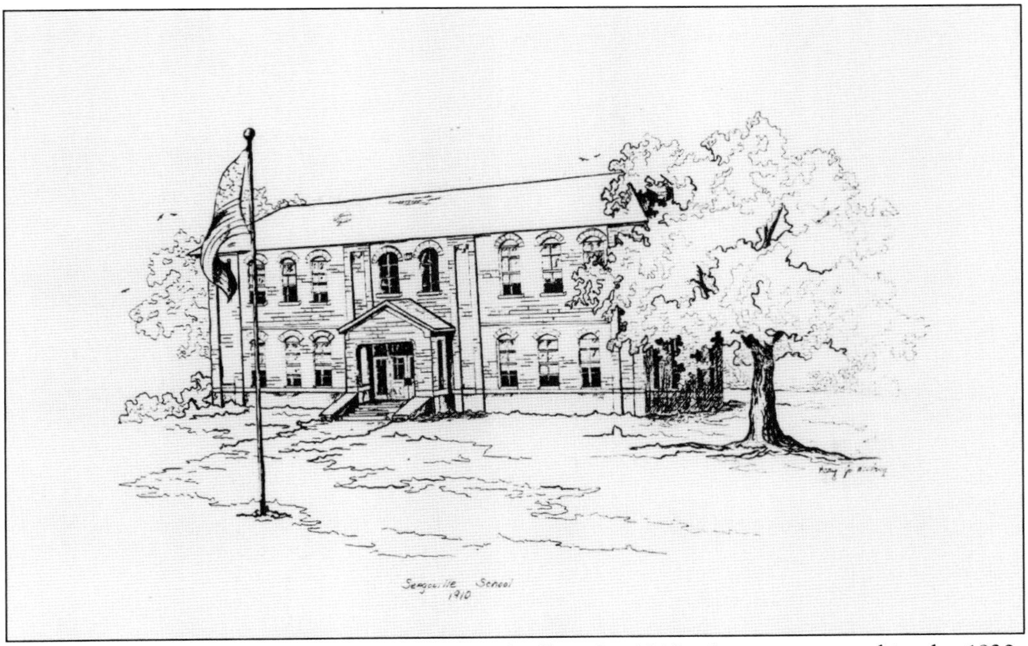

This 1910 school was sketched by Joann Woodruff in the 1980s. It was renovated in the 1930s and used continuously until a new building was constructed in 1986. This newer school building stands in back of the old school. (Courtesy of Joann Woodruff.)

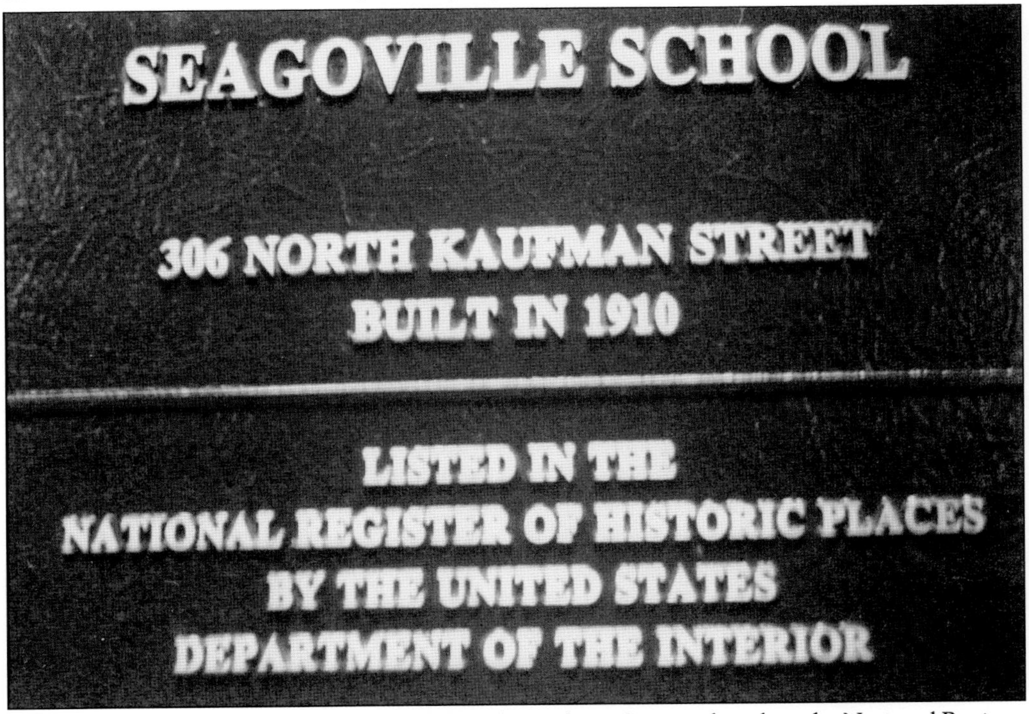

Built in 1910, the Seagoville School at 306 North Kaufman Street is listed on the National Register of Historic Places by the United States Department of the Interior. This honor was awarded August 10, 2005. Many folks got their early education in this grand old building. (Courtesy of Billie Frank Phillips.)

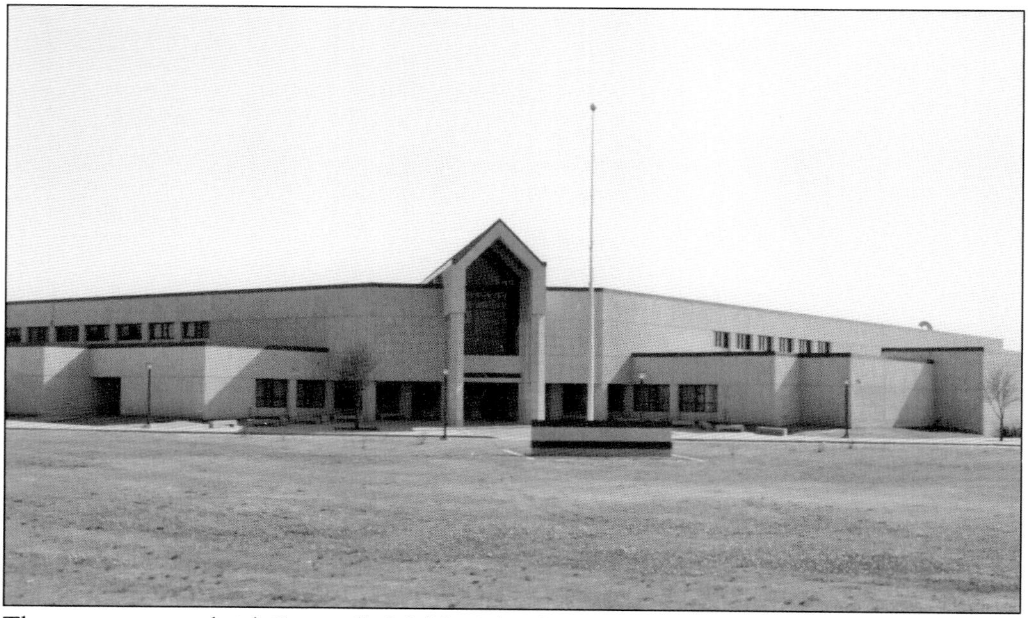

The new two-story brick Seagoville Middle School was built on the corner of Woody Road and Seagoville Road in 1988, at a cost of $5.5 million. It was built on the same tract of land that the high school was built on. When constructed, the middle school housed grades seven and eight. Now it includes sixth through eighth grades. (Courtesy of Carol Franks.)

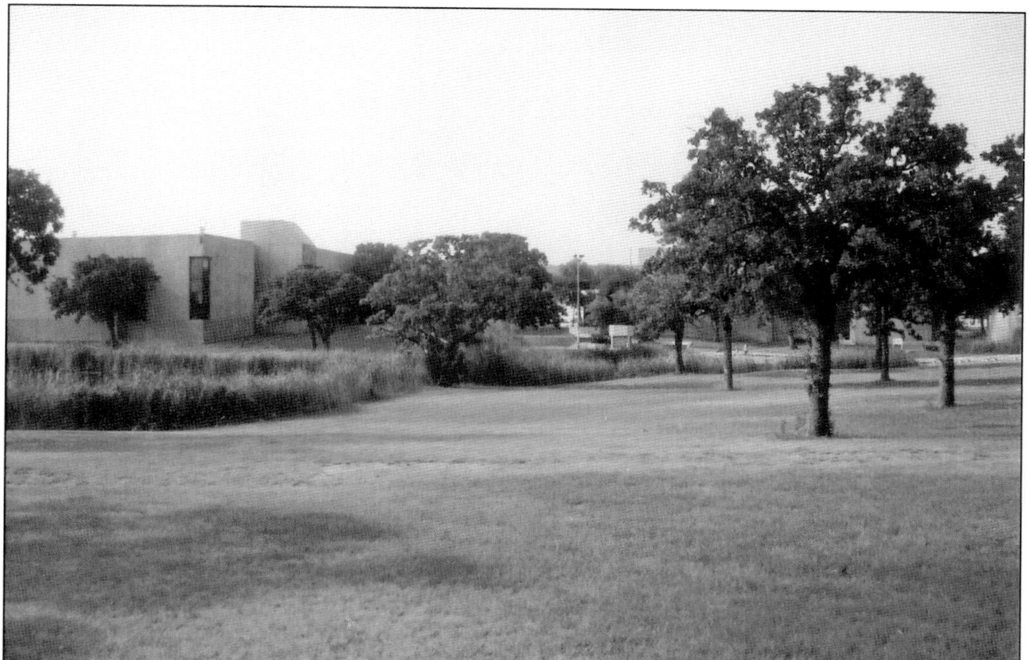

Several years after the consolidation of school systems, a bond was approved that resulted in four new schools in Seagoville. In 1979, ground was broken for a new $7.2- to $10-million high school on 100 acres of land between Woody and Stark Roads on Seagoville Road. Classes started in fall 1980, with the class of 1981 holding graduation ceremonies in the new auditorium. (Courtesy of Carol Franks.)

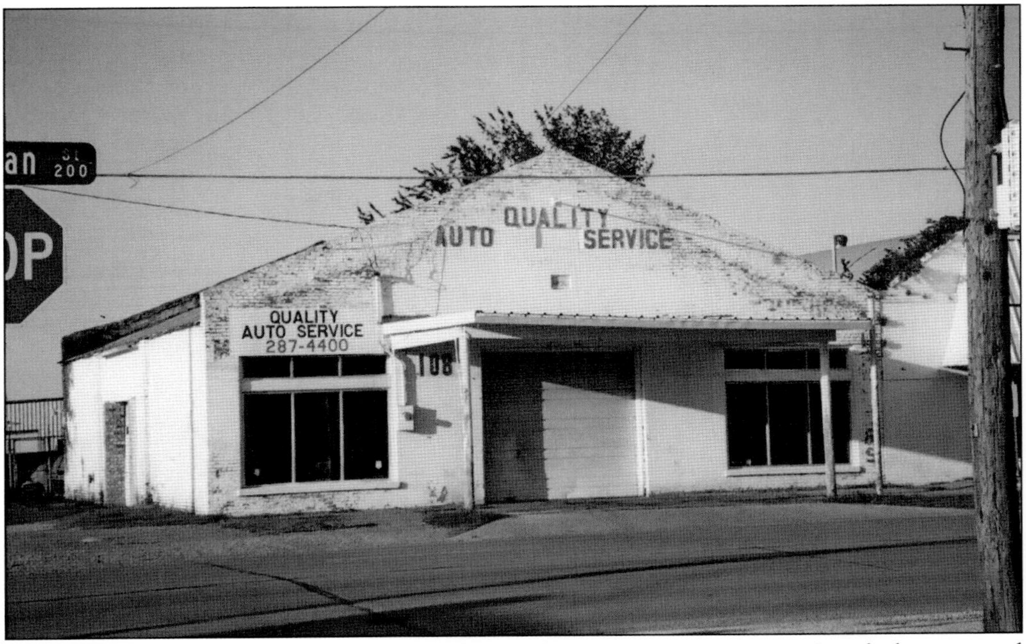

The oldest continuously operating business in Seagoville dates back to 1924. B. M. Crawford constructed a garage along with a few other buildings on Kaufman Street. W. A. (Buck) Ballard operated the Ballard garage for several years and then his son-in-law operated it for a while. In 1985, Gary Wilson bought the business and changed the name to Quality Auto Service. (Courtesy of Carol Franks.)

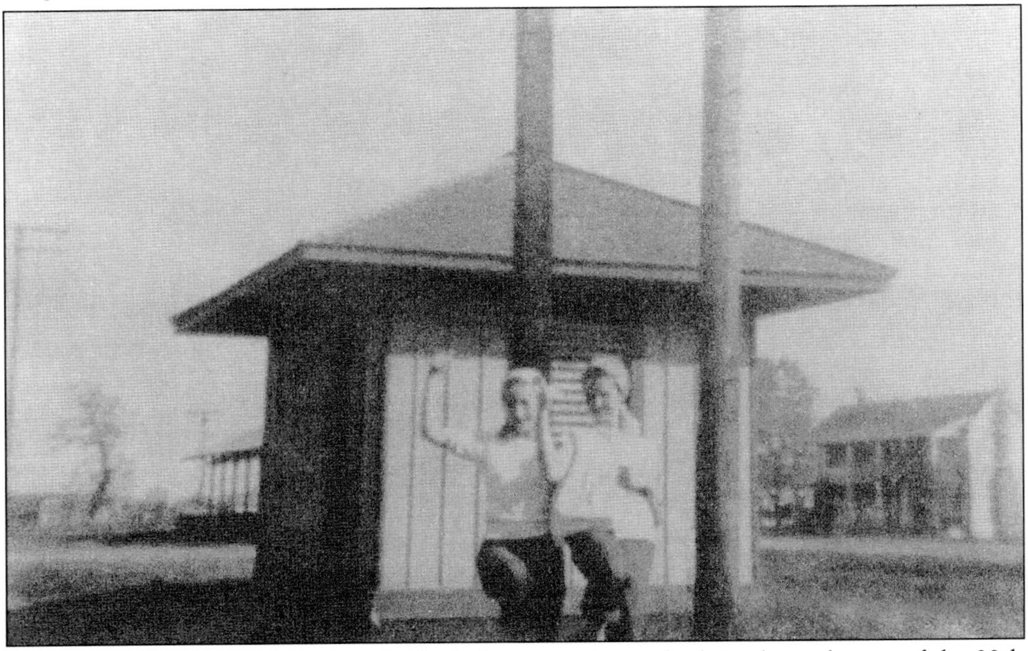

The Seagoville Hotel is shown in the far right corner. It was built in the early part of the 20th century. In the early days, the train was usually filled. Frank Hurt provided a buggy service to the drummers (salesmen) arriving on the train and wishing to go to nearby towns. The hotel was bought by Alice Petty in the 1920s. She closed it soon after the train stopped carrying passengers. (Courtesy of the Phillips family.)

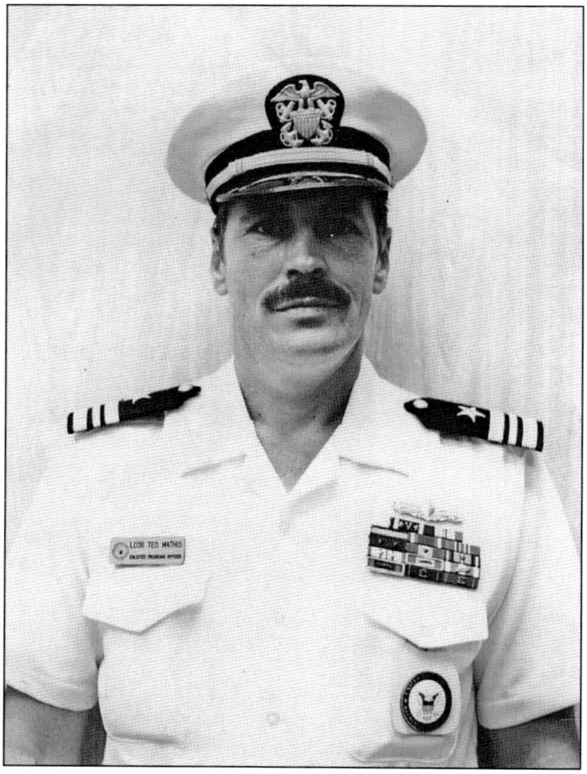

Lt. Comdr. Troy Eddie (Teddy) Mathis Jr. was born March 5, 1938, to T. E. and Pauline Kirby Mathis. He graduated from Seagoville High School in 1956 and joined the U.S. Navy on October 4, 1956. While in the U.S. Navy, Teddy received an appointment to the U.S. Naval Academy, but marriage took precedent over the appointment. However, during his service, he received an electrical engineering degree from Purdue University. In Officer Candidate School at Newport, Rhode Island, he was first in his class of 1,400. (Courtesy of Patricia Mathis.)

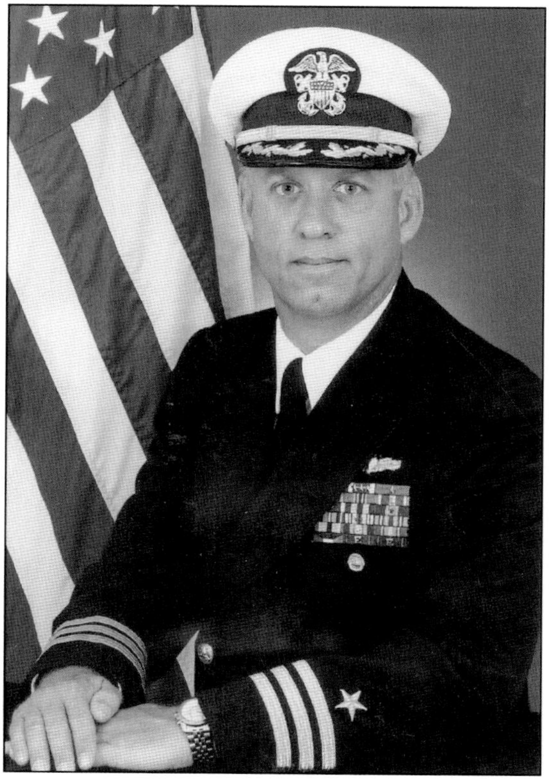

Michael Hale, the son of Mr. and Mrs. Ernie Hale, graduated from Seagoville High in 1976 and attended the University of Texas before enlisting in the U.S. Navy. He returned to the university after his enlistment as a naval reservist, completed his studies, and was commissioned at the Officer Candidate School in Newport, Rhode Island. He attained the rank of commander, retired in 2007, and is head of the Texas Naval Junior Reserve Officers' Training Corps. (Courtesy of Ernie Hale.)

Alice Ada (Seago) Starnes was born January 16, 1889, to John Thomas Seago and Margaret Van Harding. She was a great-niece of T. K. Seago. On December 16, 1906, she married John Stephenson Starnes, and they had seven children—Wallace, John, Lucille, Margie, Fowler, and twins Bill and Bob. After living in Seagoville for many years, she died on February 12, 1973, and is buried in Lee Cemetery. (Courtesy of Betty Starnes.)

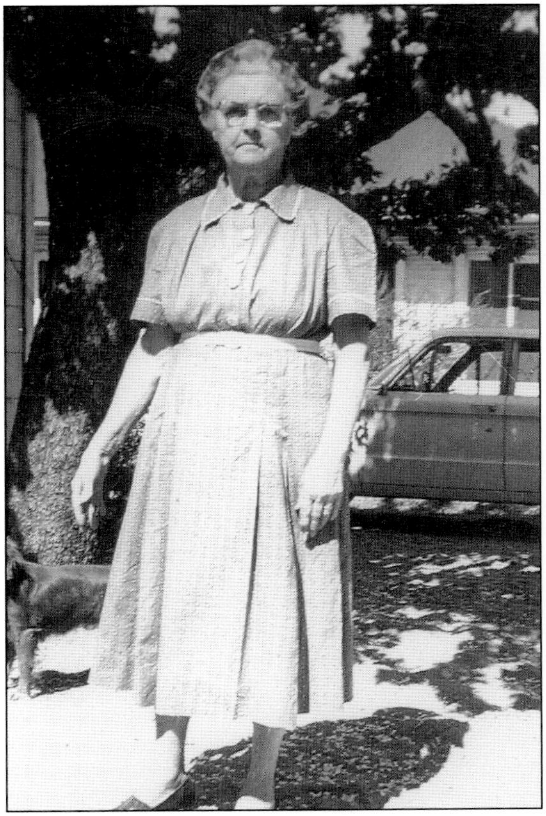

Pictured are four students standing close to the 1910 High School. This photograph was taken in 1912 across the fence from where the home of Bill and Ouida Hurt was built in 1915. Alice Petty is standing on the far right. These girls grew up together and went to the high school on the second floor of the 1910 school. Alice Petty later owned the hotel in Seagoville. (Courtesy of R. L. Glenn.)

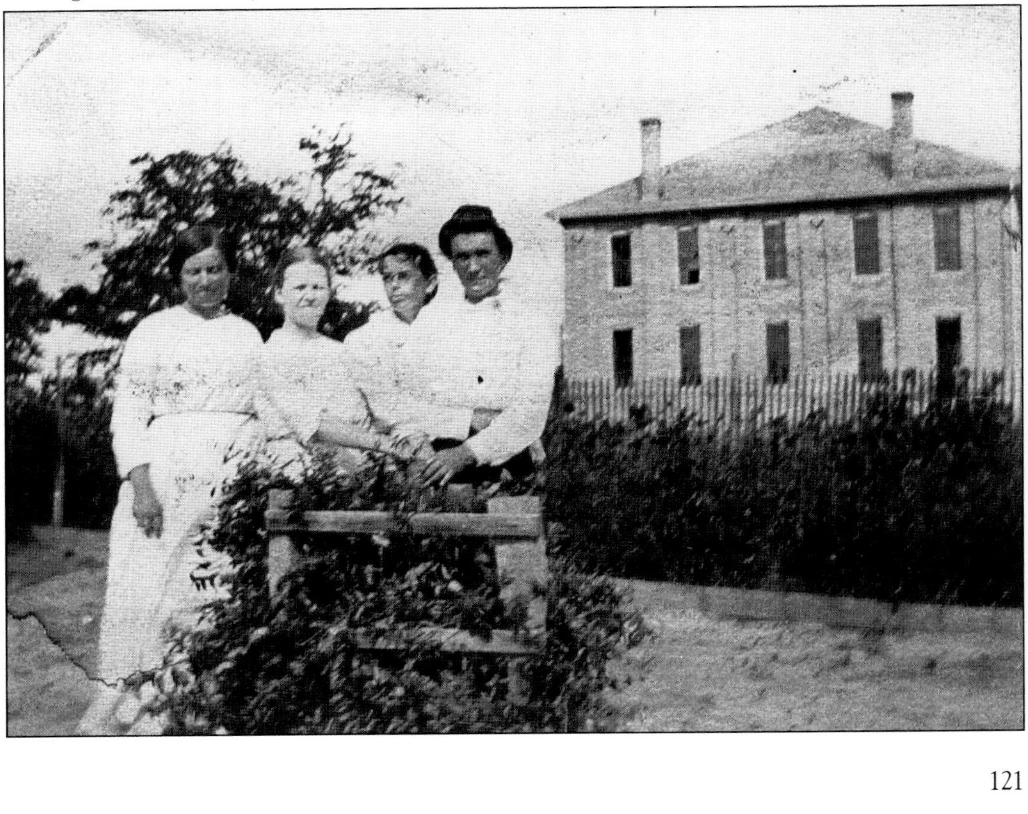

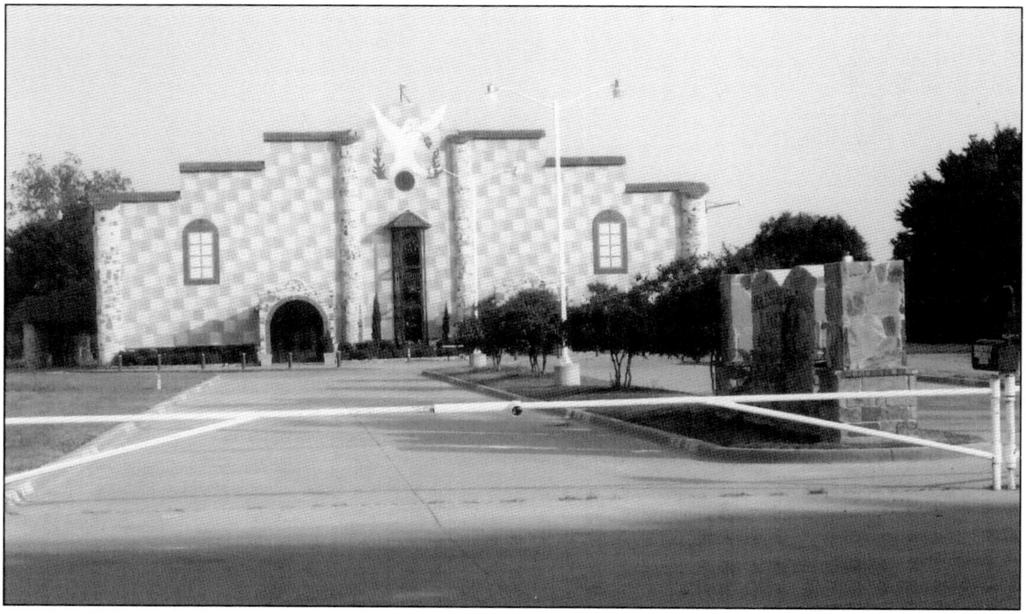

Pictured is the Iglesia Del Dios Viviente Church (Church of the Living God). The pastor of this magnificent church is Joaquin Hernandez. He was chaplin at the Federal Correctional Institute for 13 years. Starting in 1986, Hernandez held services in a frame building on Simmonds Road. That same year, construction was started on the church pictured above. All labor on the church was volunteer. (Courtesy of Billie Frank Phillips.)

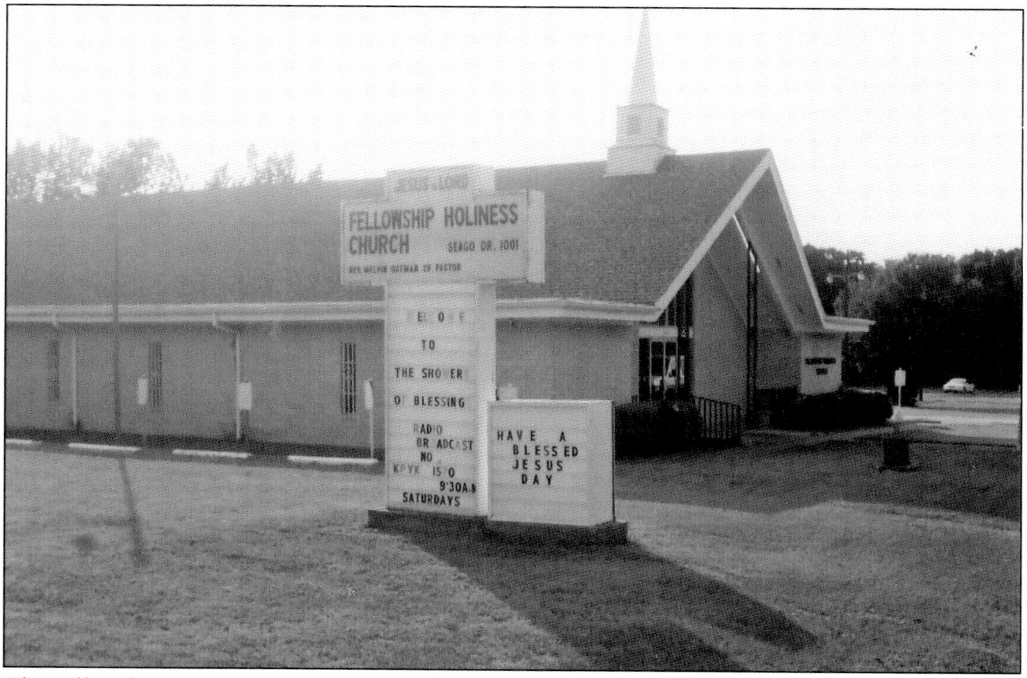

The Fellowship Holiness Church was first built in 1960. This frame church was under the guidance of Rev. Melvin Oatman Sr. He was the guiding light of the present brick structure built in 1975. Rev. Melvin Oatman Jr. assumed pastoral duties on the retirement of his father. (Courtesy of Billie Frank Phillips.)

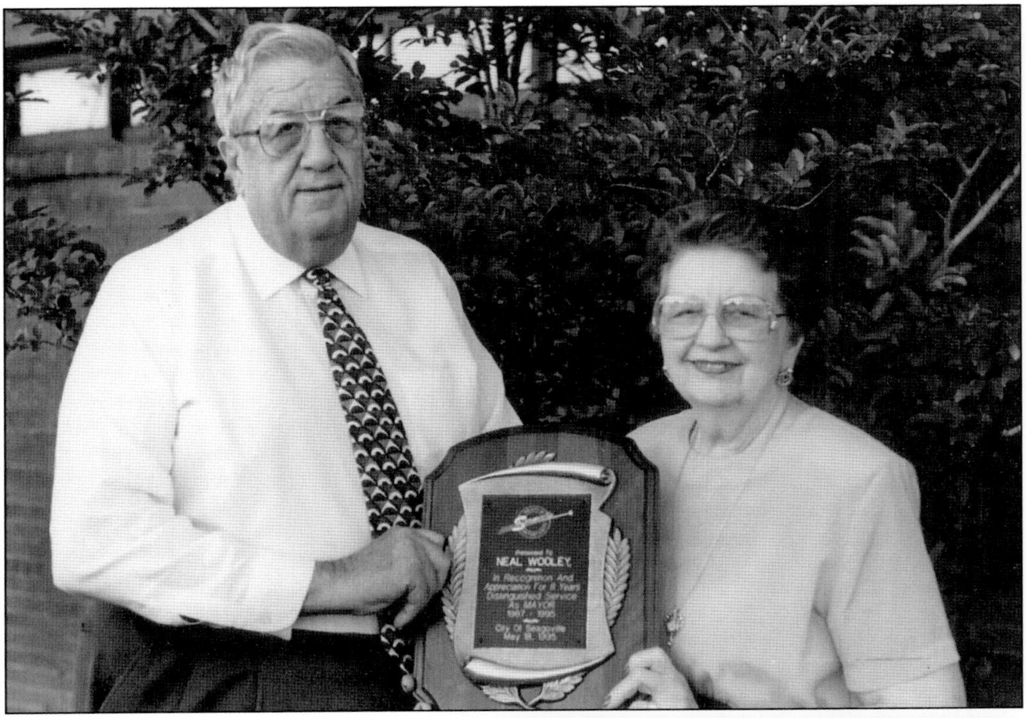

The Wooley family—Neal and Lois (above) and son Jerry—published the first edition of *Suburbia News* in 1972. Besides being the owner and publisher, Neal held many more positions. He was a mayor of Seagoville, city council member, World War II veteran, an Eagle Scout, Lions Club and Kiwanis member, a founding board member of both the Seagoville Chamber of Commerce and the Seagoville Senior Citizens Housing Association, and a member of the former Seagoville Independent School Board. Lois Wooley's sister, Grace Garrett (right), became their typesetter and held this position for several years. After 35 years of publishing the paper, the Wooleys sold to Pugh Media LLC in 2006. From the early 1900s, other local newspapers have been the *Seagoville Herald*, *Seagoville Star*, *Seagoville News*, and *Seagoville Sun*. Short-lived newspapers were the *Gazette* and *Tribune*. (Courtesy of the Wooley family.)

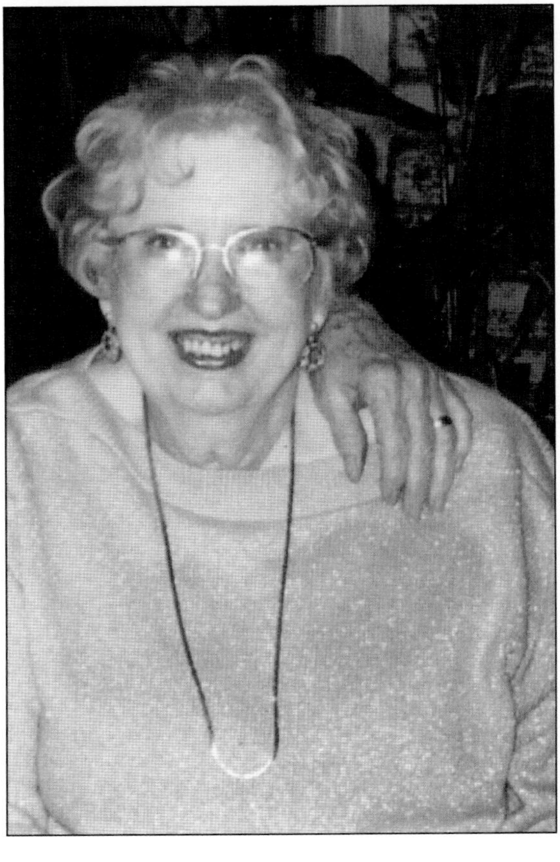

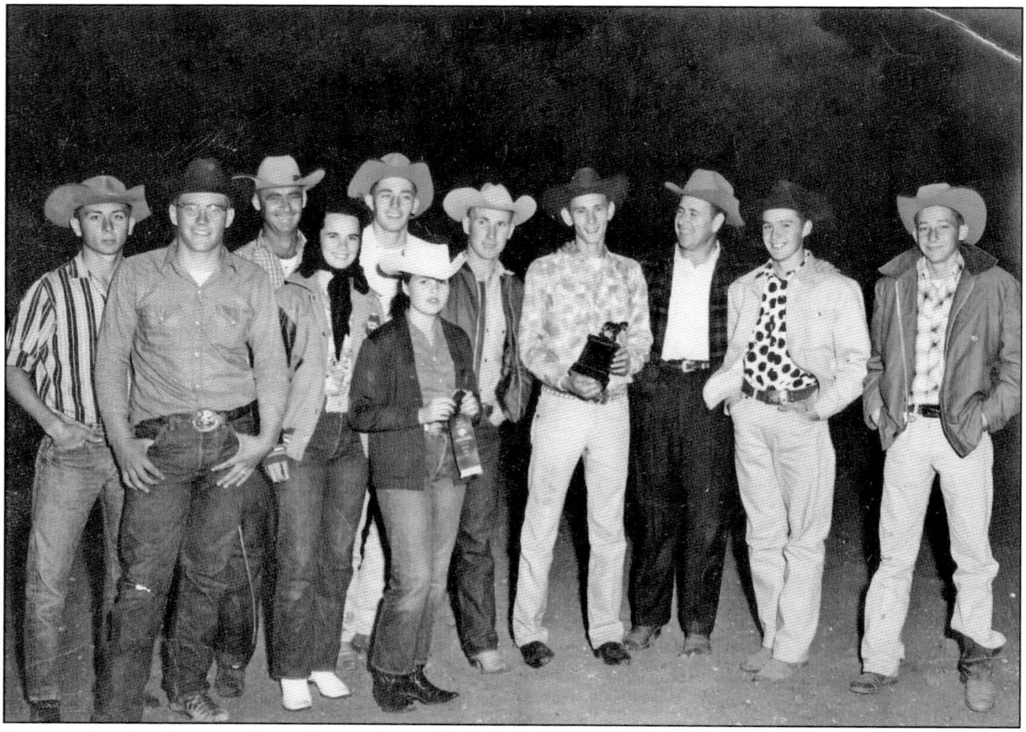

Pictured is the Seagoville rodeo team at the FFA rodeo in Wilmer Hutchins. Rodney Yarbrough was the all-around cowboy, and the team won the most points. From left to right are Omer Browning, horseback; Ron Hoffman, bull dogging; Bud Ogletree, coach; Barbara Ogletree, barrels; Wendel Schoenberger, steer riding and dogging; Pam Hart, barrels; Leroy Dixon, dogging; Rodney Yarbrough, roping, bull riding, and dogging; Wayne Phillips, advisor; Ricky Cooper, roping; and Ron Schoenberger, bull riding. (Courtesy of Wayne Phillips.)

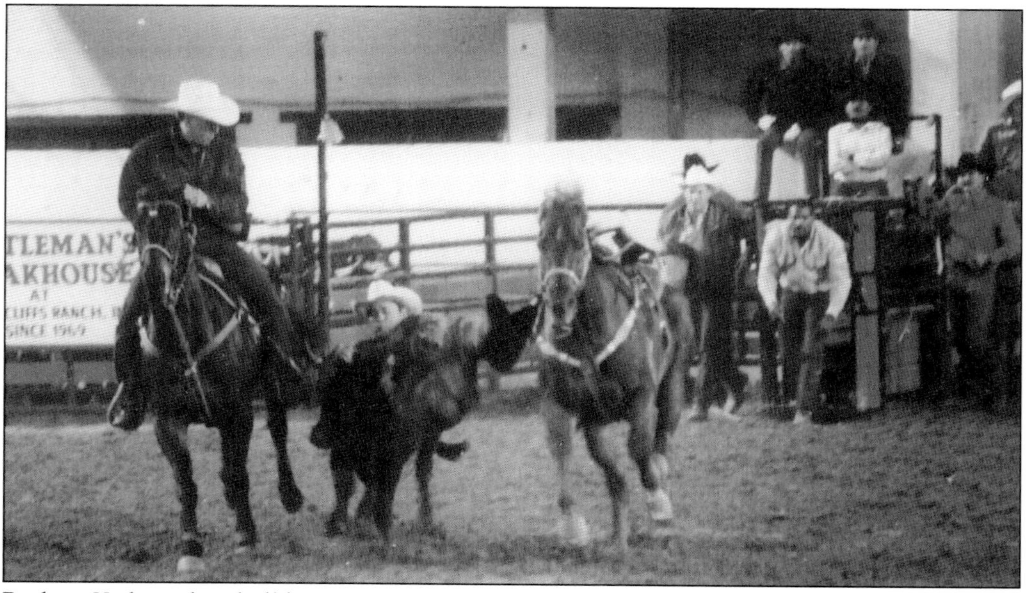

Rodney Yarbrough is bulldogging at the finals in El Paso in November 1993. Ricky Watson is hazing. (Courtesy of Barbara Yarbrough.)

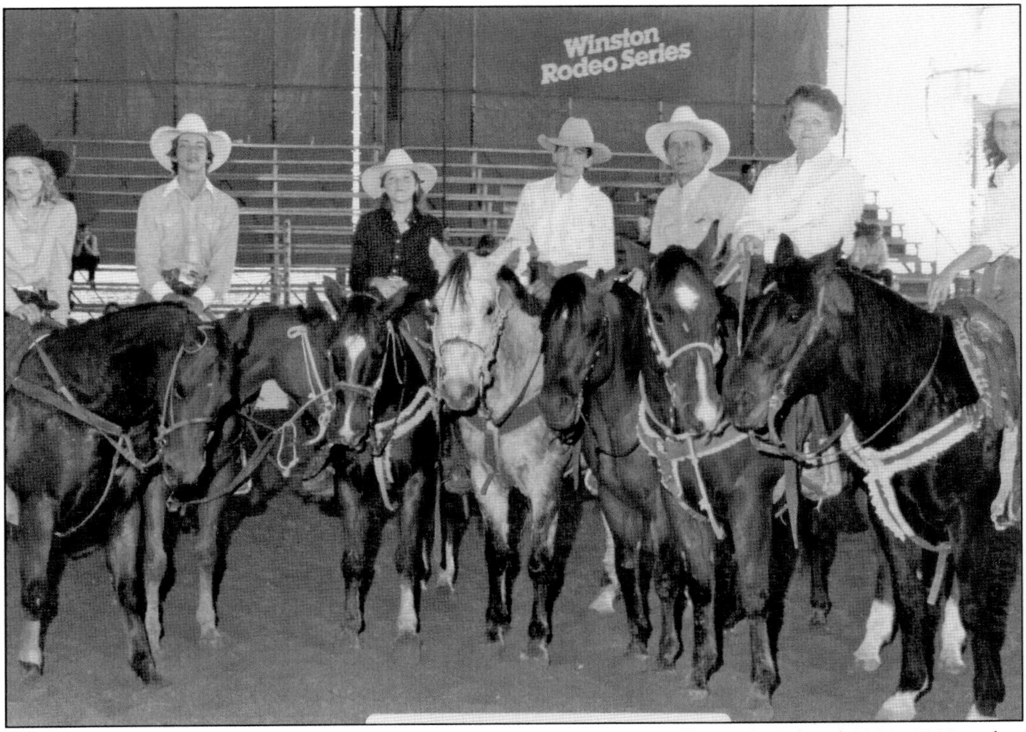

Sponsor Billie Frances Ogletree poses with a group of her Seagoville High School 1981–1982 rodeo team. Billie Frances was a sponsor for many years and was cofounder of the Lone Star Association. In this photograph are, from left to right, Laurel Landess, Trent Ward, Julie Munnerlyn, Guy Yarbrough, Rodney Yarbrough, Billie Ogletree, and Bobbi Yarbrough. (Courtesy of Barbara Yarbrough.)

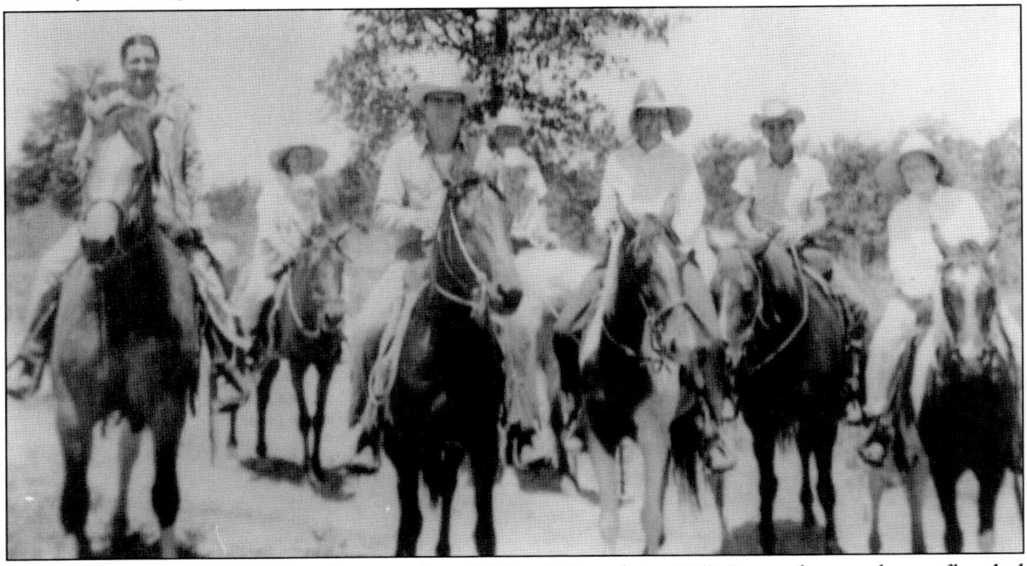

Pictured is the Glenn family riding on their Mabank Ranch in 1957. Later the ranch was flooded by Cedar Creek Lake. The riding party consisted of, from left to right, (first row) Claudine Petty Glenn, mother; Roy Petty; Lorene Hall Petty; Reagan L. Glenn; and Ada Hurt Petty, 72-year-old grandmother; (second row) Lavon Kirby Petty, Gail Petty, J. F. Petty, and Bennie Roy Petty. (Courtesy of Barbara Yarbrough.)

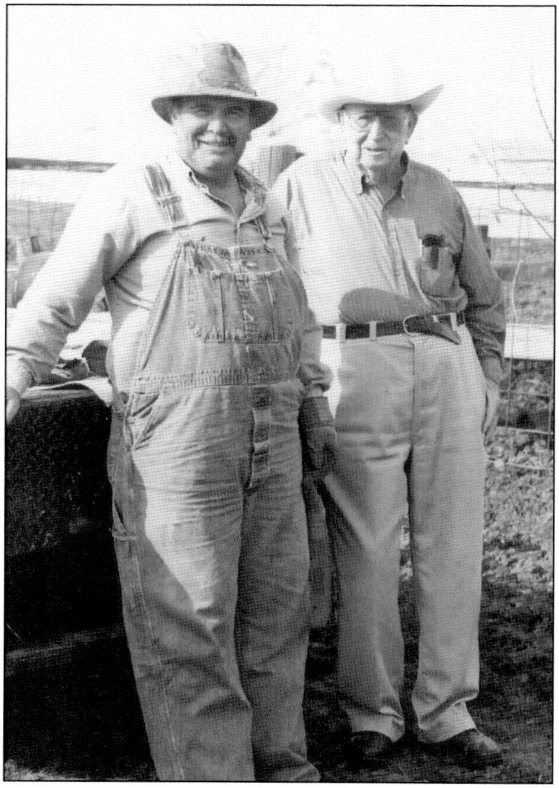

There is a story with this picture of two farmers in 1990. Their smiles tell the reader that they have sold their cattle at a good price, their maize made a bumper crop, they got a good rain, or maybe all of the above. This photograph of Jack and Reagan Glenn is rare because there are few local second- and third-generation farmers. Greg Waldrum and Johnny Whitley are the only others in Seagoville. (Courtesy of R. L. Glenn.)

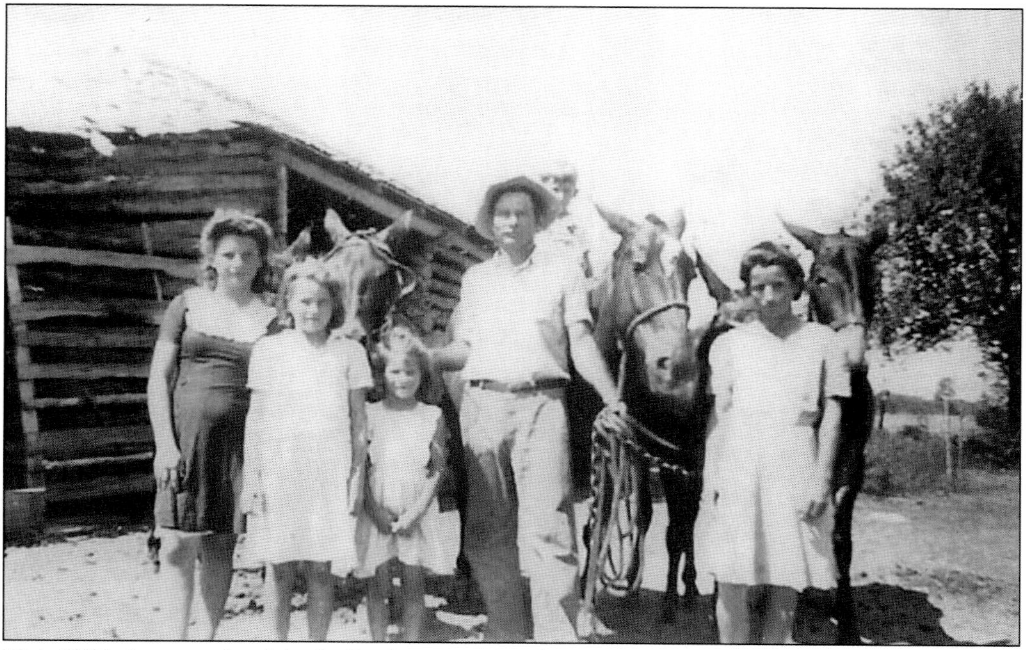

This 1935 photograph of the L. D. Gragsone family is typical of many farm families of the era. Living expenses were not excessive as most of the food was raised. Gragsone had a milk cow that birthed 17 calves. When someone saw Gragsone driving his mules, he always had a big smile, which let everyone know he loved his work and his mules. (Courtesy of Floy Ballantine.)

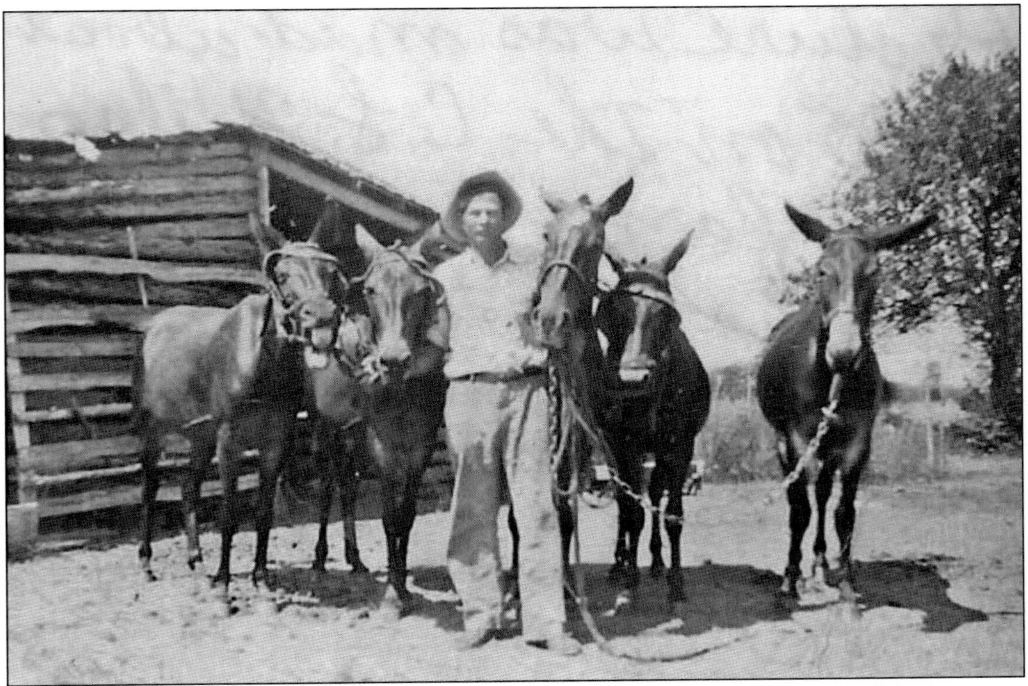

The picture above is L. D. Gragsone with his mules in 1935. L. D. always drove a well-broken team of mules. He used them for all sorts of agricultural enterprises and to pull logs to the sawmills. Of course, they were used to plow, mow, and work a wagon. It seemed L. D. preferred a small mule, but he got lots of work out of them—and always with a big smile. (Courtesy of Floy Ballantine.)

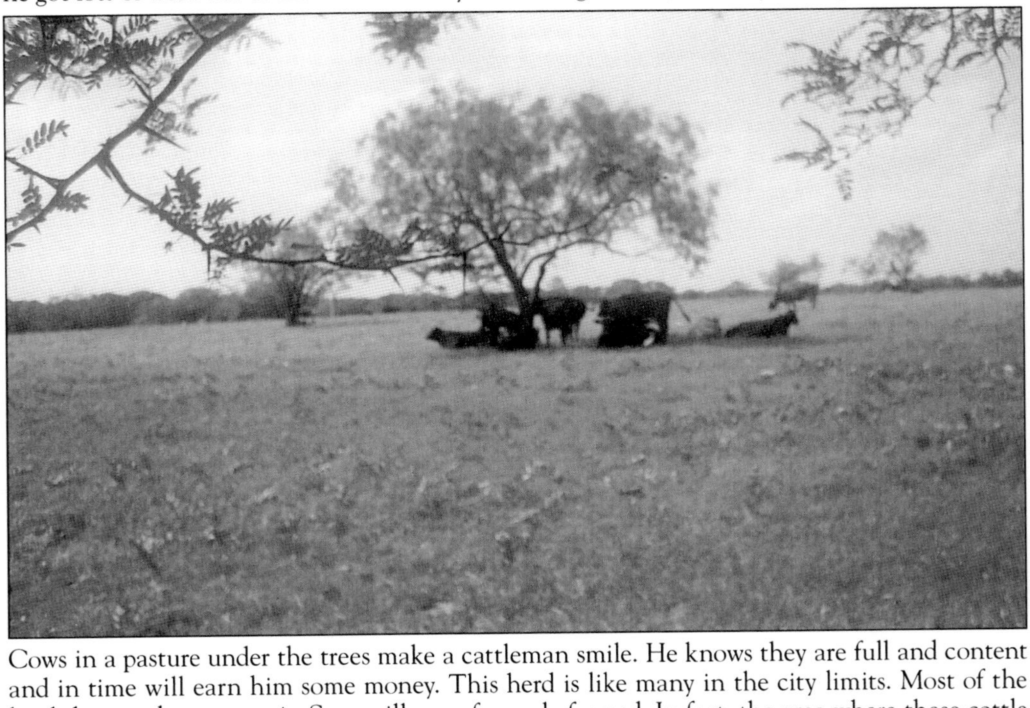

Cows in a pasture under the trees make a cattleman smile. He knows they are full and content and in time will earn him some money. This herd is like many in the city limits. Most of the land that cattle graze on in Seagoville was formerly farmed. In fact, the area where these cattle are was once a peach orchard. (Courtesy of the Phillips family.)

www.arcadiapublishing.com

Discover books about the town where you grew up, the cities where your friends and families live, the town where your parents met, or even that retirement spot you've been dreaming about. Our Web site provides history lovers with exclusive deals, advanced notification about new titles, e-mail alerts of author events, and much more.

MADE IN THE USA

Arcadia Publishing, the leading local history publisher in the United States, is committed to making history accessible and meaningful through publishing books that celebrate and preserve the heritage of America's people and places. Consistent with our mission to preserve history on a local level, this book was printed in South Carolina on American-made paper and manufactured entirely in the United States.

This book carries the accredited Forest Stewardship Council (FSC) label and is printed on 100 percent FSC-certified paper. Products carrying the FSC label are independently certified to assure consumers that they come from forests that are managed to meet the social, economic, and ecological needs of present and future generations.

FSC
Mixed Sources
Product group from well-managed forests and other controlled sources

Cert no. SW-COC-001530
www.fsc.org